AF469758

The Law and Social Work

This reader forms part of The Open University course *Social Care, Social Work and the Law (England and Wales)* and the chapters are related to other materials available to students. The course aims to develop skills, values and knowledge for those working in the social care, social work field. If you are interested in studying this course, or related courses, please write to the Information Officer, School of Health and Social Welfare, The Open University, Walton Hall, Milton Keynes, MK7 6AA, UK. Details can also be viewed on our web page http://www.open.ac.uk.

Opinions expressed in the reader are not necessarily those of the Course Team or of The Open University.

Also published in association with The Open University:

SOCIAL WORK: THEMES, ISSUES AND CRITICAL DEBATES
Edited by Robert Adams, Lena Dominelli and Malcolm Payne

COMMUNITY CARE: A READER Second Edition
Edited by Joanna Bornat, Julia Johnson, Charmaine Pereira, David Pilgrim and Fiona Williams

THE CHALLENGE OF PROMOTING HEALTH
Edited by Linda Jones and Moyra Sidell

DEBATES AND DILEMMAS IN PROMOTING HEALTH
Edited by Moyra Sidell, Linda Jones, Alyson Peberdy and Jeanne Katz

MENTAL HEALTH MATTERS
Edited by Tom Heller, Jill Reynolds, Roger Gomm, Rosemary Muston and Stephen Pattison

PROMOTING HEALTH
Edited by Jeanne Katz and Alyson Peberdy

SPEAKING OUR MINDS
Edited by Jim Read and Jill Reynolds

HEALTH PROMOTION
Angela Scriven and Judy Orme

HEALTH AND WELLBEING
Edited by Alan Beattie, Marjorie Gott, Linda Jones and Moyra Sidell

CHILDREN IN SOCIETY
Edited by Pam Foley, Jeremy Roche and Stanley Tucker

The Law and Social Work

Contemporary Issues for Practice

Edited by

Lesley-Anne Cull and Jeremy Roche

at The Open University

palgrave in association with The Open University

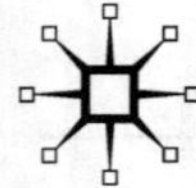

First published 2001 by
PALGRAVE
Houndmills, Basingstoke, Hampshire RG21 6XS and
175 Fifth Avenue, New York, N.Y. 10010
Companies and representatives throughout the world

PALGRAVE is the new global academic imprint of St. Martin's Press LLC Scholarly and Reference Division and Palgrave Publishers Ltd (formerly Macmillan Press Ltd).

ISBN 0–333–96126–9 hardback
ISBN 0–333–94587–5 paperback

This book is printed on paper suitable for recycling and made from fully managed and sustained forest sources.

A catalogue record for this book is available from the British Library.

Cataloging-in-Publication Data is available from the Library of Congress

Editing and origination by
Aardvark Editorial, Mendham, Suffolk

10 9 8 7 6 5 4 3 2 1
10 09 08 07 06 05 04 03 02 01

Printed and bound in Great Britain by
Creative Print & Design (Wales), Ebbw Vale

Contents

List of Contributors

Jane Aldgate is Professor of Social Care at the School of Health and Social Welfare, The Open University. Her research spans many aspects of social policy and social work relating to children and families. She is co-author, with Marie Bradly, of *Supporting Families Through Short Term Fostering* (1999) and has just completed for the Department of Health an overview of research on the Children Act 1989.

Alison Brammer is a Lecturer at the Department of Law at the University of Keele. She previously practised as a solicitor in local government. Her main areas of interest are registered homes and institutional abuse, the construction of elder abuse, and the law relating to adults with learning disabilities. She has published widely in these areas and is the Legal Editor of the *Journal of Adult Protection*.

Suzy Braye is Reader in Social Work at Staffordshire University. She has previously worked in local authority social services as a social work practitioner, trainer and manager. She teaches and has written on social work law, community care policy and values in professional practice. She is engaged in evaluative research on services for children in need and support systems for carers. She is co-author, with Michael Preston-Shoot, of *Practising Social Work Law* (1997) and *Empowering Practice in Social Care* (1995).

Isabelle Brodie is a Research Fellow in the Department of Applied Social Studies, University of Luton. Her research mainly concerns children looked after by local authorities and children excluded from school. She is co-author, with David Berridge, of *Children's Homes Revisited* (1998).

Tanya Callman is a Barrister specialising in education law and public law in the Inner Temple, London. She is the Editor of *Education Public Law and the Individual* and frequently writes and lectures on matters relating to education law, judicial review and human rights.

Sarah Chand is a Senior Practitioner with Warwickshire Probation. Her main areas of interest are developing effective practice within the changing scene of probation and working with drug-using offenders. She is the author of *HIV and AIDS in Prisons: Probation Responses* (1995).

Andrew Cooper is Professor of Social Work at the Tavistock Clinic and University of East London. With Rachael Hetherington and others, he has participated in a range of comparative European child protection research programmes and jointly authored a number of books and papers in this field.

Jeremy Cooper is at Middlesex University, where he is Professor of Law and Director of the Disability Law Research Centre. He has written and researched extensively on disability rights and access to justice. His books include *The Legal Rights Manual* (1994), *Disability and the Law* (as co-author with Stuart Vernon) (1996) and, as editor, *Law, Rights and Disability* (2000).

Nicki Cornwell has abandoned professional and academic social work for the pleasures of writing. Her academic publications range from therapeutic work to statementing, social policy issues, anti-discriminatory practice and intercultural social work practice. She has added poetry to the list and hopes that it will soon include a children's novel.

Lesley-Anne Cull is a Lecturer in the School of Health and Social Welfare at The Open University. She is a practising barrister and has researched and written widely in the areas of child and family law.

Ann Dale-Emberton is a Tutor on the Diploma in Social Work Programme at Ruskin College, Oxford and formerly an Associate Lecturer on several Open University courses. Ann has over 25 years' experience of working within the Probation Service and local authorities, undertaking a number of different roles, as well as experience of working in the field of social work education. Ann is also a guardian *ad litem*. Her current research is assessing the student's perspective of social work training, its effectiveness and relevance to practice.

Guy Dehn is the founding Director of Public Concern at Work, an independent charity that promotes good governance in the public, private and voluntary sectors. The charity was closely involved in advising on the scope and detail of the Public Interest Disclosure Act 1998. He is also a practising barrister, and from 1986–92, as Legal Officer to the National Consumer Council, he advised the Council on legal and Parliamentary matters and was responsible for a wide range of policy issues.

Ratna Dutt is Director of the Race Equality Unit, an independent organisation providing race equality training, consultancy, research, development and publications in social care. She is a social worker by profession and has written extensively on social care and race. She is co-author of a chapter on the assessment of black children in the Department of Health's Practice Guidance *Assessing Children in Need and their Families* (2000).

Philip Ells is a Solicitor at Alan Edwards & Co. in London and was formerly the Legal and Educational Officer of Public Concern at Work. He is the author of *The People's Lawyer* (2000). His interests include employment, human rights and sports law.

Stephen Gilmore, LLB, LLM, Barrister, is Senior Lecturer in the Law School at the University of East London, where he teaches family law and child law. He has taught law to social workers on DipSW courses, and has been a visiting tutor on the MA in Advanced Social Work at the Tavistock Centre.

Duncan Gore is currently the Training and Development Co-ordinator for the National Association of Child Contact Centres. Prior to this, he was a family court welfare officer in Birmingham for seven years.

Peter Harris is a Barrister and was, until he retired in 1999, the Official Solicitor to the Supreme Court. He is the Chair of the National Council for Family Proceedings, an Associate Senior Research Fellow of the Institute of Advanced Legal Studies, University of London and Chair of the Family Law Working Group of the Society of Advanced Legal Studies, which has recently published its report on the

Cross Border Movement of Children (1999). He is co-author of *The Children Act 1989 – A Procedural Handbook* (1995) and writes for legal and mental health journals. He also lectures to professional audiences on the law relating to children and mental health.

Ruth Hayman is studying at Peter Symonds' College, Winchester. Her course aims to achieve her three GCE A levels in chemistry, human biology and sports studies. She was in care from the ages of 14 to 17 and now works hard to improve services for other young people who are looked after.

Jeanette Henderson is a Lecturer in the School of Health and Social Welfare at The Open University, having previously practised as an Approved Social Worker in the north of England. Her research interests include the construction, meaning and experience of care in mental health. She has written on power in social work education and women's experiences of the mental health system.

Rachael Hetherington is Director of the Centre for Comparative Social Work Studies at Brunel University. In the last decade, she has initiated and implemented a wide range of research projects that compare the child protection and welfare practices of European countries. This work has given rise to a range of books and shorter publications, many of them co-authored with Andrew Cooper and other colleagues.

Leonie Jordan is a Solicitor who has practised in local authorities, private practice and the voluntary sector. Until recently she was Legal Adviser at the Family Rights Group. She has also developed with colleagues a multi-disciplinary approach to training and practice.

Denzil Lush has been the Master of the Court of Protection since 1996. Before that, he was a chairman of Social Security Appeals Tribunals and a solicitor in private practice. He is the author of *Cohabitation and Co-Ownership Precedents* (1993) and *Elderly Clients: A Precedent Manual* (1996), as well as co-author of *Enduring Powers of Attorney* (1996).

Ann McDonald is at the School of Social Work and Psychosocial Studies at the University of East Anglia, Norwich. She has a particular interest in community care, social work with older people and the relationship between social work and the law. She is co-author of *The Law and Elderly People* (1995) and author of *Understanding Community Care: A Guide for Social Workers* (1999).

Paul Nixon is Commissioning Officer (Family Group Conferences) for Hampshire County Council Social Services Department. His main interests are partnership practice, community involvement and family support. He is co-author of *Empowering Practice? A Critical Appraisal of the Family Group Conference Approach* (1999).

Nigel Parton is Professor in Child Care and Director of the Centre for Applied Childhood Studies at the University of Huddersfield. He has been writing and researching in the areas of child welfare and child protection for over 20 years, his most recent books including: (as editor with Corinne Wattam) *Child Sexual Abuse: Responding to the Experiences of Children* (1999) and (with Patrick O'Byrne) *Constructive Social Work: Towards a New Practice* (2000).

Michael Preston-Shoot is Professor of Social Work and Social Care at Liverpool John Moores University. He has researched and written widely on social work law, including *Practising Social Work Law* (2nd edn) (with Suzy Braye, 1997) and *Acting*

Fairly (1998). His other research focuses on how service-users experience social work, both community care and childcare provision. He is editor of the journal *Social Work Education.*

Jacki Pritchard is an independent consultant, trainer and researcher who specialises in working with abuse, risk and violence. She has written widely on elder abuse issues, her most recent publications being *Elder Abuse Work: Best Practice in Britain and Canada* (1999) and *The Needs of Older Women: Services for Victims of Elder Abuse and Other Abuse* (2000).

Jeremy Roche is a Lecturer in the School of Health and Social Welfare at The Open University. He writes and researches in the field of children's rights and the law, and is co-editor of *Youth in Society* (1997) and *Changing Experiences of Youth* (1997).

Belinda Schwehr is a Solicitor-advocate at the London law firm of Rowe and Maw, specialising in adults' social services law, health law and human rights. Her particular interest is in the legal relevance of an authority's shortage of financial resources for the discharge of all its social services duties and discretions. She collaborated with the author of *Community Care Practice and the Law* (1994) and with the Local Government Association regarding its introductory pocket booklet on the UK's Human Rights Act 1998.

Anna Souhami is funded by the Economic and Social Research Council (ESRC) to do her PhD on 'Communication and Compliance in Youth Justice' at the Department of Criminology, Keele University.

Judith Timms OBE is a Chief Executive of the National Youth Advocacy Services and an Honorary Research Fellow attached to the Centre for the Study of the Child, the Family and the Law, Faculty of Law, University of Liverpool. She is Vice President of the Family Mediators Association as well as author of the Department of Health publication *Manual of Practice Guidance for Guardians ad Litem and Reporting Officers* (1992) and of *Children's Representation: A Practitioner's Guide* (1995).

Stuart Vernon is at the School of Law, University of East London, where he teaches law, criminology and social work students. His research interests are in social work law and youth justice. He is the author of three editions of *Social Work and the Law*, most recently published in 1998.

Helen Watson is head of the multi-agency Youth Offending Service in Sunderland. The Service has been a government pilot area and is now a Youth Justice Board Pathway Site. She has written various articles on the experience of piloting for periodicals such as *Local Government Management.*

Penelope Welbourne is at the Department of Social Work and Social Policy, Plymouth University. Prior to that, she was a social worker and social work manager in children and families' social work, mostly in North and East London. Her interests include child victims in the criminal justice system and children who abuse children.

Anne Worrall is at the Department of Criminology, Keele University. Her research interests are women and crime, punishment in the community, youth justice and comparative criminal justice. She is author of *Offending Women* (1990) and *Punishment in the Community* (1997).

Introduction

The Law and Social Work – Working Together?

Lesley-Anne Cull and Jeremy Roche

In editing this collection we have been conscious of the breadth as well as the complexity of the legal issues that impact on the world of social work.

Social work has been at the centre of much debate over the past two decades, and the consequences have included a different emphasis on the law in social work education and the creation of new relationships of accountability to service-users and the law. Yet individuals working in social work are still faced on a daily basis with dilemmas over what they can and should be doing. Despite the new role accorded to law within social work, the law does not and cannot provide an answer to the complex human questions that lie at the centre of the social work task. In many senses, however, the law is an indispensable partner for social work. The law regulates social work practice, holding it to account and providing social workers with the powers and duties they need to do their job properly; it provides social workers with the authority they need as professionals. The law also structures their discretion through providing them with specific legal powers and duties in a range of situations and with 'advice' in the form of guidance. In addition, the law, like social work, is a dynamic and human process constantly changing and impacting on the lives of service-user and professional in different ways.

The law thus provides authority and a structure for decision-making, rather than solutions; it provides the framework within which individual social workers have to act. In other words, while social workers have discretion in the action they decide to take, this is not an unconstrained discretion. Social workers have to act within the law and in the light of their contractual obligations as employees. They should also work within a framework that is committed to treating all service-users with an equality of concern and respect. Social workers are in a position to make a judgment about the needs of service-users by virtue of the fact that it is the social worker who engages with the service-user on such matters. This raises issues concerning how the social work task is accomplished as well as the scope of social work powers and duties. So it is not simply a matter of deciding whether the action taken is lawful, that is the very least one can expect, or whether the social worker was acting within his or her powers and duties. It also entails a concern with the process whereby decisions are made and action taken.

Effective and ethical practice relies upon a commitment to develop and consolidate legal knowledge. It can make a crucial difference to your ability to act as an effective advocate for service-users if you are confident in your knowledge of the law. Such knowledge is also important because it can impact on the choices you have available as a professional. This entails being clear about the legal principles that inform an area of practice, as well as knowing where to go for more specialist advice or to keep yourself up to date. The law and regulations lay down what can and cannot be done in certain sets of circumstances; in addition, guidance provides advice regarding practice. Furthermore, the courts from time to time provide guidance on how the local authority social services department should proceed in certain situations. For example in *Re J (Minors)(Care: Care Plan)* [1994] 1 FLR 253, the High Court outlined the information it wanted to have provided in the care plan when considering whether or not to make a care order.

It is often, however, the court or tribunal that has to make a final decision in a particular case and in this sense the law and institutions of the law such as courts and tribunals can be seen as partners in social work decision-making. When compulsory powers are at issue, the role of the social work profession is to provide such impartial decision-making forums with the information to allow them to make decisions in accordance with legal requirements. In family proceedings, for example, the court's decision on whether or not to make a care order or supervision order is made in part on the basis of the information provided by the local authority.

One of the challenges facing practitioners, as well as any student of law, is the need to keep up to date with changes in the law. The difficulty of accomplishing this is compounded by the fact that legal change takes a number of forms and is the result of quite different kinds of activity. For example, the courts as well as Parliament develop the law. Some of these changes have their origins in forces external to the world of social work while others are internal. Demographic changes whereby more people are living longer and are in need of care and medical services, how care and medical services for the elderly are financed and the proper balance to be struck between private responsibility and public welfare are key issues in contemporary social care debates. Similarly, because of shifts in the public debate on crime, especially youth crime, social workers now have an expanding role in the youth justice system. The

Crime and Disorder Act 1998, which set up youth offending teams, was passed in response to a perceived need to pursue an effective multi-agency approach to tackling juvenile crime and delinquency that bore down particularly on largely disadvantaged communities. Finally, voluntary sector organisations and service-users are increasingly expressing their political demands for improvements in services in the language of rights rather than simply welfare or needs; there are demands not only for different procedural and substantive rights, but also for fair and respectful treatment.

Internal changes include government-inspired initiatives such as Quality Protects and best value reviews that have arisen out of the government's perception that social service providers had failed effectively to promote good practice and to provide a quality service. Now the emphasis is on evidence-based and research-led practice (DoH, 2000a, 2000b) as well as on evidence of effective implementation via audits, 'best value' reviews and inspection. In the area of work with children and families, the current emphasis on supporting parents and 'improving the lives of disadvantaged and vulnerable children' (DoH, 2000a) is in part a result of a reflection on the uneven impact of the Children Act 1989 on social work practice. Responding to emergencies as opposed to developing innovative and supportive preventative strategies in partnership with families and communities had continued to be the norm despite the philosophical underpinnings of the 1989 Act.

It is, however, misleading to push too far this division between external and internal drivers for change. Service-users' demands for clearer and effective rights to services can be seen as a direct result of their disenchantment with the quality of professional service provided by social workers. At the same time this feeds off and connects back into an emergent language of rights within the political sphere, for example the passing of the Human Rights Act 1998 incorporating into the UK the provisions of the European Convention on Human Rights.

This edited collection is divided into three parts exploring conceptual and thematic issues, giving an overview of areas of law and social work practice and providing first-hand practitioner accounts.

The first part considers conceptual and thematic issues that shape the law's engagement with social work practice today. As such the contributions cover a range of issues, including the changing and contingent character of the idea of welfare, emergent forms of accountability and the concept of risk. Overall, this section seeks to set the intellectual and policy scene within which contemporary social work practice takes place. The second part has a different rationale, focusing on the relationship between social work practice and the law in a number of specific environments. The chapters here either provide an overview of an area of law and social work practice, such as community care law, or raise questions about particular legislation such as the Public Interest Disclosure Act 1998 and its impact on social work. The third part consists of personal accounts of the practice experience. These provide an insight into the daily dilemmas experienced by social welfare professionals and others. This section is thus concerned with complementing the theoretical analyses of the law in Part I, and the consideration of law in practice contexts in Part II, with the voices of those directly involved as service-users and professionals working in different ways in the social work and social care system.

Our overall aim in bringing together the contributions in this reader has been to enrich the debate surrounding the role of law in modern social work practice by raising questions about the significance, in terms of policy and practice, of the increasing prominence given to the law in social work education and practice. This introduction has aimed to set a context for the arguments in the following chapters rather than outlining a summary of these arguments. These debates are important, the relationship between the law and social work, in the light of recent legislative and organisational developments, being likely to continue to be a key issue in the foreseeable future.

References

Department of Health (2000a) *Framework for the Assessment of Children in Need and their Families*, London, Stationery Office.

Department of Health (2000b) *Assessing Children in Need and their Families: Practice Guidance*, London, Stationery Office.

List of Abbreviations

ADSS	Association of Directors of Social Services
ASW	Approved Social Worker
CCETSW	Central Council for Education and Training in Social Work
CPN	Community psychiatric nurse
CRE	Commission for Racial Equality
DDA	Disability Discrimination Act 1995
DETR	Department for the Environment, Transport and the Regions
DFEE	Department for Education and Employment
DHSS	Department of Health and Social Security
DoH	Department of Health
DRC	Disability Rights Commission
ECHR	European Convention on Human Rights
ECtHR	European Court of Human Rights
FGC	Family group conference
FLR	Family Law Reports
LCD	Lord Chancellor's Department
NACCC	National Association of Child Contact Centres
NHSCCA	The NHS and Community Care Act 1990
NISW	National Institute for Social Work
NSPCC	National Society for the Prevention of Cruelty to Children
OFSTED	Office for Standards in Education
PSI	Policy Studies Institute
REU	Race Equality Unit
SIO	Specific Issues Order
SSI	Social Services Inspectorate
UNCRC	United Nations Convention on the Rights of the Child
YOT	Youth Offending Team

Part I

The Law and Social Work: Key Themes and Issues

1

A Critical Perspective on the Welfare Principle

Stephen Gilmore

Introduction

In *Re T (Wardship: Medical Treatment)* [1997] 1 FLR 502, the Court of Appeal held that it would not be in a child's best interests to have a life-saving liver transplant, despite unanimous medical opinion advocating such treatment. A successful outcome also depended on the child's mother's cooperation, and it was held that it was not in the child's interests to direct his mother to commit herself to a procedure that she opposed. This case is illustrative of the difficult decisions facing the courts in children's cases. Such cases are decided according to the 'welfare principle' in s.1(1) of the Children Act 1989,[1] which is the subject of this chapter. In what follows, I set this provision in its wider social and legal context, examining its historical background and criticisms of the concept. I also advance tentative suggestions for the law's role in decision-making concerning children.

The emergence of the welfare principle

Decisions relating to children have not always been taken on the basis of their welfare. In the early nineteenth century, the law upheld the right of the father to make decisions for his child: 'the father knows far better as a rule what is good for his children than a court of justice can' (Bowen, L.J. in *Re Agar-Ellis* (1883) 24 Ch. D 317, at 338). The father, as the natural guardian of his legitimate child, could enforce his right of custody in the common law courts by issuing a writ of *habeas corpus*, and he would be successful unless the child were in danger of being exposed to 'cruelty or contamination by some exhibition of gross profligacy or corruption' (*R* v. *Greenhill* (1836) 4 Ad and E 624, at 640, per Lord Denman CJ).[2]

A number of societal changes prepared the way for the emergence of the welfare principle – a rise in individualism, affective relationships, companionate marriage (Stone, 1977) and the emergence of a concept of childhood (Aries, 1962). A number of interconnected factors were also influential: a growth in philanthropic and State concern for children (Platt, 1969; Packman, 1975; Maidment, 1984; Parton, 1985, 1991), an increased emphasis on maternal care (Brophy, 1982) and a movement towards more subtle and pervasive forms of State intrusion into the family in the form of 'psy-experts' (Donzelot, 1979). The Court of Chancery introduced the interests of the child as a justification for interfering with the father's rights. (See, for example, *De Manneville* v. *De Manneville* (1804) 10 Ves 54 and *Wellesley* v. *Duke of Beaufort* (1827) 2 Russ. Rep 1. For a general review of the emergence of the welfare principle see Hall, 1972; Bainham, 1998.) By the early 1890s, the welfare of the child had become the 'dominant matter' (see *R* v. *Gyngall* [1893] 2 QB 232 and *Re McGrath* [1893] 1 Ch 143).[3]

The Guardianship of Infants Act 1886 provided that the child's welfare was to be a consideration for the court in custody disputes. The Guardianship of Infants Act 1925 provided that the child's welfare was to be the 'first and paramount' consideration. These developments owed 'more to the fight of women for joint guardianship over their children during marriage than to a child protection philosophy' (Maidment, 1984).

The House of Lords in *J* v. *C* [1970] AC 668, held that the welfare principle was not confined to disputes between parents, but applied equally between parents and third parties. The court held that it was in a Spanish boy's best interests to remain in England with his long-term English foster parents. The words 'first and paramount' were interpreted to mean:

> more than that the child's welfare is to be treated as the top item in a list of items relevant to the matter in question… they connote a process whereby when all the relevant facts, relationships, claims and wishes of parents, risks, choices and other circumstances are taken into account and weighed, the course to be followed will be that which is most in the interest of the child's welfare as that term has now to be understood. That is… the paramount consideration because it rules on or determines the course to be followed. (per Lord MacDermott, at 710–11)

There is recognition here that perceptions of welfare may change over time. An illustration is afforded by *Re M (Child's Upbringing)* [1996] 2 FLR 441, CA, in which, based on facts very similar to those of *J* v. *C* (above), a Zulu boy was returned to his parents in South Africa. The difference may arguably be an increased awareness, in the intervening quarter century, of the importance of a child's cultural heritage. However, an international recognition of children's rights (see below) has brought into sharper focus potential conflicts between children's welfare and certain cultural practices (An-Na'im, 1994; Freeman, 1995).

The welfare principle was strengthened in the Children Act 1989 by the removal of the word 'first'. The principle developed in case law and emerged in statute as a byproduct of a struggle to equalise the position of mothers and fathers in relation to the guardianship of their children. Its scope and meaning were enlarged by judicial interpretation. As Alston comments:

> despite its very limited jurisprudential origins, the principle has come to be known in one form or another to many national legal systems and has important analogues in diverse cultural, religious and other traditions. (Alston, 1994)

Indeed, it has gained an international consensus, most notably, but not exclusively, in art. 3(1) of the United Nations Convention on the Rights of the Child (UNCRC) 1989 which provides:

> In all actions concerning children, whether undertaken by public or private social welfare institutions, courts of law, administrative authorities or legislative bodies, the best interests of the child shall be a primary consideration. (UN General Assembly res 45/118, 1989).

(See generally McGoldrick, 1991; Olsen, 1992; Alston, 1994.)

A comparison of art. 3(1) with the welfare principle reveals that the latter is stronger in its adoption of children's welfare as 'the paramount' as opposed to 'a primary' consideration,[4] although its scope is narrower, being confined to decisions in relation to a child before a court rather than all actions concerning children (Parker, 1994). Indeed, s.1(1) will only apply where the welfare of a child who is the subject of an application[5] is *directly* in issue.

Even in this strongest of forms, the principle commands a broad consensus of support, and it is rare to encounter explicit justifications (Reece, 1996). Thus the pervasive nature of welfare and the consequent difficulty of getting beyond this paradigm must be recognised.[6]

Why welfare?

Herring comments:

> The strength of the welfare principle is that it focuses the court's attention on the person whose voice may be the quietest both literally and metaphorically and who has the least control over whether the issue arrives before the court or in the way it does. The child may also be the person with whom the court is least able to empathise. (Herring, 1999)

Yet a child's wishes and feelings can be important contributions to ascertaining where the child's welfare lies. There is, however, undoubtedly a complex interplay between children's rights and their welfare (Eekelaar, 1994). There are considerable difficulties in recognising children's rights (Smith, 1997a) or giving a voice to children (O'Donovan, 1993; Piper, 1999; Roche, 1999). The danger of the welfare principle is that it may impede a consideration of issues from the child's perspective. Welfare can all too readily be something that is done *to* children.

The welfare principle has important rhetorical and symbolic functions, although Altman (1997) suggests that 'overstating the importance of a child's welfare prevents parents, judges and legislators from systematically undervaluing it'. Nevertheless, it:

> represents an important social and moral value that children, being vulnerable, impressionable and dependent, must be protected from harm and given every opportunity to become successful adults, while at one and the same time it may be used to justify almost anything. (King, 1987)

The nature of welfare decision-making: predictive, value laden and indeterminate

One criticism of the welfare principle is that it affords too wide a discretion to the judge. Whereas most legal decision-making claims to reconstruct past events and apply the law to those events, decision-making in children's cases is 'person oriented not act oriented', involving an evaluation of persons as social beings (Mnookin, 1975). Decisions are consequently predictive rather than simply concerned with the determination of past events (although prediction may of course involve a consideration of past events). A feature of person-orientated, predictive decision-making is its indeterminacy. Taking a relatively uncomplicated example of a custody dispute between parents, Mnookin points out that, to reach a rational decision, one would need to:

1 Specify possible outcomes, which requires considerable information.

2 Ascertain the probability of those alternative outcomes. Here one encounters the difficulty that there are 'numerous competing theories of human behaviour' (Mnookin, 1975). Even if a consensus were possible or desirable, one seems unlikely to be achieved when theorists posit plurality of knowledge and ways of seeing and question claims to know, especially when the claim is about others.

3 Assign values to inform choice. How, for example, is one to choose between a warm interpersonal environment and one which favours self-sacrifice and discipline? Is one to take a long- or a short-term view?

Parker (1994) has pointed out that value judgments are evident at all three of the above stages, and it is not surprising therefore that welfare decisions have been criticised as being subjective or arbitrary. These criticisms must, however, be evaluated in the light of an assessment of the comparative efficiency of discretion as against rule-based adjudication (Schneider, 1992).

The advantage of discretion is its flexibility, but it may make the prediction of decisions difficult and thus encourage litigation. The investigation of children's individual circumstances may cause delay and be costly. Parties may not be given any guidance in advance on how they should conduct themselves, or the opportunity to address issues that were seen as important in the judge's mind when coming to his or her decision (Mnookin, 1975; Elster, 1987). Some writers have argued that, in custody disputes, a primary caretaker rule (or presumption) would cut down decision costs and, looking backwards, would better serve the justice of such cases (Fineman, 1989). A random mechanism, such as flipping a coin, has also been canvassed (Mnookin, 1975; Elster, 1987). The dangers are that this denies the importance of human difference, as well as denying parties a process/forum in which their anger and aspirations can be expressed (Mnookin, 1975; see also Day Sclater and Yates, 1999, for evidence of the importance of these processes). Furthermore, as King points out:

> the paradox that must be confronted is that the more clearly the law defines what factors should be considered and what objectives should be achieved... the more there will be to argue about and the less effective the welfare principle will be as a non-denominational, class-free, apolitical, race- and gender-neutral principle to which everyone may pay lip-service. (King, 1987)

It can be argued that the Children Act 1989 retains a wide discretion while providing a structure to the exercise of discretion by introducing a checklist of factors in s.1(3).

Overcoming indeterminacy – appealing to a consensus

One way of addressing the problem of indeterminacy is to draw on a consensus, particularly on what does not promote children's welfare (Mnookin, 1975). A child's welfare may, for example, be assessed according to how closely his or her upbringing accords with 'the norm'.[7] Reece (1996a) argues that such approaches impede the debate about appropriate lifestyles and may stigmatise children living in 'unusual' families.

It may be necessary, therefore, to question the alleged neutrality of the welfare principle. First, the manner in which children's welfare is promoted is contingent on a vast array of historical and political decisions relating to how we are governed, for example our individualist approach to child-rearing as opposed to a collectivist one, and Parliament's preference for 'significant harm' rather than a simple welfare criterion as a precondition to State intervention to protect children . These choices form the backdrop against which specific welfare decisions are taken. How the welfare of a particular child is viewed may differ considerably depending on whether the decision is taken in a society which considers that family privacy and autonomy should be prized highly and thus sees a minimal role for the State (see, for example, Goldstein *et al*., 1979; cf. Freeman, 1983a) or one that sees a more enlarged and very public role for the State in child-rearing (Parker, 1994).

It would be a mistake, however, to see the State's influence as being confined to its explicit political-juridical decisions. The family is not politically neutral (Olsen, 1985); the State equally governs the structures and roles within the family, some of which may be characterised by marked, and ideologically self-reproducing, inequality (Archard, 1993). We must be careful to note the connection between the underlying structures within our society and our understanding of consensus. We must therefore be vigilant to ask ourselves, 'Whose shared understandings? Whose consensus?' (Okin, 1989).

Looking to child welfare science

Law has looked to 'child welfare science' for guidance on what is likely to promote children's welfare, and this of course has been subject to change over time (for a summary, see Maclean and Eekelaar, 1997). Deferring to child welfare science is, however, not universally admired. Fineman and Opie (1987) argue that social science conclusions are 'thoroughly embedded in the culture and professional practices which produce them' and Fineman comments that:

> What has been lost under the current practice of deferral to the helping professions are legal procedural values such as due process and public decision-making, in addition to the undervaluing of nurturing and caring. (Fineman, 1989)

Is the welfare principle unjust?

A further strand of criticism is that the welfare principle is unjust in its focus solely on the child (Elster, 1987; Reece, 1996). It is arguable that, if we were constructing a principle for the first time, our starting point would be equality (Parker, 1994), and we would then adopt some principles of distributive justice. Elster (1987) suggests that while we would recognise the child's need for special protection, justice would require that small gains in the child's welfare were not achieved at the expense of large losses in parental welfare. There is at the least a case for justice considerations where welfare considerations are evenly balanced (Hall, 1977; Murphy, 1991).

Reece (1996) seeks an explicit justification for the exclusion of adults' interests, concluding that the welfare principle should be abandoned. She identifies and questions a number of assertions commonly advanced to justify it. First, children have a right to have their welfare prioritised. This is sometimes justified by drawing attention to the fact that adults have created children and that self-sacrifice is in the nature of parenting. Reece argues that these justifications are not self-evident, and the argument fails 'because it assumes what is to be justified, namely a special position for children' (Reece, 1996).

Second, it is suggested that children are more vulnerable. Reece identifies the fallacy that protection for children necessarily involves a prioritisation of their welfare over all other considerations.

Third, children must be given the opportunity to become successful adults. Reece views this argument as self-defeating because, broadly speaking, it promotes the future at the expense of the present, and more narrowly, 'if decisions are made which sacrifice adults' interests to children's interests there is little point in becoming a successful adult'. The argument here is put rather too highly. First, even a decision-making criterion that took account of adults' interests might conclude in particular circumstances that those interests were outweighed by a child's interests. Second, there are many differences in the respective lives of children and adults to justify the opposite conclusion that there is a point in becoming a successful adult even if some aspects of that life are subordinated to children's interests.

Rather than abandon the principle, Herring (1999a, 1999b) prefers to reconceptualise it in a way that recognises the child's need to learn mutual respect and social obligation. This would be only to the extent of not demanding excessive sacrifice in return for minor benefits. It seems, however, that this simply alters the paradigm in which conflict will continue, that is, what constitutes an appropriate 'benefit' or 'sacrifice' or what is excessive. I remain unconvinced by a formulation of the welfare principle that fails to take any account of adults' interests and treats adults simply as a means to the promotion of children's welfare.

The recurrent theme in this analysis of the welfare principle is that, in children's cases, law may be abdicating its own distinctive role in ensuring due process, challenging evidence and ensuring justice for the participants in disputes. Indeed, it may suggest that what is required in general is a clearer picture, and mutual appreciation (Murch, 1995), of the respective roles of professionals involved in children's cases.

Notes

1 S.1(1) provides: 'When a court determines any question with respect to – (a) the upbringing of a child; or (b) the administration of a child's property or the application of any income arising from it, the child's welfare shall be the court's paramount consideration.'

2 Thus in *R* v. *De Manneville* (1804) 5 East 221, an 8-month-old baby was retained by the father who had snatched it from the mother's breast, yet in the case of *Shelley* v. *Westbrooke* (1817) Jac. 266, the poet Shelley lost custody of his children because he was an atheist.

3 In this case, for the first time, the court attempted to explain what was meant by welfare. It was 'not to be measured by money alone, nor by physical comfort only. The word welfare must be taken in its widest sense. The moral and religious welfare of the child must be considered as well as its physical well-being, nor can the ties of affection be disregarded' (per Lindley LJ). Maidment (1984) notes that given that scientific interest in children was still in its infancy and practices that did not promote the ties of affection were common, 'where [the judiciary's] beliefs came from and why they were suddenly expressed in 1893 is unanswerable, except that a more sensitive approach to children and their needs was generally evident at the time' (Maidment, 1984).

4 There is a range of formulations in both domestic and international provisions, from treating children's welfare as paramount (for example, s.1 CA 1989; art. 21 UNCRC), to first consideration (s.25(1) Matrimonial Causes Act 1973; s.6 Adoption Act 1976), to simply regarding children's welfare as one consideration (art. 9, 18, 20 UNCRC) (see Parker, 1994 and Alston, 1994). Any discussion may, therefore, need to distinguish between criticisms that are generally applicable and those which are directed to particular formulations of welfare criterion.

5 See *Birmingham City Council* v. *H* (No. 3) [1994] 2 AC 212, and for a comment, see Douglas (1994) and Bainham (1995).

6 As Fineman (1988, p. 36) has pointed out in the context of child custody policy: 'Asserting that a professional or political position conforms to, or is advanced in a manner designed to advance, the best interests of the child has become the rhetorical price of entry into the debate.'

7 See, for example, *C* v. *C (A Minor) (Custody: Appeal)* [1991] 1 FLR 223, CA, in which it was said that, all other things being equal, heterosexual parents rather than homosexual parents were to be preferred.

2

Social Work Values and the Law

Jeremy Roche

Introduction

In this chapter, I explore the relationship between social work values and the law. I argue that there is significant common ground between the values underpinning social work practice and those underpinning the law. These legal values include a respect for the individual, a commitment to formal equality, the ending of prejudice and discrimination, and a concern with procedural fairness. While these are not the only legal values, issues of individual liberty and human rights are increasingly dominating the legal agenda. I argue that there is much in the law, in terms of its rules and procedures, including the law's insistence on certain forms of accountability, that can be supportive of social work, and therefore that the law, and the associated language of rights, should be seen by social work as a critical friend or partner.

In this chapter, I consider the recent history of the relationship between the law and social work before moving on to explore social work values and images of law. I then consider the importance of the language of rights and conclude with a consideration of why law and the language of rights are important to social workers and service-users alike.

Social work and the law

There are three aspects of the social work and law relationship that require some introductory comment. First, the law provided the mandate for social work practice in that it accorded the local authority wide-ranging discretionary powers to intervene and regulate family life, for example to protect children. At the same time, in cases involving children in care, the courts refused on public policy grounds to be drawn into reviewing local authority decision-making: statute having given the local authority powers and duties, it was not for the courts to intervene and usurp the functions of the local authority (*A* v. *Liverpool C.C.* [1982] AC 363). The law was not seen as being important in social work education (Vernon *et al.*, 1990), and 'good practice' did not see the law as a key reference point. In other words, the law provided the authority upon which professional social work activity took place, and within which professional discretion could be exercised, but the law itself and a knowledge of the law were not seen as being integral to social work practice on a day-to-day basis.

Second, in the 1980s and 90s, in part as a result of a series of scandals about the ways in which local authorities discharged their social service functions, the relationship between social work and the law was radically redrawn. Now the law and a knowledge of the law are seen as a fundamental part of good practice. The law has an ever-increasing importance in social work education as well as day-to-day professional practice.

Third, the way in which professional social workers see and understand the law is important to their practice. Many social workers and academic commentators see the law as complicated, lawyers as unsympathetic if not hostile and the courts as an unwelcoming and inappropriate environment for dealing with the complex human problems that lie at the centre of social work practice (King and Trowell, 1992). Furthermore, the courts are in the position of standing in judgment on social work decision-making. It is important to acknowledge that the calling of social work practice to account, which is integral to many cases, can be very unsettling and uncomfortable for the social work professionals involved. From the service-user perspective, however, legal accountability might bring some benefits, for example as a result of making a complaint, having a decision reversed and receiving services that the service-user believed he or she was entitled to in the first place. Some social workers have acquired a competence in operating in the court system and are thus able to advance the interests of service-users.

So the law has come to assume a significance to social work practice that would have been hard to predict in the 1980s. Today, social work students are required to demonstrate their competence in applying the law. The argument of this chapter is that this is not merely a technical activity but an ethical one, an ethical activity framed by disagreements over values both within social work and the law.

Social work values

There are a number of different ways in which social work values are written about in the social work literature. In the Central Council for Education and Training of Social Workers (CCETSW) Revised Rules and

Requirements (1995) the section on 'Values of Social Work' makes it clear that meeting the core competences can only be achieved through the satisfaction of the value requirements. The position is that 'values are integral to rather than separate from competent practice' and that 'practice must be founded on, informed by and capable of being judged against a clear value base'. The 'Values Requirements' include the need for students to 'identify and question their own values and prejudices and their implications for practice' and 'promote people's rights to choice, privacy, confidentiality and protection, while recognising and addressing the complexities of competing rights and demands'. These are self-evidently complex and contradictory tasks; the promotion of the client's right to privacy may, for example, conflict with another client's right to protection, and both may be shaped by the social worker's own values.

Braye and Preston-Shoot (1997) see the value base as being central to social work but also see its definition as open. It might refer to 'a commitment to respect for persons, equal opportunity and meeting needs' or, more radically, to a 'concern with social rights, equality and citizenship'. They are not the only commentators who have identified an uncertainty in the meaning of social work's value base. Banks (1995) has observed that 'values' is 'one of those words that tends to be used rather vaguely and has a variety of different meanings'.

Shardlow (1998), however, takes the argument further. It is not just a question of the openness or vagueness of the word 'values', he argues, but that 'no consensus exists about value questions in social work'. He refers to debates within social work over whether the contract culture empowers clients, the extent to which social work is predicated on a respect for the individual person, the significance of ideology in social work (for example, the impact of feminism on social work knowledge and practice in the 1980s and 90s) and the extent to which social workers should be held responsible when something goes wrong. Shardlow writes:

> These debates are inevitably open-ended where social work itself is intrinsically political, controversial and contested, and where the nature of practice is subject to constant change. (Shardlow, 1998)

The controversial and changing nature of social work's value base is taken up by Smith (1997b), who argues that the application of values is not without difficulty and notes the change in 'values talk' that has taken place, for example the reference to service-users rather than clients. Nonetheless, whatever is the significance of such shifts in language, Smith argues that it is still the case that a respect for persons and self-determination remain central to social work practice. The complexity of the social work task relates in part to how the professional social worker negotiates the tension between these values and the decision-making dilemmas that are integral to social work. Smith's concern is that 'rights are in danger of becoming dislocated from values' such that values become invisible; what is required is a confirmation of the relationship in particular terms. While Smith sees values and rights as conceptually distinct, she also sees in the idea of fundamental human need, itself predicated upon a respect for the person, a positive link in the values–rights relationship. She argues that a renewed commitment to values does not entail ignoring rights and that values and rights are proper partners in the social work project.

So it is possible to identify agreement on three issues. First, there is no dispute that values are central to social work practice. Second, these values are at times contradictory, and in themselves do not resolve the dilemmas inherent in the social work task. Third, there have been significant changes over the past few years, one of which is the increasing importance accorded to law within the education and practice of social workers.

This said, there is almost a note of regret in the writing, as if social work has taken a wrong turning. As the law has come to assume a greater importance in both social work education and practice, with increasing accountability to the courts, some would argue that it is this trend which threatens to undermine good practice. How can social workers get on with their job if they are always having to look over their shoulders? The complaint is that 'defensive practice' is the result of law's new prominence, of the new relationship between the social work profession and the courts. This is, however, only one dimension of the law–social work relationship, one that is constantly subject to change. Before exploring this further, I want to consider some key images of law and the significance of the language of rights.

Images of law

Just as I have argued that there are competing images of social work practice, the same can be argued about the law. There is a debate about the values underpinning social work and how these find expression (or otherwise) in everyday practice; similarly, the law is properly characterised by contest and change. In other words, law is, like social work, a dynamic and contested set of discourses.

There are a number of ways of seeing the law. The law can be viewed as a means by which the socio-economic status quo is maintained and guaranteed. The machinery of justice can be viewed as a charade or a genuine attempt to grapple with complex issues and arrive, however imperfectly, at a reasoned decision. Judges can be seen as disinterested adjudicators of disputes whose only allegiance is to the law or as biased individuals whose decisions reflect their class interests and preferences.

The law can also be seen as a champion of the unprivileged and dispossessed. Within this tradition, contests around the law are part of the struggle for social justice, for example for equal treatment. Williams sees law and the language of rights as playing a part in the fight against discrimination:

> For the historically disempowered, the conferring of rights is symbolic of all the denied aspects of their humanity: rights imply a respect that places one in the referential range of self and others, that elevates one's status from human body to social being. (Williams, 1991)

This progressive imagery of the law is strangely absent from social work. So the law is not just about, for example, the right to property: it also concerns human rights such as the right to liberty and the right to a fair trial. In this sense, the law concerns us all, irrespective of our social identity and location.

When it comes to discussing the meaning of rights, there is no less debate. Positivists argue that the law is simply those rules laid down by the proper law-making procedures. There is thus no necessary moral content to the law – in the past, some legal regimes have sanctioned slavery, others the 'rights of man'. For utilitarian thinkers like Bentham, the question of 'what the law is' is distinct from the question of 'what the law ought to be'. A critique of the law was not to be confused with an accurate account of what *was* the law. Events in the twentieth century, however, rendered this neat distinction problematic. The State in Nazi Germany had all the trappings of the rule of law (referred to as the 'tinsel of legality'), yet unimaginable horrors were committed.

Natural law thinkers such as Fuller and Dworkin argued that unless the law satisfied certain criteria in terms of its content and procedures, it could not properly be called law. While Fuller (1969) was mainly concerned with procedural questions, for example whether the rules of law were known to those who were required to obey them, whether they were comprehensible and whether obedience to them was possible, Dworkin addressed the issues of law's content. Dworkin (1980) argued that, in a democracy, individuals require rights and that the interests of the minority cannot be sacrificed to those of the majority. He then argued that such a belief in the importance of rights requires a respect for persons and a commitment to political equality. It is this commitment to an equality of concern and respect that makes rights so important. While Dworkin does concede there are circumstances in which rights can be overridden, for example because it is necessary in order to uphold another's rights or because the cost of not doing so is excessive, it is only if rights are seen as special that there can be said to be any real constraint on the power of government.

This argument is important because it opens up a number of issues, two of which concern us here. First, it alerts us to debates surrounding State power. When the State proposes new legislation in the field of social care, it often raises controversial issues concerning, for example, a redistribution of resources or new powers to intervene into the private sphere. Second, it serves as a reminder that when we are talking about social work and the law, we are also talking about human relationships in which a commitment to an equality of concern and respect is important. However, what also needs to be made explicit is the idea that the public power of the State may be needed in order to correct a past injustice, to prevent discriminatory and oppressive behaviour in the 'here and now' and, practically and symbolically, to signal that certain forms of behaviour are not acceptable.

All legal systems have a value base. The important question about the law is what are the values upon which the laws are built. Some legal regimes have been built on values that have been explicitly discriminatory, for example the law in Apartheid South Africa or the legal regime in Nazi Germany. In the UK, the law with the passing of the Human Rights Act 1998 has embraced more directly the fundamental freedoms in the European Convention on Human Rights (ECHR). The freedoms contained in the ECHR are those commonly associated with Parliamentary democracies, for example the right to a fair trial and the right to family life, both of which are issues central to social work practice.

The question of rights

According to some, however, rights talk does not progress the interests of the disadvantaged in our society. The Critical Legal Studies movement argues that rights talk is unable to address structural oppression and often serves to depoliticise social issues.

For some feminists, the law and the language of rights is suspect. Smart (1989), while recognising the role that rights rhetoric has played in the history of the women's movement, believes that its potential is 'exhausted' – it may now indeed even make things worse. Feminist critiques of rights analysis include the charge that they are abstract, impersonal, atomistic and induce conflict. Others suggest that rights talk 'obscures male dominance' while its strategic implementation 'reinforces a patriarchal status quo and, in effect, abandons women to their rights' (Kiss, 1997).

Perhaps the most sustained arguments against the language of rights come from those who embrace an ethic of care, influenced by the work of Gilligan, with which they seek to supplement or even supplant the ethic of rights. The ethic of care is based on the idea of connectedness and thus focuses on caring as moral action (see Tronto, 1993; Heckman, 1995). As such, an ethic of care is as concerned with welfare as it is with justice – what is important is the ambiguity and context of the action in question rather than simply the application of abstract legal principles. Thus the proper response to dependency and vulnerability is a rethinking of caring relationships. Sevenhuijsen argues for the recognition of vulnerability to be 'incorporated into the concept of a 'normal' subject in politics'. She observes, however, that:

> Clearer ideas about what constitutes necessary care can be gained by granting those who are the 'object' of care cognitive authority over their needs and giving them the opportunity to express these in a heterogeneous public sphere which allows open and honest debate. (Sevenhuijsen, 1998)

Minow and Shanley (1997) agree with feminist critics of rights theory 'that a political theory inattentive to relationships of care and connection between and among people cannot adequately address many themes and issues facing families'. However, they go on to observe that rights-based views require 'public articulation of the kinds of freedoms that deserve protection and the qualities of human dignity that warrant societal support' and that 'rights articulate relationships among people'.

There are a number of important distinctions to be made about the different ways in which rights are considered. First, at a theoretical level, rights can be a source of protection, allowing one to make claims on others, for example for services, and allowing people to change relationships, via, for example, divorce law. Kiss argues that rights can also be seen as being concerned with mutual obligations:

> There is nothing isolating about a right to vote, to form associations, or to receive free childhood immunisations. And while many rights, like political rights and rights to free expression, do enable people to express conflicts, they also create a framework for social co-operation… Rights define a moral community; having rights means that my interests, aspirations and vulnerabilities matter enough to impose duties on others. (Kiss, 1997)

Kiss (1997) argues that the problem is not so much with rights but with 'the tendency to cast the State in the role of exclusive rights violator': employers, service-users and colleagues can all threaten one's rights. What we need to consider is the effect of rights – whether or not they make a practical and valuable difference to people's lives and the quality of their relationships. It is in the political aspects of rights that the link with social work values becomes most clear cut. How, for example, are we to understand the failure of social work to engage with service-users in the sense of showing respect for them and their choices? Braye and

Preston-Shoot (1998), in their discussion of social work and the law, provide the following instance in which it is social work and its organisational and managerial context, rather than the law, that is undermining of social work values. They write:

> Social Workers attending law workshops have recounted experiences of being instructed not to inform service users of their rights, and of users being charged for services which fall outside the legal mandate to charge. (Braye and Preston-Shoot, 1998)

It is clear from their discussion that they see part of the social work task as having the skill to challenge unfair or illegal policies and procedures. This leaves the question of how social work values are to be translated into practical action and what might the law's role be.

Conclusion

Social work and law are properly characterised as contested and multiple discourses. The value of law and rights resides not in the idea that the law has the answer or that the language of rights makes social conflict disappear – on the contrary, the latter is a key part of making it visible. Rights talk is the language in which differently positioned people can articulate their own definitions of their needs and interests. I would thus argue that law and the language of rights is a necessary but not sufficient condition for good practice. As Banks argues:

> The law does not tell us what we ought to do, just what we can do... most decisions in social work involve a complex interaction of ethical, political, technical and legal issues which are all interconnected. (Banks, 1995)

The law by itself cannot and does not provide a clear guide to action in a whole host of complex circumstances. To argue that it did would be to misrepresent the importance of law. The law is open textured and contested, and when this is considered, alongside the detail of social work decision-making, it is clear that the law cannot and does not provide the answer. Instead, it provides the framework within which social work knowledge is applied.

Nor, it must be conceded, does the law always provide an immediate practical remedy – often, some would say too often, the law lags behind failing to support anti-oppressive practice. Thus the law might at times deny the legitimacy of a claim, for example proscribing discrimination on the basis of age. At other times, however, it is not the law that fails to provide a remedy, but the actions of officials working within the authority of the law that deny the remedy, as in, for example, police inaction over instances of domestic violence. However, because the law can be seen as among other things an expression of the power of the State to meet certain outcomes, and one which can be mobilised to secure a wide range of objectives, it is important not to underestimate its power. Individual decisions of the courts, some existing practices of the legal system and indeed some statutory provision might all be vulnerable to criticism when considered in the context of social work's commitment to respect for persons and self-determination. Yet, like social work itself, the law is the site of contest and debate, and one must not lose sight of the fact that one of the distinctive aspects of modern developments is the deployment of the language of rights by service-users and service-user organisations.

For social work today, the relation between social work values and rights need not be seen in negative terms. This is not to deny that there are court decisions that disadvantage the socially marginal or to claim that recourse should always be had to the courts and lawyers. It is instead to recognise that, for some service-users and professionals, the language of rights is the only means by which their perspective can be heard. The language of care might not allow the object of care to break free of their dependent, being-cared-for status. The language of rights is also about values – not necessarily in the form of a preferred list of 'correct' values but through the recognition of different viewpoints and through the hearing of different and perhaps unfamiliar voices on questions of need and respect.

3

Racism and Social Work Practice

Ratna Dutt

Introduction

The issue of racism in social work is not new. The subject has both been written about and been on the agenda for social service departments, social work practice/practitioners and educators for a considerable period of time. Despite the acknowledgement and recognition of racism in social work and ongoing attempts to address the issue, it is a sad but true fact that social work has not rid itself of racist practice. This chapter considers the extent of racism in social work practice, providing evidence from research and literature to substantiate this claim. The chapter starts with a brief look at the wider context of racism and moves on to address the issue of racism in social work. It then explores the role of law in counteracting racism and identifies some measures that need to be taken to address it.

Wider context

To understand racism in social work practice, it is crucial to understand the wider societal context within which social work and social work practitioners operate. This is because, as Naik (1991) observes, social work 'is systematically related to the social scene. It is a reflection of the forces in society.' This means not only that social work needs to understand the impact of wider societal values on social work knowledge base and individual value systems, but that it cannot control its practice in any area of social work 'without reference to surrounding conditions' (Naik, 1991).

Racism is not a side issue in Britain. If there had been any doubts about this fact, the death of Stephen Lawrence, the black teenager killed by racists on the 22 April 1993, and the subsequent report into the investigation of this murder, should remove any such doubts.

Stephen Lawrence's murder and the subsequent investigation report do two things. First, they refocus our thoughts on the issues of racial abuse, and second, they reinforce the fact of institutional racism. In relation to the former, we know from evidence that the incidence of racial abuse is on the increase. The report on statistics on Race and the Criminal Justice System (Home Office, 1999), for example, shows an increase in the number of incidents 'reported to and recorded by the police from 11,010 in 1993/94 to 13,878 in 1997/98 and 23,049 in 1998/99'. This does not of course tell us anything about the number of actual incidents as many incidents do not get reported to the police, but it does give us a flavour of the problem.

In relation to the latter, the report into the investigation of the death of Stephen Lawrence (Macpherson, 1999) acknowledges the existence of institutional racism in all institutions in this country. The report states:

> we feel it is important at once to state our conclusion that institutional racism, within the terms of its description set out in paragraph 6.34 above, exists both in the Metropolitan Police Service and in other Police services and other institutions countrywide. (Macpherson, 1999)

The report defined institutional racism as:

> The collective failure of an organisation to provide an appropriate and professional service to people because of their colour, culture or ethnic origin. It can be seen or detected in processes, attitudes and behavior which amount to discrimination through unwitting prejudice, ignorance, thoughtlessness and racist stereotyping which disadvantage minority people.

The report states that institutional racism persists:

> because of the failure of the organisation openly and adequately to recognise and address its existence and causes by policy, example and leadership. Without recognition and action to eliminate such racism it can prevail as part of the ethos or culture of the organisation.

The evidence that all major institutions in Britain discriminate against black and minority ethnic people and are institutionally racist is now well documented. (In the context of this chapter, 'black' refers to people of African-Caribbean and Asian descent.) Only a very brief overview of that evidence is highlighted here.

The evidence of institutional racism

According to the Social Exclusion Unit (1998), 'Ethnic minority groups are more likely than the rest of the population to live in poor areas, be unemployed, have low incomes, live in poor housing, have poor health and be victims of crime.'

If we look at poverty first, the fourth national survey of ethnic minorities conducted in 1994 by the Policy Studies Institute found that black people were more likely than white people to experience poverty. The survey found that 84% of Bangladeshi, 82% of Pakistani, 45% of Indian, 41% of African-Caribbean and 39% of African-Asian households had an income that was below half the national average. This was in comparison to white households, for which the percentage was 28 (PSI, 1997).

In relation to unemployment, the survey found that the unemployment rate among Bangladeshi, Pakistani and Caribbean men under retirement age was the highest, at 42%, 38% and 31% respectively. An article in the *Guardian* (2000) states that 'A total of 24% of black people in Spring 1999 were in workless households, compared with 12% for white people.'

When one looks at health research, evidence shows that black and minority ethnic communities experience poorer health and, furthermore, that the infant mortality rate is higher among poorer black communities (Nazroo, 1997; Smaje, 1999).

Finally, in relation to education, evidence clearly points to the fact that black children, particularly those of African-Caribbean origin, are four times more likely to be permanently excluded from school than white children (Kundnani, 1998).

Racism in social work

Unlike the position with other institutions in the UK, the assertion by the Macpherson report that all major institutions in this country are institutionally racist comes as no surprise to social care agencies and social work/care professionals. This is because the existence of racism, both institutional and personal, has been acknowledged by social work for well over two decades, this acknowledgement being well documented (ADSS/CRE, 1978; Dominelli, 1988; Ahmad, 1990; Dutt and Phillips, 1990, 1996; Macdonald, 1991; Jones and Butt, 1995; Dutt and Ferns, 1998).

Although this acknowledgement has led to a change in the policy, practice and curriculum content of social work education and training, it has unfortunately not resulted in equitable social care provision to Britain's black communities.

The evidence

The evidence of institutional racism in social care is highlighted by a recent survey on the future of social care for black communities. The survey concludes:

> There is a growing body of research which examines both the social care needs of black communities and their experience of accessing services. While the research often paints a complex picture, it is the case that two debates appear to dominate. First why do black people often appear to be over-represented in the controlling aspects of social care provision, for example secure units in psychiatric hospitals. Second why do they appear to be under-represented in the supportive aspects of social care provision, for example counselling (Baylies *et al.*, 1993). It is difficult not to conclude from these debates that there continues to be a lack of provision of supportive or appropriate services. (Butt and Box, 1998)

It is not possible here to highlight the evidence of over- and under-representation as it exists in all areas of social work/care, and I will therefore limit my comments to childcare/protection only, highlighting the way in which racism in social work results in black children being over-represented in the care system and under-represented in relation to supportive and preventative services.

Racism in childcare

Before looking at the evidence of over- and under-representation it is, however, worth saying something about research itself and the way in which mainstream research has, in the main, failed adequately to address the experiences of black children. There are numerous examples of the way in which race and racism are marginalised by mainstream research, but in many ways the most striking is *Child Protection: Messages from Research* (DoH, 1995b), not least because this contains the results of research commissioned by the Department of Health (DoH). Concerns about the failure of 'Messages' to address race adequately is aptly described by Butt *et al.*, when they state:

> We have seen the appearance of Child Protection: Messages from Research, a summary of the 17 studies funded by the Department of Health. Messages does raise the issue of race on a number of occasions, at one point acknowledging parental fears about 'external influences on their children's well-being, particularly racial abuse'. (Butt *et al.*, 1998)

Its most striking remark is, however, to assert that 'race is not as salient in these studies as some readers may have liked' (DoH, 1995b).

It is not difficult to conclude that this allows 'Messages' to side-step an important issue. If the demand from recent controversies is 'for more children to be protected more effectively' (DoH, 1995b) can we not expect the evidence to inform us on whether black children have been protected and how effectively (Butt *et al.*, 1998)?

The failure of mainstream research to record the experiences of black children has the effect of marginalising black children and indeed making them invisible. The outcome of this failure, whatever its intent, is racist in nature. The gap in our knowledge created by this failure has fortunately been compensated for by small-scale and local research, which has built up a picture of the experiences of black children. Some of that evidence is provided here.

The issue of over-representation

> Black children and children of mixed parentage have always been over-represented among children in local authority care and in schools for children with emotional and behavioural difficulties. They tend to stay in care longer than white children, a probable indication of weakened family support and consequently, of personal vulnerability. (DoH, 1997b)

The over-representation of black children in the care system has been a consistent feature of research evidence over the past two or more decades (Barn, 1993a; Barn *et al.*, 1997).

Barn, in her 1993 study, found that 'compared with their numbers in the general child population, African-Caribbean and mixed parentage children were over-represented in the care system'. This finding was repeated in the 1997 study, which also found that 'As in other studies, this study showed that the two largest groups of black looked after children were African-Caribbean and mixed parentage' (Barn *et al.*, 1997).

If we look at child protection specifically, the evidence again suggests an over-representation of black, particularly mixed-parentage, children among referrals for physical abuse (Thoburn *et al.*, 1995; Gibbons *et al.*, 1995). An important point to remember in relation to the above evidence is that it points to referrals and allegations of abuse rather than necessarily the extent of abuse.

The issue of under-representation

Under-representation refers to the lack of preventative and support services, which can not only hasten entry into care, but also leave children in a vulnerable position.

In relation to the former, there is evidence to suggest that preventative and supportive services to black children and families are limited, and where they are available, they are not appropriate to their needs. The study by Barn *et al.* (1997), for example, suggests that preventative and supportive work, which is crucial in avoiding the escalation of crisis, is 'particularly under-developed' in work with minority ethnic families. Butt and Box (1998), in their study of family centres and their use by black families, found that 'black communities do not always have access to family centres and rarely access the full range of services that are available.

In relation to children being left in a vulnerable position as a result of inappropriate and misguided practice, the most illustrative examples are of course the death of black children at the hands of their family. The Inquiry reports into the death of Jasmine Beckford (London Borough of Brent, 1985), Tyra Henry (London Borough of Lambeth, 1987) and Sukina Hammond (The Bridge Child Care Consultancy Service, 1991) all highlight the way in which under-reaction by practitioners contributed to the children being left in vulnerable and dangerous family situations.

Another area of under-reaction that leaves black children vulnerable is that of racial abuse and harassment. As Dutt and Phillips note:

> Racial abuse and harassment on the whole receives a 'no-reaction' response from social work professionals. Although many social services departments have developed policies on racial attacks and harassment, there is little evidence to suggest that the issue of racial abuse is a priority for departments or that practice is beginning to take into account the reality of racial abuse. (Dutt and Phillips, 1996)

Yet there is evidence to suggest that racial abuse has a very damaging effect on children both physically and emotionally. This is how a study by Childline on children and racism describes how children feel about being racially bullied and harassed:

> They felt hated and they felt despised. These feelings were exacerbated by the sense that the views embodied in the harassment were widely held. It is extremely difficult to maintain a sense of self-worth against such relentless persecution as the children here described. (Childline, 1996)

Discussion

Black children, like white children, need to be protected from abusive families, and, as with white children, there will always be circumstances that will make it a necessity rather than an option for black children to come into the care system. This does not, however, explain the extent of the over-representation of black children in the care system, nor does it explain how some black children are left in a vulnerable situation, or why supportive services are rarely made available to black families with children. The explanations, I believe, lie in the racial stereotyping of black families, an over-reliance on what is seen to be culturally sensitive practice as well as the inability of practitioners to take on board the reality of racism in work with black families.

Racial and cultural stereotyping, both negative and what appears to be positive, has been shown to work against black children and families. For example, the study by Barn *et al.* (1997) highlighted the way in which stereotyping can lead to over-reaction, which can in turn lead to children being removed from their families. The study quotes the example of a black mother whose children were removed early one morning by four white men, two police officers and two social workers, the mother being handcuffed in the police van. The example leads the researchers to conclude that 'insensitivity and/or "over-reaction" based in racial and cultural stereotype is clearly a factor in the above case'.

The stereotype of aggressive and violent African-Caribbean people in general, and men in particular, is one that is commonly held. It is as likely to be held by social care workers as it is by anyone else in society. In social work practice, this view will probably inform assessments, which in turn are likely to inform intervention. This means that a preconceived view of aggression and violence will colour judgments on, for example, whether abuse has taken place, and will also influence decisions about whether to remove a child from his or her birth family and indeed by what means, as the example by Barn *et al.* quoted above illustrates.

Racial stereotyping, which on the face of it appears positive, can also lead to at best inappropriate, and at worst dangerous, practice. One example is of course the often-quoted case of Tyra Henry, in which social services failed to provide adequate help to Tyra's grandmother to help her look after Tyra. This finally resulted in Tyra moving back to her parents, where she was killed by her father. The report of the public inquiry into the death of Tyra Henry (London Borough of Lambeth, 1987) raises the issue of 'positive' racial stereotyping and states:

> There is… a positive, but nevertheless false, stereotype in white British society of the African-Caribbean mother figure as endlessly resourceful, able to cope in great adversity, essentially unsinkable. We do think that it may have been an unarticulated and unconscious sense that a woman like Beatrice Henry would find a way of coping, no matter what, that underlay the neglect of Area 5 Social Services to make adequate provision for her taking responsibility for Tyra. (London Borough of Lambeth, 1987)

Under-reaction can sometimes be a result of the professional fear of being labelled racist, or of professionals trying to over-compensate for past insensitivity to culture by being overly dependent on culture to explain even abusive behaviour. An example is of a parent trying to explain an injury to a child by saying the injury is the result of physical punishment, and physical punishment is cultural. The problem arises when a professional accepts the cultural explanation as a fact and fails to undertake a proper assessment of the situation that led to a child receiving the serious injury in the first place. It may well be that the situation does not warrant child protection consideration, but that can only be ascertained after a careful assessment of the situation rather than by eager acceptance of cultural explanation.

It is crucial to understand that no culture condones abuse and culture does not ever explain abuse. Culture can, as Dutt and Phillips (DoH, 2000b) acknowledge, explain the context within which abuse takes place, it can explain the values, beliefs or attitudes of the parent at the time when an abusive incident took place, but it cannot provide an explanation for the parent's action in response to those values, beliefs or attitudes.

It is also important to recognise that cultural sensitivity does not mean making generalised conclusions based on individual situation, nor does it mean condoning unacceptable behaviour and action because it is assumed to be cultural. It does, however, mean recognizing that cultures are flexible and dynamic, and will vary according to class, country of origin, age, family history and so on. In the context of racism, it also means professionals acknowledging the way in which their own personal values, beliefs and views are shaped by racism, which can result in them holding negative stereotypical views of black people and their cultures. If practice is to change for the better, professionals will need to look critically at their personal practice as well as challenge the practice of other professionals and their organisations. Professionals should also, as *Working Together* points out:

> guard against myths and stereotypes – both positive and negative – of black and minority ethnic families. Anxiety about being accused of racist practice should not prevent the necessary action being taken to safeguard a child. Careful assessment – based on evidence – of a child's needs, and a family's strengths and weaknesses, understood in the context of the wider social environment, will help to avoid any distorting effect of these influences on professional judgments. (DoH/Home Office/DFEE, 1999)

This means that professionals will need not only to examine personal values and beliefs in practice with black families, but also to take on board wider environmental factors such as poverty and social exclusion and their impact on the lives of black people. Addressing wider environmental factors also means acknowledging and tackling the impact that racial abuse has on children and families.

Racial abuse and harassment can be a feature of the lives of black children in schools, in residential care, in the street and, for some children of dual heritage, in their own homes from white family members. This necessitates social care organisations developing effective policies on how this will be addressed by the organisation and by individual practitioners. Individual practitioners need to ensure that assessments consider the impact of racial abuse on children and families as well as the support needs of families in which racial abuse is a feature. Practice should also address how the racial abuse of children by family members is to be tackled and, in the context of residential care, how residential care is to become 'racial abuse' free.

Role of law in counteracting racism

I now turn to the area of law and the use of law to counteract racism and promote anti-racism. The law has not always acted as an instrument to promote anti-oppressive practice, and some would argue that legal powers and remedies 'do not always empower [social workers] to protect vulnerable people' (Braye and Preston-Shoot, 1992). In relation to black people, it can also be argued that the law (any law) has not necessarily brought about equity and justice. Ahmad states:

> If legislation alone could bring about equality and justice, and amend the discriminatory outcome of social work policies and practices, then it could have been argued that considerations of race, culture, religion and language of black children should have been an integral part of social work practice, since at least 1976. For 1976 was the year of the revitalized Race Relations Act.
>
> 'The Race Relations Act 1976' has not really been able to make the necessary link between the quality of social work for black children and their families and the equality in social work with black children and their families. (Ahmad, 1991)

Having noted this 'caveat', it is important to stress that, given that social work operates 'within a statutory framework, it is important to manage this from an anti-racist perspective', and, furthermore, to acknowledge that 'the law can offer the opportunity to promote good practice' (Dalrymple and Burke, 1995). In relation to work with children and families, the Children Act 1989 and other related documents and Guidance are the place to start, not merely because these form the basis of childcare practice, but more importantly because the Children Act 1989 and its associated documents, such as *Working Together to Safeguard Children* (DoH/Home Office/DFEE, 1999) and the *Framework for the Assessment of Children in Need and Their Families* (DoH, 2000a), include limited but crucial reference to race and culture.

The Children Act 1989, under s.22(5), requires that due consideration be given to a child's racial origin, religious persuasion and cultural and linguistic background. These are clearly crucial aspects of the life of all children and, in relation to black children and families, are 'central to group and individual identity' (DoH, 2000b). In relation to the assessment of a child's identity, for example, Dutt and Phillips suggest that the following be taken into consideration (DoH, 2000b):

- Any difficulties which a child may be having in acquiring a positive racial identity;
- The child's access to lived experience of their culture;
- The religious and spiritual needs of black children and their families;
- The extent to which black children, disabled and non-disabled have the opportunity to learn about and maintain family languages.

Working Together to Safeguard Children makes it clear that:

> The assessment process should maintain a focus on the needs of the individual child. It should always include consideration of the way religious beliefs and cultural traditions in different racial, ethnic and cultural groups influence their values, attitudes and behaviour, and the way in which family and community life is structured and organised. Cultural factors neither explain nor condone acts of omission or commission, which place a child at risk of significant harm. Professionals should be aware of and work with the strengths and support systems available within families, ethnic groups and communities, which can be built upon to help safeguard children and promote their welfare. (DoH/Home Office/DFEE, 1999)

The assessment framework makes the following suggestion for practice:

> In assessing the needs of children, practitioners have to take account of diversity in children, understand its origins and pay careful attention to its impact on a child's development and the interaction with parental responses and wider family and environmental factors.
>
> Use of the Framework requires that children and families' differences must be approached with knowledge and sensitivity in a non-judgemental way. Ignorance can result in stereotyping and in inappropriate or even damaging assumptions being made, resulting in a lack of accuracy and balance in analyzing children's needs. To achieve sensitive and inclusive practice, staff should avoid:
>
> - Using one set of cultural assumptions and stereotypes to understand the child and family's circumstances;

- Insensitivity to racial and cultural variations within groups and between individuals;
- Making unreasoned assumptions without evidence;
- Failing to take account of experiences of any discrimination in an individual's response to public services;
- Failing to take account of the barriers which prevent the social integration of families with disabled members;
- Attaching meaning to information without confirming the interpretation with the child and family members.

> The use of the framework, derived from children's developmental needs and which also takes account of the context in which they are growing up, takes on more significance in relation to children for whom discrimination is likely to be part of their life experience. Such children and their families may suffer subsequent disadvantage and a failure of access to appropriate services. (DoH, 2000a)

The practice guidance (DoH, 2000b) that accompanies the assessment framework also includes a specific chapter on the assessment of black children, so practitioners would be well advised to use both the assessment framework and the practice guidance as tools for practice.

Conclusion

> We must work together to ensure that Children's social services are equally accessible to all children in our society, regardless of their race, religion or culture. Racism must have no place in public services. (John Hutton, Health Minister, 1999)

Britain is a multi-cultural society, a society with a sizeable black population. The black population is younger, and family units with children under 16 are common for black families. In certain parts of the country, black children constitute the majority of the child population, in some forming the majority of the care population. All these factors have an implication for social work, and social work can no longer afford to push these issues to the periphery.

4

Safeguarding and Promoting the Welfare of Children in Need Living with their Families

Jane Aldgate

The Children Act 1989

> The Bill in my view, represents the most comprehensive and far reaching reform of child care law which has come before Parliament in living memory. (Hansard, 6 December 1988, 2nd reading, col.488)

Such claims were made by the Lord Chancellor as the Children Bill passed on its journey through Parliament in 1988 to become the Children Act 1989. It was indeed different from previous legislation in that it provided a unifying framework for most aspects of legislation relating to the care and upbringing of children in England and Wales.

This chapter is concerned with the role of the law in safeguarding and promoting the welfare of children in need and their families, one of the key principles of the Children Act 1989:

> There are unique advantages for children in experiencing normal family life in their own birth family and every effort should be made to preserve the child's home and family links. (DoH, 1989b)

To begin with, it may be helpful to explore just why the Act places such store by keeping children with their families. This principle was founded on a cumulative knowledge of the importance of families to children's sense of identity and the relevance of secure, continuing attachments to children's development and well-being (see, for example, Rutter and Rutter, 1992; Haggerty *et al.*, 1996). It was also founded on research in the

1980s relating to the negative impact of the alternative to growing up in families in the community – growing up in care – which launched young people to premature independence, isolated from their families, with poor health and poor educational attainment (DHSS, 1985). However, the research also reported that the care system could be used positively and creatively to support families in the short term. Many families reiterated to researchers the value of short-term fostering or respite care, the latter a service often used for children with disabilities (DHSS, 1985).

Bearing in mind these research findings, it is equally important to remember that the Children Act's definition of 'family' is deliberately wide in recognition of the part played by significant others where children are not brought up by two birth parents. Indeed, the diversity of family life in England and Wales at the beginning of the twenty-first century is firmly recognised in the Children Act 1989:

> Although some basic needs are universal, there can be a variety of ways of meeting them. Patterns of family life differ according to culture, class and community and these differences should be respected and accepted. There is no one perfect way to bring up children and care must be taken to avoid value judgements and stereotyping. (DoH, 1989b)

The concept of parental responsibility

Nevertheless, all those who are engaged in the upbringing of children have duties and responsibilities for their welfare. The Children Act seeks to recognise these in its concept of parental responsibility:

> The Act uses the phrase parental responsibility to sum up the collection of duties, rights and authority which a parent has in respect of this child. That choice of words emphasises that the duty to care for the child and raise him to moral, physical and emotional health is the fundamental task of parenthood and the only justification for the authority it confers. (DoH, 1989a)

Any rights that parents, or others acting in a parental role, might have under the Children Act flow from their duties towards their children; they are not vested in *a priori* rights that follow from their status as parents. In any contest between the rights of parents and those of children, the children's welfare comes first.

Supporting parents to provide a nurturing environment is a logical consequence of the philosophy of valuing what families mean to children. There are two important points here. First, the extended family and close links with other significant adults may have a part to play in preserving families for children:

> If young people cannot remain at home placement with relatives and friends should be explored before other forms of placement are considered. (DoH, 1989b)

Second, where children are separated from their families, parental responsibility should continue:

> Parents should be expected and enabled to retain their responsibilities and to remain as closely involved as is consistent with their child's welfare, even if that child cannot live at home either temporarily or permanently. (DoH, 1989b)

Thus the parental responsibility of absent parents is not extinguished where children live in reconstituted families. Its continuation is also encouraged when children are looked after by local authorities, even in cases where children are subject to care orders. It is only extinguished by adoption and even here, open adoptions are a possibility.

This retention of responsibility marked a radical change from previous law, which allowed for the assumption of parental rights by the local authority. The Children Act recognises that the birth family holds a symbolic and important place in the lives of individual children, a factor reconfirmed by several recent research studies that elicited the views of children looked after by the local authority (DoH, 2000e). It therefore follows that working with parents is held in the Children Act to be important in order to preserve children's links with their families and promote children's welfare.

Partnership with parents

The context of Children Act thinking warrants some explanation. The importance of working with parents evolved in the mid-1980s, supported by research suggesting that many parents, whose children were in public care prior to the Children Act, had felt that their legitimate interests had been denied and their links with their children had been wittingly or unwittingly severed (DHSS, 1985). Child placement research had also drawn attention to the fact that the outcome for children's welfare was often better when parents participated in the decision-making (Thoburn *et al.*, 1986).

The research recommended a more participatory approach to parents: parents were to be actively involved in decision-making relating to their children (DHSS, 1985). This approach came to be known as working 'in partnership' with parents and was extended to parents in many circumstances, including families who needed preventative help. The rationale for such an approach is summarised in a 1995 guide on working in partnership, issued by the Social Services Inspectorate (SSI):

> The fact that they can take part in decision-making helps build up their self-esteem and encourages adults and children to feel more in control of their lives. Professional practice which reduces a family's sense of powerlessness, and helps them feel and function more competently, is likely to improve the well being of both parents and children. (DoH, 1995a)

With hindsight, the term 'partnership' was perhaps unfortunate, subject to much variation in interpretation and unable to convey the tension that surrounds social work intervention in cases of child maltreatment. It is worthy of note that nowhere in the Children Act does the term 'partnership' appear. 'Participation' might have had a more precise and measurable meaning. However, the intention was clear: to include parents in decision-making concerning their children who were in receipt of child welfare services.

Working in 'partnership' with parents

Much has been written about the nature of partnership with parents within the child welfare system. A key factor is that partnership is a *process* rather than an *event*, the desired outcome being the strengthening of parental responsibility. Some of the key features of successful 'partnership' with parents are:

- a shared commitment to negotiation and actions concerning how best to safeguard and promote children's welfare
- a mutual respect for the other's point of view
- recognising the unequal nature of power between parents and professionals
- recognising that parents have their own needs that should be addressed
- good communication skills on the part of professionals
- the establishment of trust between all parties
- integrity and accountability on the part of both parents and professionals
- shared decision-making
- a joint recognition of constraints on the services offered
- a recognition that partnership is not an end in itself.

It is argued by several recent research studies that the outcomes of working in a participatory manner justify the effort needed to make it work, especially where compulsory action is warranted (see DoH, 2000e).

Balancing children's and parents' needs

Working in 'partnership' with parents is not without its tensions. There will be cases in which social services take compulsory measures to safeguard children because parents are not adequately exercising their responsibility. Issues of partnership may seem rather thin to those on the receiving end of the power of the statutory services at such times.

Reconciling this tension with meeting the needs of children is not new to social workers and others working within the framework of different post-war childcare legislation. Issues concerning children will always require balance and judgment. The Children Act 1989 reflects these two important concepts in its structure and philosophy. The Children Act is clear that it is only in court cases that children's welfare is paramount. Where children are living with their families, a balance has to be struck between the short-term needs of parents and children to ensure that children's welfare is safeguarded and promoted in the long term. There is also the balance between compulsion and voluntariness in any intervention. This applies to children living with their families as much as it does to children in other circumstances away from home.

Additionally, the Children Act introduces another dimension to this balance by creating a continuum between being at home or elsewhere through the inclusion of accommodation as part of family support services. No longer is there the responsibility 'to diminish the need to receive children into care'; instead, voluntary arrangements in the form of accommodation are intended to be seen as part of services to support families.

Weighing the balance between children's long-term needs and parents short-term needs, between voluntary and compulsory action and between children being at home or elsewhere, is part of the real world of decision-making that social workers and other professionals working with children face every day. What the Children Act 1989 does is to provide a framework within which those decisions can be made and carried out. Central to this framework are the intertwining principles of safeguarding and promoting children's welfare.

Safeguarding and promoting the welfare of children in need

Safeguarding and promoting welfare are dealt with differently here compared with previous legislation in several respects. No longer is there a separation of protection from prevention: any intervention at any level within the Children Act has to consider both prevention and protection simultaneously. Exploring the concepts of safeguarding and promoting welfare may help to explain the policy intentions behind their usage.

Within the Children Act 1989, safeguarding has two elements:

- a duty to protect children from child maltreatment
- a duty to prevent the impairment of development.

These demand a knowledge and understanding of child development. The prevention of impairment is only part of what is needed to ensure that children have the chance of developing to an optimal level. Action will be needed on the part of parents and others to ensure that children's welfare is promoted, this, as well as the need to safeguard, being the legal basis for any decision-making and interventions.

Like safeguarding, the promotion of welfare has several elements:

- understanding and helping to provide the necessary building blocks of child development for a particular child
- understanding the importance of children's families to their development
- understanding and helping to ensure that the quality of a child's life will contribute to the outcomes and life chances that a child will have in adult life.

Translated into practice, this means that opportunities should be created to enable children to grow up in circumstances consistent with the provision of safe and effective care. The Children Act seeks to maintain a balance between children's needs and the means by which these needs may be identified and met, recognising the importance of families to children and taking a view, based on previous research, that compulsion should be used judiciously and that the State should, wherever possible, seek to work in partnership with families on a voluntary basis.

Safeguarding children with the Children Act 1989 should not be seen as a separate activity from promoting their welfare: the two concepts are mirror images. However, safeguarding and promoting the welfare of children in practice are bound to create an inherent tension in some circumstances. As early guidance on the Act suggests:

> The Act seeks to protect children both from the harm which can arise from failures or abuse within the family and from the harm which can be caused by unwarranted intervention in their family life. There is a tension between these objectives which the Act seeks to regulate so as to optimise the overall protection provided for children in general. (DoH, 1989a)

The link between safeguarding and promoting welfare and services

The concepts of safeguarding and promoting welfare are linked to the duty of the local authority to provide services for children who might be deemed to be in need of them. 'The provision of services to help maintain the family home is a requirement of the Children Act 1989 [Schedule 2, paras. 8, 9, 10]' (DoH, 1989b).

Part III of the Children Act 1989 is very much concerned with the provision of services, either coordinated by or directly provided by social services departments for all children in need and their families, irrespective of whether they live with their families or elsewhere. For the first time in child welfare legislation in England and Wales, specific services to support children and families are named. These include advice, guidance and counselling, activities, home helps, day care and family centres, and accommodation and financial assistance in certain circumstances. Family centres are especially valued as a non-stigmatising service. They seem to work best when they offer an open-door approach and include parents in decision making about how the services are run (Smith, 1996). Social work in the form of casework, which combines direct counselling and the linking of families to other services, is much valued by children in need and their families (DoH, 2000e).

The widening of the boundaries of the family support services to include accommodation was made in response to the research findings mentioned above (DHSS, 1985). The promise of accommodation as a first resort service has been fulfilled, albeit modestly, in the provision of short-term or respite arrangements. There is strong evidence from at least two studies on family support that children are not harmed by the experience of planned, short-term accommodation provided that they are well prepared and supported throughout the placements by their parents, carers and social workers (Aldgate and Bradley, 1999). Working in partnership with parents simultaneously with the provision of short-term accommodation can help to strengthen their parenting capacity to respond to their children's needs in the longer term. Furthermore, adequate safeguarding can be provided by a combination of short-term accommodation and other support services for the majority of children at risk of significant impairment and for a selected number at risk of significant harm (Aldgate and Bradley, 1999; Thoburn *et al.*, 1999).

The use of full-time accommodation is, however, not as straightforward. On the positive side, families who might previously have faced lengthy court proceedings have benefited by voluntary arrangements. On the negative side, the tension remains concerning the use of accommodation for so many children who need protection and for those youngsters who present challenging behaviour. The evidence from several studies of the coercive use of accommodation as a diversionary tactic to avoid court proceedings would seem to be a misuse of the 'no order' principle and may in a minority of cases have caused a damaging delay in ensuring the safeguarding of children through court action (Packman and Hall, 1998; Hunt *et al.*, 1999; Cleaver, 2000).

It must be stressed that, alongside these Part III services, it is the expectation of the Children Act that children in need will require such other services as health and educational services and those from other agencies or parts of the local authority. Section 27 of the Children Act specifically gives social services the power to call upon other agencies to help them to safeguard and promote the welfare of children in need. Such a step has been made significantly easier since 1996, when the intentions of the Children Act to operate within a multi-agency approach were strengthened by the introduction of Children's Services Plans. By 1999, legislation had also been passed to allow the health and social services to pool their budgets for the benefit of children in need.

Eligibility for services: children in need

In order to receive services from the local authority, children have to be defined as being 'in need'. A child is in need if:

> a) he is unlikely to achieve or maintain, or have the opportunity of achieving or maintaining, a reasonable standard of health or development without the provision for him of services by a local authority;
>
> b) his health or development is likely to be significantly impaired or further impaired without the provision for him of such services;
>
> c) he is disabled. (Children Act 1989, s.17(10))

Accessing services is achieved by processes of assessment, through either a voluntary route of self-referral or referral by professionals under s.17 of the Children Act 1989, or via enquiries to establish whether or not children are at risk of significant harm under s.47. Even families whose children are subject to court orders will continue to need services if their children are placed under care orders and looked after by the local authority, whether the plan is to return them home or to seek alternative permanent families for them. Parents will need services to maintain appropriate contact or to relinquish their children.

Accessing services through s.17 or s.47

The s.17 definition of 'in need' was new within childcare legislation because it related need to the multi-faceted nature of children's development. Furthermore, services to support children and families are inextricably linked to the definition of 'in need'. It was the intention in the Act that the narrow eligibility criteria of *prevention*, present in previous legislation, should be replaced with a broader concept of *family support*. However, as research on the implementation of the Children Act has shown, the concept of family support linked to the definition of 'in need' created a paradox. Services available under the auspices of family support were increased by the Act, but the eligibility for them was variable across the country and tended to be narrowed to include only children for whom the local authority held concerns about child protection or already held responsibility for their welfare, such as accommodated children (Aldgate and Tunstill, 1995).

The emphasis on child protection was hardly surprising since, during the 1980s, social services had been targeted by the media as failing to protect children. Several high-profile cases in the 1980s had added to social services' concerns to ensure that they were seen to be actively identifying child abuse. The Children Act was asking them to do something more than identify abuse – to think about the impact of abuse on children.

So driven were social services by the investigation of suspected child abuse that statutory duties were seen as mainly being concerned with child abuse and children 'in care'. Consequently, a major definitional problem linked to the concept of need arose from this biased interpretation of 'statutory duties', although official guidance on this was clear that such a narrow vision would be illegal under the Children Act:

> The definition of 'need' in the Act is deliberately made to reinforce the emphasis on preventive support and services to families. It has three categories; a reasonable standard of health or development; significant impairment of health or development; and disablement. It would not be acceptable for an authority to exclude any of these three – for example, by confining services to children at risk of significant harm which attracts the duty to investigate under Section 47. (DoH, 1991)

A good example of the confusion arose in relation to disabled children. In a study on the early implementation of the Children Act, just under half of the 102 authorities surveyed in England said that disabled children, as defined by the Act, would not be a group allocated a high priority for services unless a further risk of significant impairment was present in the form of child maltreatment concerns (Aldgate and Tunstill, 1995).

There has also been ongoing confusion over the past nine years about the use of s.47 enquiries, which, in some local authorities, have continued to be seen as an end in themselves, contrary to the clear intentions of the Act:

> The aim of an inquiry should be to establish whether the authority need to exercise any of their powers under the Act with respect to the child (s.47(3)). They may decide that an application should be made to a court, for example for a care or supervision order, or they may decide to offer services to the child or his family under Part III of the Act. (DoH, 1989a)

Even where authorities have made links between s.47 and the provision of Part III services, the continuing emphasis on the identification of child maltreatment has resulted in local authorities continuing to use s.47 enquiries as the main gateway to family support services (Brandon *et al.*, 1999). Even when s.17 assessments are used as such, there has remained a very narrow eligibility criterion in some cases, which has pushed families and social workers to slant the content of their problems to fit a child protection agenda (Aldgate and Tunstill, 1995; Thoburn *et al.*, 1999).

However, the use of s.47 enquiries to safeguard and promote children's welfare offers a route to services that the Act intended should be seen as parallel to s.17 assessments. The difference between s.17 assessments and s.47 enquiries is that the former are voluntarily made but the latter are triggered by an expression of concern on the part of social services or others. Both are the means to the same ends: to safeguard and promote children's welfare and to shift the agenda from the identification of risk to the identification of the impact of that risk on children's development.

This shift from risk to need is very important in signalling a relationship between the identification of the nature of significant harm or impairment and the power to respond to children's needs through Part III services. Not surprisingly, however, the implementation of s.47, as with that of s.17 assessments, has seen a resistance towards making this shift. Brandon *et al.*, for example, noted that in most child protection conferences:

> what appeared to be an unconscious avoidance of discussion of the nature of 'significant harm' to the child in question, in favour of discussion of specific acts of abuse or neglect and categories for registration. (Brandon *et al.*, 1999)

The study by Brandon *et al.* (1999) suggested that, several years into its implementation, child protection conferences still concentrated on measures to counteract specific acts of maltreatment or neglect and tended to produce protection plans that ignored important causes of harm to the child. Domestic violence, for example, was present in nearly half the cases in the study but was rarely mentioned in child protection plans. This was in spite of the DoH's initiative in the mid-1990s to refocus the resources given to children's services away from the identification of risk and towards meeting children's needs through supporting families (DoH, 1995b).

Brandon *et al.*'s research echoes the DoH's refocusing initiative by questioning whether such a heavy-handed approach to formal s.47 enquiries is justified and cost-effective. The researchers claim that a more prominent use of s.17 assessments might have led to an earlier provision of services for children in need, thereby preventing some situations deteriorating into potential significant harm. Additionally, there seemed to be a considerable variation in the use of compulsion in similar cases between different local authorities.

Most importantly, Brandon *et al.* (1999) conclude that there was no obvious differences in outcome after one year between similar cases in which compulsion in the form of placing children on a child protection register was used and those in which it was not. Forty-three per cent of children placed on a child protection register could have been dealt with by voluntary means. The authors conclude that:

> This reduction in workload, costs and stress to all concerned would have been achieved at no cost to the welfare and protection of the children. (Brandon *et al.*, 1999)

Brandon *et al.*'s study, along with several others, suggests that a more discerning approach is needed, placing more emphasis on the matching of children's needs to appropriate services and recognising a wider definition of safeguarding that embraces concerns about children's development (DoH, 2000e).

Other research, reported in 2000, gives cause for optimism that family support services are beginning to be used more broadly for other groups of children in need of services inclusive of a wider definition of safeguarding. These include children with behavioural problems at home and at school, those in families in which there are parental problems such as drug and alcohol misuse and domestic violence, and those whose families are subject to issues of family poverty (Thoburn *et al.*, 1999; Tunstill and Aldgate, 2000).

A framework for assessing children in need and their families

The confusion over who are the children in need of services and the lack of standardisation of definitions of safeguarding and promoting welfare has evolved in individual local authorities to the detriment of the broad eligibility criteria for family support services. Almost nine years after the implementation of the Children Act, the intentions of policy-makers to focus on the development of children as the defining factor that places them 'in need' may at last be realised.

In April 2000, the DoH introduced an assessment framework acknowledging the links between assessment and the provision of services to meet children's needs. In this framework, the contribution to children's welfare of factors in the children themselves, the parents, the wider family and community is seen as important in the assessment of need. The framework recognises the parallel contribution of s.17 and s.47 in the assessment process and firmly moves the identification of risk to the identification of need caused by a wide range of factors. In short, the framework takes a positive, ecological approach to assessment and confirms the value of working in partnership with parents to strengthen their capacities (DoH, 2000a).

The framework also restores the principle that a broad range of services, provided by different agencies, is highly desirable to support children in need and their families. The Children Act always intended that social services should work together with other agencies, such as health and education, to provide services for children in need with 'the whole child' in mind. It remains to be seen whether, in the first decade of the twenty-first century, the aims of safeguarding and promoting the welfare of children 'in need' brought up by their families will actually be attained.

5

Social Work Practice and Accountability

Suzy Braye and Michael Preston-Shoot

Introduction

Accountability is central to social work practice as well as to the organisational contexts in which it takes place. This chapter identifies ways of understanding accountability as a concept and explores contemporary concerns about its effectiveness. The legal framework is presented, along with a consideration of mechanisms that it provides for holding social work to account, concluding with the implications of this analysis for future directions in accountability.

Defining accountability

Accountability is a complex territory, the word itself having multiple meanings in a variety of contexts. Hunt (1998) considers that it is about 'a preparedness to give an explanation or justification to relevant others for one's acts and omissions'. This encapsulates the twin concepts of 'accountability to' – to those on whose authority professionals act – and 'accountability for' – for the range of activity that is open to scrutiny. Leat (1996) points out that accountability is multiple and may be owed to different people for different things, to different people for the same things, and to the same people for different things. Her analysis is helpful in differentiating between forms of accountability: *explanatory accountability*, to those who are owed justification for actions (in the social work context this might include other professionals or the public); *accountability with sanctions*, to those who have power to coerce (for example the courts or employing agencies); and *responsive accountability*, to those who should be consulted but not necessarily be obeyed (perhaps service-users). There are thus distinctions between accountability that is voluntarily accepted and that which can be imposed.

There is room here for tension and conflict. Social work draws its legitimacy not only from the agency within which it is practised, but also from professional values. These require a responsiveness to service-user aspirations, which may run counter to the agency's goals, and a commitment to challenging inequality and oppression, which may be perpetuated by the agency's role. Local authorities are mandated by the local electorate but must answer to central government. Independent organisations owe multiple allegiance to trustees and users as well as to funders of their activities, whether under contract, through charitable donation or, in the case of private companies, as investors.

Lines of accountability may run both vertically, through the hierarchies within and between organisations, and horizontally, between equal parties. The emphasis varies at different levels in an organisation, managers prioritising accountability upward through the hierarchy, in contrast to professionals looking outward to service-users (Lawton, 1998). The delegation of budgets characteristic of new public management has brought an emphasis on financial accountability at levels in organisations at which professional rather than managerial culture would previously have prevailed (Exworthy and Halford, 1998). Professional staff may prioritise accountability for how individuals' needs have been met, whereas managers may be more concerned with achieving equity between groups. Users will be interested in what works, whereas funders may want to know what works quickly.

Challenges to accountability

At the level of definition, it is possible to identify two broad models of accountability – a citizenship model and a consumerist model. Both are seen to be failing in respect of social care provision, to the extent that Hunt (1998) refers to a 'crisis of accountability'. A citizenship model of accountability requires the local authority to account for its management of the political processes of resource allocation between competing interest groups, for the collective benefit. It demands accountability for what is not done as well as for what is, and to those who have a social and moral interest in those decisions, even if they are not direct beneficiaries.

This model has traditionally relied on representative democracy to ensure that the interests of key stakeholders are heard in the debate. Yet with voting turnout in local elections in Britain averaging 40 per cent, and being on occasion as low as 6 per cent, there is a severe deficit in the mandate. In relation to services, monopolistic State bureaucracies have been dismantled, provision increasingly being located in organisations that are not controlled at all by elected bodies (Barnes, 1997). Montero (1998) claims that representative democracy has ceased to be a service to the community but has become the servitude of the community to its representatives, who invert the meaning of the mandate and become owners of power.

Tackling these issues is on central government's agenda for modernising local government (DETR, 1998). A greater accountability may be achieved through participatory democracy, which can encompass a range of activities such as citizens' forums, focus groups and referenda, facilitating the dialogue on which accountability depends. Such participation is not easy to achieve. Barnes (1997) points out that community action and community development have a long history, but have failed to promote dialogue between citizens and the State, perhaps because of the defensiveness of institutionalised power structures and a failure to establish coherent collective agendas. Many people may just not be interested. Nonetheless, New Labour overtly links participatory democracy with accountability and is critical of local authorities' failure in this respect (Blair, 1998).

Participation has long been a defining feature of social work's values, seeking to involve people in individual service provision, strategic planning and management (Braye, 2000), yet such approaches have arguably failed to promote greater accountability, service-users commonly being denied both consultation and explanation, and having no sanctions to impose. Despite its aspiration, social work has no tradition of reaching to its client base for endorsement and legitimation, looking instead to the State for both (Jones, C., 1998).

In contrast, consumerist accountability derives from the belief that the marketplace generates accountability explicitly through participants' status as customers. It emphasises individuals' levels of satisfaction with their own consumption of service, providing mechanisms for representation and redress through complaints procedures and processes of legal challenge to decisions.

The marketisation of welfare has had a number of effects. Differentiation and diversity in the marketplace raise unavoidable problems of accountability. In the 'complicated and almost incomprehensible structures' of commissioner and provider organisations, confusion can reign over who is responsible for what (Jones, C., 1998). Provider agencies may have neither user representation nor electoral influence and may be preoccupied with commercial survival. In voluntary organisations, the traditional broad-based governance of unpaid management committees has been replaced by a need for greater technical expertise, and accountability has developed to purchasers of the agency's services rather than to its trustees (Lewis and Glennerster, 1996). Equally detrimental has been the trend away from voluntary organisations representing and giving 'voice' to marginalised groups, their campaigning and innovatory ethos ceding to the influence of the purchaser.

Associated with the market economy, and bringing its own challenge to accountability, is the rise of managerialism in the public sector, which in its search for economy, efficiency and effectiveness has borrowed substantially from the business techniques of commercial 'for-profit' management. Accountability has become more opaque, and it is unclear whose goals and interests shape the behaviour of managers (Flynn, 1998). Barnes (1997) expresses concern that accountability has become conflated with that key tool of managerialism, performance review, practice being matched to standard measures. This represents the mechanisation of accountability, satisfied by quantified achievement.

Despite the drive to marketisation in social care, consumerist accountability has arguably failed to become established. Haynes (1999) finds that the transfer or sharing of market power with users is undeveloped in social care planning. The users of social work enjoy neither purchasing power nor consumer protection. In any event, the accountability mechanisms accompanying consumerism are largely reactive problem-solving measures rather than genuine recalibrations of power relationships (Braye and Preston-Shoot, 1999).

The crisis in accountability has been further fuelled by the failure of its mechanisms to ensure standards in public sector services. This has two main strands: standards of service and standards of conduct. Local authorities are seen as putting the needs of service providers before those of service-users, and 'the government will not hesitate to intervene directly to secure improvements where services fall below acceptable standards' (Blair, 1998). This may include removing from a local authority the responsibility for providing the service. Substandard services are attributed to a failure of the accountability structure in agencies (Laming, 1998). Renewed attention is focused by the report of the Waterhouse Inquiry (DoH/Welsh Office, 2000) into abuse in children's homes and foster care in North Wales, detailing evidence of children's lives 'grossly poisoned' by a system purporting to care for them.

A further challenge to accountability arises from the sheer complexity of the social issues with which social work engages as well as the 'complex multi-form maze of institutions' (Rhodes, 1997) that constitute the response environment. Accountability is traditionally characterised by functional specialism in the structure of services – health authorities are concerned with health, education departments with education, housing departments with housing and homelessness, social services with vulnerability. These separate domains are accountable for their own service inputs and outputs, which they provide in accordance with their own rationalities but not for the outcome in terms of whole citizens' real lives.

There are barriers here to creative collaboration. Funding frameworks, planning cycles, legal and policy mandates, patterns of professional culture and affiliation and, arguably, the attempt to manage complexity by limiting rather than broadening agency vision all conspire to limit the ability to produce joined-up solutions. Traditional notions of accountability can prevent creative things happening. Agencies act defensively, encouraged by the ethos of managerialism, to protect budgets by acting within narrow interpretations of their remit. Fragmentation and conflict characterise service-users' experience. Some of these concerns may be addressed by the statutory duty of partnership created by the Health Act 1999.

Accountability in law

Social care and social work practice is increasingly being challenged in the courts and through submissions to the Commission for Local Administration (the Ombudsman).

Statutory duties and powers are placed on local authorities, which, in turn, delegate authority to their employees. Employers are therefore liable for the actions of their employees, even when without their knowledge and consent, unless employers have taken all practicable, reasonable steps to prevent such acts. Employees must act within the authority delegated to them (*R* v. *Kirklees MBC, ex parte Daykin* [1996] 3 CL 565). Some social workers may, however, be designated by their local authority to perform certain statutory functions, such as Approved Social Worker (ASW) duties. On these occasions, practitioners carry individual liability for their actions.

Employee accountability must take precedence where the employer's interpretation of the statutory mandate is defensible. If it is not, employees may draw on their accountability to legal, professional and/or service-user mandates. The Public Interest Disclosure Act 1998 offers protection from victimisation for employees disclosing information about criminal offences, failure to comply with legal obligation, miscarriages of justice, danger to the health and safety of individuals or damage to the environment where there has been an attempt to cover up any of these. Its provisions clearly contain the potential to strengthen accountability where it is being obscured.

The powers and duties assigned to local authorities are contained in statute and elaborated through secondary legislation, such as Regulations and Policy Guidance, the latter issued under s.7 of the Local Authority Social Services Act 1970 (LASSA 1970). Practice guidance provides additional advice on the nature, extent and implementation of social work intervention, case law also providing direction. Practitioners have a duty to take reasonable care, for example in the provision of advice (*T (a minor)* v. *Surrey* CC [1994] 4 All ER 577) and supervision (*Vicar of Writtle* v. *Essex CC* [1979] 77 LGR 656). Similarly, standards for decision-making have been prescribed (*R* v. *Devon CC, ex parte Baker* [1995] 1 All ER 72; *R* v. *Barnet LBC, ex parte B* [1994] 1 FLR 592).

Authorities must consult when proposals are still being formulated. The reasons for any proposals must be explained and the people affected given time to make representations, which must be considered. The reasons for any decisions taken should be given, which must themselves be reasonable.

In the search for accountability and quality, there has been a proliferation of statutory guidance (Ward, 1996). The requirements in the Regulations and in the policy guidance issued under s.7 (LASSA 1970) must be followed by the local authority unless there are exceptional circumstances. Judicial reviews have quashed decisions taken in breach of these requirements, for example concerning charges for residential care (*R* v. *Sefton MBC, ex parte Help the Aged and Charlotte Blanchard* [1997] 1 CCLR 57) and arrangements for reviewing community care services (*R* v. *Gloucestershire CC, ex parte Mahfood* [1995] 160 LGR 321). Practice guidance, which is advisory, on for example how need should be assessed, reviews managed and care plans produced, is vulnerable to the impact of resources, even though its importance has been emphasised (*R* v. *Islington LBC, ex parte Rixon* [1996] 32 BMLR 136). The standards and principles outlined by policy and practice guidance have unfortunately not guaranteed good practice in personal encounters between workers and service-users.

Moreover, regulation might ironically undermine good practice if it promotes defensive or procedural practice, or removes a sense of individual responsibility. What is lost then is sensitive and flexible practice, based on informed professional judgment, partnership, and relationships with service-users (Blaug, 1995; Drakeford, 1996; Prins, 1996). Procedure takes precedence over professional knowledge as the legitimation for practice (Marsh and Triseliotis, 1996; Powell, 1998). Asserting professional knowledge and values can bring qualified staff into conflict with their employing agencies (Karban and Frost, 1998).

Managers and practitioners alike appear to be more concerned with how to cope with statutory responsibilities than with the aims of legislation and regulation (Lawler and Hearn, 1997). Policy guidance is more honoured in the breach than in observance, its significance often being unknown to practitioners and managers (Braye and Preston-Shoot, 1999). As a regulator of practice, it is too distant. It does not prevent local authorities disregarding their statutory duties. Indeed, the inability of policy guidance to ensure that local authorities act lawfully has been implied by the confirmation in primary legislation (Community Care (Residential Accommodation) Act 1998) of the judicial review decision against Sefton's unlawful policy on charging for residential care. Judicial review against one authority does not mean, however, that other local authorities will follow suit.

While judicial review can act to enforce policy guidance, to control local authority decision-making and to clarify the law, it is a discretionary remedy with a narrow focus on whether organisations have acted lawfully, rationally and with procedural propriety. When challenging the rationality of decision-making, complainants must prove not only unreasonableness, but also utter unreasonableness. When disputing procedural appropriateness, they must demonstrate a significant breach in the requirements of natural justice (Guthrie, 1998). The courts have proved reluctant to intervene in local authorities' use of discretion, unless clearly exercised unreasonably, because their resources are limited and subject to competing claims, and because they have a limited knowledge of the weight that should be attributed to demands on local authorities (Braye and Preston-Shoot, 1999).

Historically, the courts have also been reluctant to allow local authorities to be challenged in actions for negligence in the performance of statutory duties (*X and Others* v. *Bedfordshire CC* [1995] 3 All ER 353). This protection is, however, being eroded. The courts are recognising that local authorities might be vicariously liable for failures by practitioners to exercise a professional standard of care in giving advice, information or guidance, on which others might be expected to rely. Individual practitioners might additionally be held accountable for their practice (*Barrett* v. *Enfield LBC* [1999] 3 All ER 193; *W and Others* v. *Essex CC and Another* [2000] 2 All ER 237).

The influence of the European Convention on Human Rights and Fundamental Freedoms, and of the Human Rights Act 1998, which integrates this into UK law, can be detected here. The European Commission has heard an application from the children in the Bedfordshire case and declared both the original failure to protect them from inhumane and degrading treatment, and the local authority's subsequent immunity from claims, to be in breach of the Convention. The case will now be heard by the European Court, with a potentially far-reaching impact on the accountability of social services.

The Commission for Local Administration can conduct broader inquiries than judicial review, but it too is a discretionary remedy and a lengthy procedure. Moreover, the Commission cannot require a local authority to alter its decisions or to compensate a complainant for maladministration. Nor can it follow up cases to establish whether its recommendations have been implemented. Nonetheless, Commission reports, which are public documents, do represent unwelcome publicity for hard-pressed authorities.

The law also provides mandates for accountability through the participation of users, carers and other agencies in the planning and provision of services, as well as the availability of safeguards. The effectiveness of these mechanisms has been patchy, and they are located predominantly within a consumerist model of accountability.

Information

A prerequisite for effective accountability is access to information. Statute (Chronically Sick and Disabled Persons Act 1970, Disabled Persons (Services, Consultation and Representation) Act 1986 and Children Act 1989) and related guidance provide the necessary mandate. However, the provision of information raises the likelihood of increased expectations and demand in a context of constrained resources. Unsurprisingly, therefore, service-users are critical of the availability of information (Preston-Shoot, 2000), while social services departments do not routinely have information policies (Fryer, 1998). While the provision for access to information held in personal files potentially promotes accountability, it is hedged with exceptions that constrain its effectiveness (Feintuck and Keenan, 1998).

Involvement and consultation

There are duties to consult with organisations of users and carers in respect of service planning (Disabled Persons (Services, Consultation and Representation) Act 1986 and NHS and Community Care Act 1990). Reference to working in partnership with individual users and families is found extensively in guidance on both the NHS and Community Care Act 1990 and the Children Act 1989. The goal, as identified in practice guidance, is empowerment (DoH, 1991a). Across different user groups and service sectors, however, users and carers express scepticism and cynicism about consultation, doubting whether their experiences will result in fundamental change (Preston-Shoot, 2000). There are examples of systematic consultation about service development and quality of provision, and of individual involvement in assessment and care planning. Many users and carers, however, appear unaware of their entitlements.

Inspection

Guidance (LAC(95)12 and LAC(94)16) and statute (Registered Homes Act 1984, Children Act 1989 and NHS and Community Care Act 1990) outline a framework of duties, powers and responsibilities for registering and inspecting services, for protecting service-users and for maintaining standards. Accountability is to be achieved through consultation with service providers and users concerning the creation and monitoring of standards, open reports and lay involvement in inspections. A long-standing picture has, however, emerged of ineffective inspection procedures (Sinclair and Payne, 1989; SSI, 1993a, 1994a, 1995; Anderson *et al.*, 1998; Wellard, 1999):

- Statutory requirements have not been met.
- Abuse and poor practice have been missed.
- Recommendations have not been adequately enforced.
- Standards have been variable and/or unclear.
- Liaison between inspection units and other parts of the social services departments has been poor.

Gaps in the registration and inspection framework are to be closed (DoH, 1998a), with, for example, the inclusion of small children's homes and domiciliary care services. The independence of inspection and consistency in standards will be enhanced through the creation of regional Commissions for Care Standards. It is difficult to see, however, how the new arrangements will make the system more visible and accessible for service-users. Infrequent inspection visits are unlikely to promote trust between inspectors and service-users or create the relationships necessary to encourage the disclosure of abuse or poor practice. Sadly, they are unlikely to act as deterrents or change organisational cultures where staff feel isolated, powerless or devalued, or where resource constraints distort policy goals and quality standards.

Complaints procedures

Statute (Children Act 1989 and NHS and Community Care Act 1990) provides the framework for service-users to challenge organisational decision-making. Policy Guidance (DoH, 1991c) adds the substance and aims to create a culture in which people can voice concerns and local authorities are held to account.

Ordinarily, service-users must commence any challenge against local authority decision-making and practice through its own complaints procedures (*R* v. *Birmingham CC, ex parte A* (1997) *The Times*, 19 February) because they have a broader investigative scope and provide a speedier remedy. The findings of complaints procedures are, however, not binding on a local authority, although any departure from them must be reasonable (*R* v. *North Yorkshire CC, ex parte Hargreaves* [1997] 1 CCLR 104; *R* v. *Avon CC, ex parte M* [1995] Fam Law 66). Additionally, the regulations that established the detail of complaints procedures have been criticised for their ambiguity (Simons, 1995) and for the areas of local authority practice that are excluded from their remit (Schwehr, 1992).

Research findings (Preston-Shoot, 2000) indicate that service-users are often unaware of the existence of procedures and are anyway deterred from complaining. This reluctance appears to be related to the possibility of adverse consequences – a loss of services and/or relationships with professionals, concern about how the complainant will be perceived and feeling daunted by the procedures (Braye and Preston-Shoot, 1999). It is also related to low expectations about services and to a scepticism that complaints will be taken seriously because of the limited independent element within the procedures.

Inspections (SSI, 1993b, 1994b, 1996) have also revealed problems. These concern variations in the interpretation of the regulations and a lack of follow-up and enforcement. Inspections have found a delay in responding to complaints and a lack of information for service-users. Criteria for decisions have sometimes appeared unclear, and reasons have not uniformly been given for decisions. Staff reactions have been noted to be defensive, while complainants have felt reluctant to complain, fearing a loss of service or a collusion between staff members involved and their line managers.

Future directions

There is now increasing recognition that working with and through other organisations is required and that single agency priorities are unrealistic because no one agency can produce a solution that responds to the complexity of experience. This requires accountability relationships to transcend organisational boundaries and traditional structures.

It is arguably impossible to organise into static structures the complex networks that are needed to address multi-faceted issues that are themselves subject to rapid change and require flexibility of response. It may be more productive to view these networks as complex adaptive systems, seeking to understand their processes of self-organisation, co-evolution and evolving cooperation, and to build accountability mechanisms into these processes. In such a system, there is no hierarchy of authority, no legitimate chain of command and compliance. Rhodes (1997) refers to the need for a new operating code based on persuasion and negotiation, one akin to diplomacy. Hunt (1998) proposes a model of networked accountability, based on a series of checks and balances built into a service system rather than on hierarchical relationships. Such systems involve partnerships and alliances, operating not necessarily in consensus but with reciprocity. Partners have both individual and mutual interests. Accountability is held individually and reciprocally for enabling the satisfaction of individual interests, and is held jointly for the products of the cooperation, which may be in the interests of an external beneficiary. It is more likely to be satisfied by many little accountability relationships than one overarching one.

There are, however, dangers here in the relativity of multiple accountabilities. If social work cannot please everyone, is it sufficient to please someone, and does it matter who that is? There is a risk here of replicating established hierarchies of power and influence. Rhodes (1997) considers that citizen participation in the new networks through which accountability is expressed is even more essential because of the failures of representative democracy. Yet while there is evidence that negotiated and participatory accountability relationships, based on trust and respect, have developed between contracted parties in the mixed welfare economy, the casualty appears to have been accountability to service-users, which has a lower profile in these arrangements (Kumar, 1997).

At a more individual level, practitioners and managers will daily negotiate the legal and ethical minefields of accountable practice. How decisions are made is a key aspect of this negotiation. What factors are weighed in the balance? How are values ascribed to alternative outcomes? Whose views are considered and prioritised? Employing agencies clearly have a claim on social work's accountability but, as Wilmot (1997) argues, in situations where allegiance conflicts with achieving ethical practice in relation to an individual, the moral accountability is to the person rather than to the agency.

New structures are being created in the search for accountability. The Care Standards Bill, introduced in December 1999, creates a General Social Care Council in England and a Care Council for Wales, non-departmental public bodies to promote a high standard of conduct and practice among social care workers and in their training. Suitably qualified workers will be registered. Staff unsuitable to work with vulnerable adults will be listed, as already are those unsuitable to work with children. A National Care Standards Commission will regulate services in England, and in Wales this power will transfer to the National Assembly. Similar bodies will be created in Scotland and Northern Ireland.

There have been long-standing arguments advanced in favour of appointing a Children's Commissioner or Minister (Hodgkin, 1998). These have been strengthened by recommendations from the Waterhouse Inquiry (DoH/Welsh Office, 2000) for such a post to be created, and there are indications that the Welsh Assembly has a strong commitment to achieving this aim (Thompson, 2000).

It will be important to acknowledge and use the new structures being put into place through legislation and policy implementation. The Human Rights Act 1998, the Public Interest Disclosure Act 1998, the Care Standards Bill when enacted and the possibility of a Children's Commissioner all hold the potential to contribute substantially to professional practice. Along with an adherence to professional values, they will help social work to respond with strength and wisdom to the factors that threaten its ability to satisfy the requirements of ethical accountability.

6

Practising Partnership

Leonie Jordan

Introduction

Social workers are told from the outset of their training that they should work in partnership with the adults and children to whom the social services department is providing services. But what does this mean? How would you know that you were working in partnership? Can you always work in partnership? And if not, does it mean that your professional practice would somehow be different? More importantly, why work in partnership with children and their families, and adult service-users? This chapter will raise issues about the principles and values of partnership practice and their influence on the methods of working with families and children.

Partnership in social work practice

Before we examine some of the reasons for working in partnership, let us consider what social workers mean by partnership. At the Family Rights Group, we have asked social workers to define what they mean by partnership – not specifically linked initially to their own practice. In other words, what words would you use to describe partnership? Key words and phrases that they list include trust, openness, giving information, sharing 'the good and bad times', equality, respect, working in the same direction, listening and supporting, making decisions together, sharing responsibility and power.

We then ask them to consider what, among all those words and phrases, describes the relationship that they have with the families and children with whom they work. We begin to see that some words have to go or to be qualified. Equality in terms of status and power does not apply. As the professional who is the gateway to accessing services for the family, you hold power to make decisions that will provide opportunities or close options for families. The family does not feel equal with you and its members are not equal to you: the families see you, the social worker, as powerful. This does not prevent professionals working in partnership with the family, but it means that we need to be aware of how we work. Working in partnership will be the goal you will want to achieve in your professional relations with families. Sometimes, however, you will not be able to work in partnership but you will be taking a partnership approach, and we will examine later some of the barriers to practising partnership.

Definitions of partnership

Partnership is at one end of the continuum of the working relations that social workers make with families and service-users. Involvement is not partnership. Involvement may develop into participation, which is again not partnership. Involvement may be passive, reflecting the family's powerlessness or disagreement with the intervention. If involvement becomes more active, with family members contributing to information-sharing and decision-making, it may become participation. But before a family can be involved or participate, let alone be in partnership with you, the family needs accurate, comprehensible and usable information. Information about entitlements, the legal framework for decision-making and rights is an essential ingredient for beginning to negotiate a working relationship and must always be given, whatever point on the continuum you have established.

Partnership is about a 'redistribution of power from the very powerful (professionals) to the powerless (families and children [and service-users generally]) (Family Rights Group, 1991). Family Rights Group has suggested a definition of partnership as follows:

> respect for one another, rights to information, accountability, competence and value accorded to each individual input. In short, each partner is seen as having something to contribute, power is shared, decisions are made jointly, roles are not only represented but backed by legal and moral rights. (Family Rights Group, 1991)

Is partnership something new to social work?

It is important to remember that partnership practice is not a new tool that social workers are expected to acquire. Instead, it is a method of working that flows from and is consistent with the values and aims of the profession. In the last decade, there has been an increased emphasis in the public sector on effectiveness and value, measuring outcome against input. Are the services that a local authority provides useful to service-users? Do they achieve the intended results? Is there a gap between the intentions of the service providers and the users' experience of the service?

Various analyses of social work practice have sought to identify what enhances effective practice. If the social work task is seen essentially as assisting problem-solving, what methods of intervention are likely to achieve a solution? Task-centred practice is an established method, but what makes this approach even more effective? We have seen a shift from professionals solving problems on behalf of families and trying to impose solutions to working on the basis of consent and cooperation. After much reservation, for example, and resistance by some childcare professionals, it is now standard for parents to be invited to attend a child protection case conference (DoH, 1999). This shift was encouraged because practitioners believed from their own practice experience, informed by research findings, that a 'co-operative working relationship between the helping services and families is essential if the welfare of the child is to be ensured' (DoH, 1995a).

Decision-making relating to which services or supports may assist the service-user is likely to be more accurate if it is based on what the needs of the service-user are. One of the core social work skills is asking about and listening to the wishes and feelings of families and children. Families and carers are an important source of information about the needs of their children and have much to contribute to effective decision-making. What families need to make the best decisions is information about what services are available. This is a key element of the model of family group conferences, in which the task of the professionals is to give families information about the services available to support the family's plan. This practice is also essential to working with vulnerable adults. Practice that empowers users to make their own decisions, and gives them control over what will happen to their family or children, helps to build self-esteem. Building upon their strengths enables families to be more competent in managing adverse circumstances with support rather than being dependent on support.

Partnership practice is consistent with the requirement that the State supports family life and that any intervention into family life is based on necessity in order to protect an individual member, with due process and accountability. The Human Rights Act 1998 will require local authorities as a public authority to ensure 'respect for private and family life' (art. 8 of the European Convention on Human Rights). Social workers exercising power on behalf of the State must practise consistently within the civil rights of individual family members and children. Working in consensus with families complies with this requirement.

The Children Act 1989 is established on the principles of partnership, with the requirements on local authorities to provide information, to consult and to give 'due consideration' to the child's and family's wishes in decision-making. Although the word 'partnership' does not appear in the Act itself, the guidance explicitly confirms the spirit of the Act to work in partnership.

Principles of partnership

Marsh and Fisher (1992), based on practice research in a local authority, have written a thoughtful and practical guide to implementing the concept of partnership in practice. They identify a set of key principles as follows:

- The investigation of the 'problem' or the cause for the referral must be based on the explicit consent of the potential user of the service. If consent is not given, any investigation or enquiries must be to the minimum level consistent with the local authority's statutory responsibilities.
- If the service user has not given their consent to social work involvement, the social worker must obtain a mandate from outside the family. Thus, where there are concerns about whether a child is 'in need' or at risk of 'significant harm' the local authority cannot intervene without permission. Under the Children Act the court is responsible for giving the external mandate, and will make the decision based on evidence to establish 'significant harm'. Unless the child is at immediate risk of harm the court is required to ensure that the parents' views are known directly and taken into account.
- As intervention must be based on the views of all the individuals directly concerned, there must be either joint or individual agreement. Any conflicts between family members with equal authority and the social worker must be resolved by negotiation or by seeking an external mandate.
- Negotiated agreement is fundamental to partnership practice so that the wishes and views of the service user are properly reflected in the type and way in which the service is provided. Service agreements cannot be based on assumptions, misinformation or prejudices about what the user may want or what would be best for them. Such practice is likely to result in deliberate or unwitting individual discriminatory practice and forms of institutional discrimination.
- Service users must have the maximum possible choice in the services offered. They must have accurate information about restrictions on services, time limits and any charges.
- If these principles are consistently applied, the intervention will be based on negotiation and consensus rather than coercion, and the outcomes measured in terms of effectiveness, empowerment and clarity of civil rights. Respect for the service user will be enhanced.

Practice skills for partnerships

Making and sustaining partnerships does not require new or additional skills, but it does require social workers and the other professionals involved with families to reframe how they approach their role. We need to be very clear about what is legally required and what authority we have for our interventions, and to shift away from seeing our role as problem-solving for service-users to that of enabling service-users to make decisions about what is likely to work best for them. We need to be confident about encouraging families to obtain independent advice, to involve other family members if they wish and to use supporters and advocates to assist them in their contact with social services.

First, there must be a shared agreement about what the problem is. What is the specific child development or child health concern? Is the child 'suffering harm', and is the harm 'significant'? To achieve this understanding, we must use ordinary everyday language to identify the problem. Concerns and worries do not convey to the family exactly what is unsatisfactory about the care that the child is getting. Where the family's first language is not English, we must give them the opportunity to have this discussion using skilled interpreters in the language of their choice. If a parent or carer has a sensory impairment, we must ensure that we have agreed a clear communication method. We must use listening as an activity to increase our understanding of the family's viewpoint and wishes.

The goal or goals agreed must be within the user's capacity to achieve with appropriate support. The goals must be explicit and one must be able to determine whether they have been achieved, with the standard by which 'success' will be measured agreed at the outset. If the concern is about the child's development, what targets are set over what time limits based on what measures to determine satisfactory development? How will the family know what is good enough? For this reason, encouraging families to use a supporter or advocate can help the social worker to be more confident that the goal is understood and agreed and that the social worker has actively accounted for the power difference between him or her and the service-user.

Second, the tasks to achieve the goals must be set up as a series of logical steps, tasks being allocated not just to the family, but also to the professionals who are providing the services. Where necessary, alternative ways of carrying out the tasks may need to be agreed. Social workers should aim to make the intervention as short as is practically possible. If longer-term support is required, they should consider agreeing the overall goal and then a series of interim goals as part of the working plan. Tasks are then allocated in stages, based on a review and shared assessment of the progress towards the overall goal. This enables workers to build on the strengths of the family as the problem-solving moves forward.

We need to record with the family the purpose of the intervention, the agreed goal and the tasks to resolve the problem. Recording is useful not only for the service-user, but also for the professional. The record can be used as a means of reviewing progress, building confidence about refining tasks to be more effective and measuring outcomes. Written records using the family's preferred language are just one means of recording agreements. We may want to use tapes, videos, photographs and drawings. The record of the agreement should, however, not become so fixed that we become unresponsive to new circumstances in the family. The agreement must contain the means to review progress and to adapt the tasks. Families want to know what sanctions will be applied to them if they do not carry out their tasks, and, as partners and even as participants, they are entitled to know what sanctions will be imposed on the professionals if they fail to deliver the support services.

Thoburn *et al.*, among others, have examined partnership in child protection practice, one of the areas of social work practice in which a family and child may not necessarily choose to be or remain service-users (Thoburn *et al.*, 1996). They found that 'the inclusion of parents as valued participants' in the case conference was more likely to result in an effective child protection outcome. This was preceded by agency policies and procedures that supported social workers to work to involve families and children. What would this practice look like? The picture to emerge would include:

- a range of information for children and families about the child protection process, information and preferably support to get independent information and support, as well as practical assistance, to help them to attend the conference
- managers giving social workers adequate time to help families to prepare for any preliminary interviews and medical assessments as well as time to prepare for the conference
- all the information from the agencies' investigations, which professionals were attending the conference and the agenda being available some days before the meeting. Families would be supported to make their own report and to have a supporter or advocate attend with them
- the chair being confident about deciding which professionals needed to be present, restricting the number to the essential personnel and also managing the impact of hurtful and devastating information
- parents participating throughout the meeting, consideration being given to how the room was set up, how people were introduced and where people sat
- the chair and the social worker being honest about any limits on the services or conditions.

Even where supportive policies and procedures are in place, there needs to be, however, at the heart of practice, a social worker and manager who believe in partnership values; professionals who believe that parents who ask for help are reasonable parents who have expertise about what they need, and that they are entitled to information about how to get the services and that, where the family's view is different from that of the professionals, they are entitled to have equal representation in any decision-making forum.

Will the service-user and the social worker always be partners?

Marsh and Fisher (1992) describe with clarity the fluid relationship between the service-user and the social worker, showing how a working relationship may shift depending on the consent of the service-user. Where the service-user either does not have the capacity to agree on what the problem is or is unwilling to accept that there is a problem, social workers must be clear about how they derive their authority to intervene. Service-users must give a mandate, and if they do not, the social worker will need to obtain an external mandate either under the legal powers given to the local authority or via a court order. Merely because a child's name is on the child protection register, the social worker does not have the right to intervene against the wishes of the family. The social worker must satisfy a court that it is necessary to intervene to 'safeguard and promote' the child's welfare based on evidence to establish 'significant harm'. The effect of the court order may, however, persuade the family to become involved and thereby enable the social worker to move towards participation even if partnership cannot be achieved.

Conclusion

Aiming to work in partnership has been criticised by some professionals because of concerns that 'it might have a negative impact on the welfare of children' (Thoburn *et al.*, 1996). Not surprisingly, the studies show the opposite, with an improved outcome for children where the main parent is involved. Parents say, in many differing ways, that what they value in their social worker is honesty, reliability, respect and support. No methodology for working in partnership will be welcomed or effective if the social worker does not hold these core values. Contrary to some of the media perceptions of social workers, families generally value the support and assistance. As Thoburn *et al.* (1996) conclude 'partnership, caring and competence are inextricably intertwined'.

7

Risk and Professional Judgment

Nigel Parton

Introduction

The rationale for the development of welfare services was traditionally articulated in terms of meeting a range of social and individual needs, even though there was considerable debate on how needs could be most appropriately defined, conceptualised and operationalised (see, for example, Bradshaw, 1972; Towle, 1973; Doyal and Gough, 1991). It is also the case that the notion of need lies at the heart of much of the legislative framework for contemporary practice in social care, particularly in terms of the Children Act 1989 and the NHS and Community Care Act 1990. It is, however, the argument of this chapter that the idea of need has in many respects been superseded by concerns about risk as the focal rationale for policy and practice in the social care field, including probation. For risk assessment, risk management, the monitoring of risk, risk insurance and risk-taking itself have become key issues for both practitioners and managers, such that notions of risk have increasingly become embedded in organisational rationales and procedures for both the delivery of services and relationships with service-users and other agencies (Parton, 1996; Kemshall *et al.*, 1997).

Estimations about risk have become key in identifying priorities and making judgments about the quality of performance and what should be the central focus of professional activities. Concerns about risk have taken on a strategic significance for rationing services and holding professionals to account in a changing political and economic context where potential need and demand, however defined, are increasing but where there are insufficient resources. An understanding of risk is thus key to providing important insights into the changing nature and role of social work and social care at the start of the new millennium.

At the same time, however, it is important to recognise that while concerns about risk are central and pervasive, the way in which these are considered varies in different areas of practice and is subject to differing interpretations by different stakeholders. In particular, I will suggest there is a major tension between competing policy objectives, especially the tension between the increased emphasis on user empowerment and rights, and the growing demand for professional accountability. While the response of central government, local authorities and other welfare agencies has been to place an increasing emphasis on the importance of monitoring, audit and various management quality control systems – particularly the introduction of more and more detailed procedures and guidance – this has had the potential consequence of reducing the role of welfare practitioners to little more than organisational functionaries. In the process, there is a danger that we fail to recognise the importance of professional judgment as lying at the core of decision-making and thus being key to addressing these tensions in day-to-day practice.

It is noticeable that the literature in social work and social care concerned with risk is of a very recent origin (see in particular Kemshall and Pritchard, 1996, 1997; Alaszewski *et al.*, 1998), most mainstream social work and social policy texts having little or no discussion of it. As Brearley (1982), in the only book that had until recently explicitly discussed the significance of risk for social work, wrote, while 'social work already had a great deal of knowledge and ideas about risk… it may not always be expressed in those terms'. Framing these issues in terms of risk is a very recent phenomenon, and its significance should not be underestimated. While increasingly central, the concept of risk is itself, however, somewhat ambiguous.

The concept of risk

Mary Douglas (1986, 1992) has argued that, as notions of risk have become more central to politics and public policy, the connection of risk with technical calculations of probability has weakened. While it continues to combine a probabilistic measure of the consequences of those events, the concept of risk in terms of public policy is primarily associated with negative outcomes. Definitions of risk are much more associated with hazards, dangers, exposure, harm and loss. The risk that is central for policy debates has now not got much to do with neutral probability calculations. 'The original connection is only indicated by arm-waving in the direction of possible science: the word *risk* now means danger; *high risk* means a lot of danger' (Douglas, 1992, original emphasis). The *Oxford Dictionary*, for example, defines risk as 'a situation involving exposure to danger', while Alaszewski *et al.* (1998), writing specifically in relation to health and welfare, define risk as 'the possibility that a given course of action will not achieve its desired and intended outcome but instead some *undesired* and *undesirable* situation will develop' (emphasis added).

Whereas a high risk originally meant a game in which a throw of the die had a strong possibility of bringing great joy or great pain, the language of risk is now reserved almost exclusively in public policy for talk of undesirable outcomes. While 'danger' would previously have been the right word, '*danger* does not have the aura of science or afford the pretension of a possible precise calculation' (Douglas, 1992, original emphasis). The language of danger, having turned into the language of risk, thus gives the impression of being calculable and scientific – of being predictable.

Douglas (1992), however, argues that this shift is not the major significance of the contemporary concerns with risk: 'The big difference is not the predictive uses of risk, but in its forensic functions.' The concept of risk emerges as a key idea for contemporary times because of its uses as a forensic resource. The more culturally individualised a society becomes, the more significant is the forensic potential of the idea of risk. Its forensic uses have become particularly important in the development of different types of blaming system, and 'the one we are in now is almost ready to treat every death as chargeable to someone's account, every accident as caused by someone's criminal negligence, every sickness a threatened prosecution'.

Thus risk is inherently related to contemporary developments that hold people to account not just for their actions, but also for the *consequences* of their actions, for the idiom of risk not only presupposes ideas of choice and calculation, but also responsibility. Whether or not the risk attitude prevails depends on the degree to which areas of social life are assumed to be fixed, inevitable and influenced by fate, or subject to human agency and control, and hence responsibility. The more we have assumed that areas of life have moved from the former category (fixed, inevitable and subject to fate) to the latter (subject to human agency and control), the more we have taken them from the sphere of the natural and God-given and made them the objects of human choice and responsibility. Thus welfare agencies and practitioners are made to account for their (in)actions when situations or cases in which they have been involved are seen to go wrong.

This is most obviously the case in the areas of child welfare and child protection, but it has increasingly been the case in the areas of mental health, work with older people and criminal justice. It is this culture of 'blame' which has been seen to dominate the policies, procedures and practices of welfare agencies in recent years and which makes it very difficult to envisage and operationalise a notion of risk that is as concerned with developing positives as it is with defending possible negative outcomes, often in the full glare of the media (Franklin and Parton, 1991; Aldridge, 1994; Franklin, 1999). The concern shifts from trying to make the *right* decision to making a *defensible* decision. In the process, the concern is not so much 'risk' as 'safety'.

Safety became the fundamental value of the 1990s, such that passions that were once devoted to the struggle to change the world for the better (or to keep it the same) are now invested in trying to ensure that we are safe (Beck, 1992; Furedi, 1997). Not only can concerns with safety be seen to characterise our contemporary social and political culture, but they can be seen to characterise the contemporary nature of social work and social care policy and practice (Parton, 1996).

What I am suggesting, therefore, is that there are a number of key elements to the idea of risk: it is future orientated; it emphasises calculability, human agency and responsibility; it gives the impression of being predictable and scientific; in public policy and practice, it tends to emphasise the negative consequences of (in)actions; and it fulfils an important series of forensic functions, with their implication for blame allocation and holding people and organisations to account.

The policy and legislative framework

A closer but selective analysis demonstrates how recent changes in legislation and policy have both reflected and underlined the importance of risk for characterising changes in social care. Not surprisingly, the area of childcare is the clearest example, for while the Children Act 1989 has 'the welfare of the child' as its overriding principle and, together with the accompanying guidance, emphasises the importance of negotiation, partnership and supporting families with children in need, thus trying to keep care proceedings and emergency interventions down to a minimum, it is important to recognise that the threshold criteria for formal State intervention has been significantly reframed. The threshold for adjudication in care proceedings, supervision orders and emergency protection orders is 'that the child concerned is suffering, or is likely to suffer significant harm' (s.31(2)). For the first time, such decisions were to include what might or was likely to occur in the *future*, based on the notion of significant harm. The necessity to identify *high risk* was embedded at the centre of the legislation.

This notion of risk was even more explicit in the accompanying guidance for agencies working together for the protection of children (Home Office *et al*., 1991). The focus of the guidance, and a central issue for the legislation itself, was to reconstruct the balance between the protection of children and the protection of the privacy of the family in order to try to maintain public and political confidence following the furore associated with the Cleveland affair (DHSS, 1988) and a series of other high-profile child abuse inquiries in the mid to late 1980s (see Parton, 1991, for a more detailed analysis). What becomes evident is that any reference to child abuse is virtually expunged from the guidance as the focus for all agencies was to become 'protecting children at risk of significant harm'. The term 'risk' played a strategic and central focus for what practitioners should be doing and for trying to make judgments about whether a family was considered safe for a child.

As has been clearly demonstrated, it is the notion of risk that lies not just at the core of attempts to reconstruct policy in the 1980s (the Data Protection Act 1984, for example, referring to 'risk of serious harm'), but also at the core of practical day-to-day professional child protection decision-making (Parton *et al.*, 1997; see also Parsloe, 1999). As a result, current attempts to 'refocus children's services' away from an emphasis on a narrowly defined forensic concern with investigations towards a greater concern for family support for children in need (Parton, 1997) have recognised that, in the current climate in the UK, this is unlikely to happen if the guidance has as its main concern 'risk' to children. Thus the most recent guidance from the DoH has framed the issues in terms of 'the assessment of need' (DoH/Home Office/DFEE, 1999; DoH, 2000a). It is too early to say whether such a strategy will be successful.

What was evident from research earlier in the decade (Aldgate and Tunstill, 1995; Colton *et al.*, 1995; DoH, 1995b) was that even those sections of the Children Act which were concerned with encouraging an emphasis on family support for children in need, particularly s.17 of the Act, were, when operationalised in terms of priorities for allocating cases and scarce resources, framed in terms of risk so that cases defined as serious or high risk were deemed the highest priority. In other words, need itself was ultimately understood and framed in terms of risk. It is also important to note that while a central focus of the recent guidance, reflecting the Children Act 1989, is the assessment of and planning for children in need, the new guidance is entitled *Working Together to Safeguard Children: A Guide to Inter-agency Working to Safeguard and Promote the Welfare of Children* (DoH/Home Office/DFEE, 1999). There is an attempt to try to balance the need to promote the child's welfare, while emphasising the importance of safety.

The Probation Service is another area in which the notion of risk has come to the fore. The Probation Service was traditionally characterised as the rehabilitative arm of the criminal justice system (McWilliams, 1987), concerned primarily with the re-integration of the offender into society. Need operated as the key organising principle, the assessment of offender need and the potential for successful rehabilitation being seen as central tasks for probation officers. Since the late 1970s, however, the prison population has increased, and there has been growing concern about the protection of the public – in a context in which there were insufficient resources and the conditions in prisons were seen as inadequate.

In these circumstances, accurately identifying and classifying the riskiness of offenders – in terms of high and low risk – has the attraction of trying to safely limit the use of custody, and other costly penal measures, while also protecting the public. As Bottoms (1977, 1980) has noted from the late 1970s, there has been an emphasis on a 'bifurcatory' response in penal policy whereby we try to differentiate between 'on the one hand, the so called "really serious offender" for whom very tough measures are typically advocated, and, on the other hand, "the ordinary offender" for whom… we can afford to take a more lenient line' (Bottoms, 1977). These issues have been even more evident in recent years with the growing concerns about violent offenders, especially violent sex offenders.

Within probation, risk has been defined by the legislative concerns of the Criminal Justice Act s.1(2)(b) to protect the public from violent and sexual offenders. The offender was recast as the perpetrator of risk to others. In due course, National Standards (Home Office, 1995), particularly on the preparation of pre-sentence reports, focused assessments on the offender's risk of recidivism and risk of harm status rather than upon the offender's risk of custody status. 'Risk estimates' were not to be 'confined to cases of violent or sexual offences where there is a risk of serious harm to the community' and signalled the desirability of assessing risk in all cases rather than just in those which threaten public safety. In effect, the categorisation of risk in s.1(2)(b) of the Act was to be pervasive (Kemshall, 1998).

This emphasis on risk in the 1991 Act marked the formalisation of a different approach to crime control, which has continued ever since. Garland (1996) has argued that the dominant rationality of crime control before the late 1980s was a social one in which the social regulation of offenders was achieved through their re-integration and normalisation. The problem of crime was constituted as essentially a social welfare one located at the level of the individual and the family in need of help and support. Such problems could be alleviated by welfare delivered through the expertise of the professional. Crime is, however, no longer seen as a problem of individual deviants or families but as a problem of opportunities for criminality and the distribution of crime risks in the population. Crime becomes a problem to be managed in which 'the competent technician has replaced the diagnostic expert, and the knowledge base of the profession has been redrawn and functionalised towards the provision of objective, scientific and effective interventions' (Kemshall, 1998), and in which the assessment and management of risk is key to both the control of crime and the protection of the public.

The relationship and balance between concerns about civil liberties and whether someone is a danger to themselves or to others have also been important issues in mental health policy and legislation throughout the century. They have, however, taken on a new significance over the past 15 years following high-profile public inquiries after the death of a number of people in the community for which it was felt that the mental health services were culpable and that there had been inadequate assessment and management of the risks posed (Shepherd, 1995). For example, the inquiry into the killing of Jonathan Zito by Christopher Clunis (Ritchie *et al*., 1994) paid particular attention to the importance of developing an effective system for identifying risk, especially when patients who had been detained in hospital under the Mental Health Act were discharged into the community under s.117 of the Act. Health authorities and social services authorities already had a duty to provide aftercare for patients who had been detained under s.3 of the Act. The inquiry recommended that procedures under s.117 should be tightened and that authorities should use a new standard form that would not only record details of agreed aftercare plans, but also include, in the case of patients who had been violent, 'an assessment… as to whether the patient's propensity for violence presents any risk to his own health or safety or to the protection of the public' (Ritchie *et al*., 1994).

What these issues point to is that the issue of risk, or rather trying to differentiate between the 'high risk' and the 'low risk', has taken on a new significance over recent years with the growing policy emphasis on community care and trying to be much more differentiated about who should be hospitalised or 'institutionalised'.

Although 'risk' is not a term that figures in the NHS and Community Care Act 1990, and hardly figures in the DoH's associated guidance, there is considerable emphasis on ideas of personal choice, independence, individuality, dignity and empowerment. While a primary motivation of the community care changes was directly financial, shifting the responsibility for assessment and management to local authorities, it is also the case that there was an explicit attempt to increase personal choice, improve independence and enhance the empowerment of users.

Clearly, however, managers and practitioners are attempting to balance a whole variety of potentially conflicting demands from users, carers, the wider community and other agencies in a context of both an increasingly older, infirm and isolated population and, crucially, in an ever-tighter financial context. As a result, as we previously noted with childcare, the notion of need that the legislation has as its core, particularly in the assessment process, is replaced by risk. As Lewis *et al*. (1995) have demonstrated from their research on the new community care provisions, 'it seems inevitable that in the main only need defined as high risk will receive service'.

What these examples from different areas of policy demonstrate is that the nature of risk varies in different contexts and that different areas of policy and practice have different concerns and priorities. Within policy, it is possible to identify three objectives: the concern to protect society against the dangers posed by some individuals; the concern to protect vulnerable individuals from harm or danger, sometimes by themselves; and the concern to integrate potentially vulnerable individuals within ordinary social relations and give them the same opportunities as others – often referred to as normalisation (Alaszewski *et al.*, 1998). The clearest example of the first objective is perhaps the area of criminal justice, of the second child protection and of the third services for people with learning disabilities. Clearly, however, it would be inappropriate to see these areas as mutually exclusive as, in each area of policy, it is possible to see each objective being simultaneously at play.

In the area of criminal justice, for example, while the priority may be protecting the public or society, we should not under-emphasise the need to ensure that attempts are made to protect vulnerable individuals, for example women and children in cases of domestic violence, or that of seriously trying to integrate criminals back into society. Similarly, in the area of learning disability while the priority may be trying to integrate or normalise individuals into society, this should not be at the cost of putting individuals in situations where they are vulnerable or a danger to others. These are clearly complex issues, and while there has been a proliferation of guidance and procedures, they are not ones that are easily resolvable in any clear-cut or categorical way: each situation needs to be addressed in its own terms and may change at any time.

Thus while legislation may give the impression of being concrete and straightforward, this is not the case. In practice, the way in which these potentially contradictory objectives are managed on a day-to-day basis is delegated to welfare professionals who have to exercise considerable judgment on what to do, how to do it and how to interpret their legislative mandates and the various procedures and guidances that inform their practice. Decision-making and professional interventions cannot operate as if there were a ready-made formula that simply has to be operationalised and based upon the accumulation of hard evidence. At the same time, however, welfare professionals are increasingly being made accountable for their actions and inactions. When things are seen to 'go wrong', practitioners are very aware that their decisions and actions can be subject to detailed interrogation, often in the glare of the media. Of course, while decisions on a day-to-day basis have to be made on the basis of judgments about the future – they are prospective – interrogations of practice are invariably retrospective and hence are informed by the 'wisdom of hindsight'. Professional judgement and decision-making is inherently uncertain. This key issue is unfortunately often forgotten both in policy debates and when professionals are called to account.

Conclusion

It is perhaps not surprising, therefore, if the way in which risk is considered and operationalised organisationally and practically is often defensive and concerned with safety. In terms of the safety of not simply the individual or the public, but the organisation and professionals themselves – it is negative, narrow and uncreative. However, as I argued at the outset, the original notion of risk was concerned with positives as well as negatives, and with trying to maximise potential as well as avoid hazard and danger. In contemporary society more widely, it is still very much accepted that dealing with and accepting risk brings great excitement and adventure not just in terms of gambling, but also in driving fast and a whole range of sports such as mountain-climbing, flying and so on. The challenges posed by taking risks, as opposed to opting for safety, are similarly seen to lie at the heart of entrepreneurship, a vibrant economy and a stimulating culture. Yet discussions of risk in social care are dominated by emotions of fear, an undermining of trust and the wish to control. This is clearly not always the case, and, as I have suggested, there are examples of where the primary concern is widening choice, increasing empowerment and increasing inclusion and diversity. It is perhaps to these examples and areas of practice that we need to look in order to move forward.

However, in the current context of practice, which we might characterise as a 'blame' culture (Parton, 1996), it is not perhaps surprising if it is this negative interpretation of risk that has come to dominate. But this is clearly not adequate. It is important that we develop an understanding, conceptualisation and operation of risk that seriously attempts a more rounded, holistic approach and is much closer to the way in which it was originally intended. Issues surrounding organisational culture, trust and mutual support are key, and the role of the media and the political climate in which practice is carried out clearly cannot be underestimated. I do feel, however, that a part of the problem and the solution is to recognise the way in which risk and uncertainty are closely interrelated.

While it is often assumed in our approach to risk that social life can be subjected to prediction and control, and that rational systems of accountability should be constructed in case things go wrong, many areas of social care practice are, in fact, much better characterised in terms of uncertainty. It is very important to distinguish between the predictable and the unpredictable, or more accurately the calculable and the non-calculable. While the former may be appropriately referred to as 'risk', the latter is, I would suggest, more appropriately understood as 'uncertainty'. It is my contention that the vast majority of social work and social care practice that is currently referred to as the assessment and management of risk is primarily concerned with the assessment and management of uncertainty. Many of the risks that practitioners are expected to assess or manage are 'virtual' in that they can neither be directly sensed (touched, heard, seen or smelt) nor subject to scientific evaluation in any quantified or probabilistic sense.

Unfortunately, our obsession with the 'scientised', calculative notions of risk has failed to recognise that much of our experience is better characterised as uncertainty. As a consequence, systems, procedures and organisational frameworks operate as if issues are resolvable in a realist, scientific or probabilistic sense. It might be much better if we recognised that much practice operates on the basis of making situated professional judgments based upon hunch, experience and 'making sense' of what is going on (Parton and O'Byrne, 2000). In recognising that risk or, as I prefer to call it, uncertainty lies at the core of practice, we underline the importance of professional judgment and the nature of the values that inform it.

Part II

Overview of Key Areas of Law and Practice

8

Human Rights and Social Services

Belinda Schwehr

Introduction

This chapter considers the impact that the Human Rights Act 1998 will probably have on social services assessment, care-planning and commissioning. We look at the European Convention on Human Rights (ECHR) and how the Human Rights Act, which incorporates the provisions of the ECHR, should work to bring about a radical change of culture in social services. The focus then turns to an informed prediction of the main aspects of social services provision that are likely to be affected by the new legal rights and remedies under the Human Rights Act. Next, we look at a number of practice issues, such as the impact of the Act on 'best value' obligations of the social services department, the question of standards and regimes in residential care, discrimination issues and adult protection. We conclude by considering whether or not the Human Rights Act is a good or a bad thing for service-users and the caring profession.

The European Convention on Human Rights

The UK government became a signatory to the ECHR in 1951. People in the UK were able to present a human rights problem to the court in Strasbourg, but only after first using the full court process in the UK. In practice, many factors have conspired to make human rights litigation a rarity. It is not taught as a mainstream part of legal education so high street solicitors are unfamiliar with it. The financial compensation awarded by the European Court of Human Rights (ECtHR) tends to be quite low, and it takes time, determination and private means or legal aid to get as far as Strasbourg.

The rights covered by the Convention are those associated with liberalism, such as rights to liberty, freedom of speech and thought, and assembly, as would be expected when one recalls that they were composed over half a century ago in the wake of the Second World War. The rights and freedoms conferred are expressed to be against the State.

The Human Rights Act 1998

In 1998 the Human Rights Act was passed and brought 'rights home' by 'incorporating' the ECHR into domestic law. As a result, human rights are now embedded into the very fabric of UK society and are binding not just upon the State, but also on every public authority as defined in the Act. It should be noted, however, that the Act stopped short of full incorporation. It makes ECHR principles *nearly* all-pervasive but allows for the unambiguous intention of Parliament (in the form of clear statutory words) to override human rights in the name of 'sovereignty'.

Section 1 of the Human Rights Act 1998 sets out the particular rights and freedoms (the 'Convention rights') that the Act adopts, the most important ones being arts. 2–12 and 14 of the ECHR and arts. 1–3 of what is called the First Protocol. Section 3(1) provides 'so far as it is possible to do so, primary legislation and secondary legislation must be read and given effect in a way which is compatible with Convention rights'.

Section 6 makes it 'unlawful for a public authority to act in a way which is incompatible with one or more of the Convention rights'. The section does not, however, apply where the incompatible conduct is positively required by the clear wording of primary legislation or by secondary legislation (see ss.6(2)(a) and (b)). In such a case, the High Court may only issue a declaration of incompatibility between the UK law and the Act, and the government is only then required to *consider* changing the law (and not with any necessary retrospective effect).

Only 'public authorities' are able to be challenged under the Act, but the definition is stretched in order to cover 'any person, certain of whose functions are public in nature.' The courts have yet to decide what that means. Under the Human Rights Act, it will not be possible for anyone to take 'the State' to court, as can be done in Strasbourg, to allege that it has failed to legislate to protect a Convention right in dealings between individuals, because art. 1 of the ECHR has not been incorporated into the UK Act's scheduled rights or freedoms.

Rights unlimited?

Most of the rights and freedoms contained in the articles incorporated into the Act contain express restrictions that require any court adjudicating upon the legality of action or decision to balance the interests of society with the interests of the complainant. The rights can be seen as those which are *absolute* (for example, no torture), those which are *limited* (for example art. 5, the right to liberty, limited in certain defined circumstances expressly set out) and those which are *qualified* (arts. 8–11, qualified according to the balance to be struck between the individual's and the wider public's competing interests). In relation to limited and qualified rights, States have been given fairly wide margins of appreciation in the past by the ECtHR, for fear, it is thought, of losing the support of those States. So long as an interference with the right is lawful, serves a legitimate purpose, is necessary in a democratic society and is not discriminatory, the action has generally been upheld – this is 'proportionality' in its widest context.

It is thought probable that courts are going to be anxious to continue to give full weight to the decision of Parliament to leave a wide range of decision-making to the discretion of public bodies, because of the extreme sensitivity of the function concerned (for example, child protection work) or the range of issues, for example, resource allocation issues, that has to be taken into consideration, inevitably beyond a judge's experience and understanding.

After the Act is brought into force, discretionary decisions of public bodies will have to be assessed in accordance with the principles of proportionality and non-discrimination in order to ascertain whether there has been a breach of any Convention right made part of UK law. This is because the Act requires all courts and tribunals to 'take account of' European Commission and Court jurisprudence where these principles are fundamental.

Claims of unlawful action are restricted to 'victims' – a concept from ECHR law that has been directly imported into the UK's regime by ss. 7(7) and 7(3). In ECHR terms, a victim is 'any person, non-governmental organisation or group of individuals' *directly affected* by the act in question. Case law reveals that the concept of being directly affected covers people who are closely or personally related to those who were affected, as well as people who are potentially affected by a *proposed* action. This means that the executors of a deceased person, or the carers, for example, of a disabled person, could bring a claim in their own right, based on the wrong to the other person having affected him or her.

The impact of the Act

This Act brings about three radical changes to the culture of decision-making in social services. First, it makes discretionary policies and decisions challengeable on the basis of an alleged breach of human rights (financial compensation might be available) as well as providing a new ground for judicial review – additional to the traditional ones of unreasonableness, illegality or procedural unfairness.

Second, the Act signals a new test for judicial intervention – that of 'proportionality'. From now on, the courts will be using a magnifying glass when scrutinising the decision-making process. Justification for council policy changes (or even an adherence to policy) will be required (rather than just lip-service being paid to the idea of accountability); justification that a judge agrees can be seen as proportionate to the social aim and the costs and benefits to individuals and communities concerned.

Third, the Act requires positive action from local authorities, in certain circumstances, in furtherance of people's human rights. Just as proportionate reasons will be required for action, so will they be for *inactivity* – and that means that budgetary control can no longer be the sole determinant of an authority's decisions.

It is important, too, to remember that if an authority is challenged over a matter in respect of which it believes that it has the defence of incompatible statutory authority (a provision that can only be read in such a way as to oblige the authority to act in the manner alleged to be in breach), it cannot make the claim go away quietly by *agreeing* a declaration of incompatibility – only the High Court can grant such an order. For this reason, if no other, local authority staff's and lawyers' efforts will need to turn to scrutinising the legislative framework under which functions are exercised much more closely.

Two predictions

Commentators expect the Act to make a difference in many areas, but two in particular in the social services field deserve attention: the impact of recording in assessment, and vulnerability to liability in negligence as well as in human rights breaches.

Recording within the assessment process

Social services functions affect people's private and family lives, hopefully for the better, but sometimes by way of intervention that is unwelcome, either in principle or because of the particular outcome of the assessment. Article 8 protects the right to respect for these areas of life and for correspondence. This right stops short of an absolute right to privacy as art. 8 allows for potentially incompatible actions or decisions if certain justifications apply, such as the protection of health or morals, the prevention of disorder or the protection of rights and freedoms of others.

These areas of justification will, if challenged, need to be established to be in play, by way of evidence from a social services authority. In addition, the action or decision must be proportionate, as described above, otherwise it will be in breach even if the authority was well motivated. Thus much greater attention to balancing risks and the benefits of intervention in a particular way or at a particular level will be required, and that balancing must, by way of reasoned documentation, be *seen* to be done if efficient use of officer time is to be achieved.

Liability issues

Local authorities have enjoyed immunity from legal action for some years now where harm was alleged to have arisen in the course of decision-making required by their statutory duties. This was because the courts could see that often impossible decisions about priorities have to be made and that authorities would be spending a ridiculous amount of officer time and money fending off litigation if challenges to high-level policy decisions were possible. However, the European Court has recently decided that blanket immunity for certain types of public authorities breaches art. 6 – because access to a court is an essential aspect of a fair determination, and immunity from action effectively completely denies access to a court. Hence it is possible that negligence actions against local authorities will re-emerge as a common occurrence – not just in relation to injuring a client in the day-to-day delivery of a service, but also in terms of much more policy-orientated decisions, such as tightening eligibility criteria, wrongly assessing people against criteria, cutting people's care packages, closing down services and so on.

Practice issues

The Human Rights Act 1998 gives rise to a number of practice issues, one overarching one being that of procedural fairness and reasoned decision-making. Article 6 provides for a fair determination of people's 'civil' rights, and once somebody has qualified for a service under discretionary criteria, they probably *have* a civil right to the service. Failure to provide the service, or a cut to it, without a lawful re-assessment, may amount to a breach of human rights if the decision, in procedural terms, has been taken in an unfair way. Thus a chance to make representations and proper reasons for the decision would have to be given, which would mean that many more people would be given the *evidence* on which to bring a judicial review under UK law, for the actual enforcement of their entitlement to services.

Best value and 'fiduciary' duties

Will the current local authority tendency to prefer the most cost-effective means of meeting people's needs have to be loosened in the light of rights to respect for home, family life and privacy under art. 8 and the general doctrine of proportionality? It is at the moment appropriate to choose the cheapest means of meeting a need as long as one has taken into account the possibility that some other way might provide better (or 'best') value. Under the Human Rights Act, enabling people to stay together in a family unit and receive services at home, or have a more limited number of carers providing personal care, may become more important and, at the very least, shift the balance of decision-making away from *generally applicable* policies to a closer consideration of individual cases and wishes, rather than just meeting the local authority criteria for 'needs'.

Relationships with contractors and partners

Contracting officers may have to take on board that if the private sector is contracted to contribute towards the provision of a service, on behalf of the authority, or to provide a service under public sector typical statutory duties to 'make arrangements' for the provision of a service, the content of the service might be challengeable on human rights grounds (for example, art. 3 and art. 8 principles). Thus conditions and standard-setting will become more important. While indemnities are traditionally sought when social services departments contract with providers, it is not possible to seek an indemnity against the authority's *own* breach of human rights in failing to exercise its contracting or grant-monitoring functions in order to *prevent* providers actively or inadvertently breaching users' rights.

Inhuman treatment: standards

Is it inhuman or degrading to be tagged electronically if one has dementia and has lost the capacity to consent to being tagged? What about restraint and bed-guards, and locks beyond the capability of residents? The ECtHR has given medical professionals a very wide margin of appreciation when considering allegedly 'therapeutic' regimes. Interference is allowed under art. 8(2) for the protection of health. On the other hand, the ECtHR has more recently said that degrading treatment includes acts of a serious nature designed to interfere with the dignity of a person; there is no justification available for a breach.

Might aspects of the regime in a care home amount to inhuman treatment under art. 3? Can factors such as room size, an authority's insistence that 'standard' accommodation means sharing a room, and the provision of *only* communal meals in a home be consistent with art. 8 rights? The economic well-being of the local government area concerned is a factor that can be cited by way of justification, but only if it is proportionate.

Adult protection

There must be a line beyond which intervention for the purposes of the protection of people lacking capacity becomes unlawful because of excessive or 'inhuman or degrading treatment', or an unjustified interference with the person's right to liberty. Thus even if social work professionals enjoy a 'best interests' power by virtue of their statutory role (an issue that is not yet clear in UK law), it cannot justify disproportionate treatment.

As for guardianship, requiring a person to live somewhere is a plain interference with patients' right to respect for their private lives. Stopping someone being visited by a member of their family, under the 'best interests' implied power, or physically taking someone to residential care seem equally clear cut. Indeed, the power to obtain the patient's forcible return to the chosen residence might be seen to amount to *detention*, although not in the ordinary physical sense of the word.

However, the right merely to 'respect' under art. 8 and the express qualifications to that right give rise to a potential justification for interfering with the human rights of those lacking mental capacity. Those exceptions to the right relate to legitimate social aims necessary in a democratic society, as long as they are in accordance with the law. The right to freedom of association is similarly qualified, and the right to liberty is expressly qualified in the case of persons of unsound mind.

Discrimination

Article 14 of the ECHR, although it appears to contain an absolute ban on discrimination, is only capable of being successfully established if the less favourable treatment is not regarded as justified. An age cut-off for certain services, or a lower cost ceiling for the over-65s, could potentially constitute discrimination in the amount of respect accorded to the private or family lives of the elderly. Alternatively, the latter may be able to be justified by reference to the *greater* cost of providing for supervision or stimulation that a learning disabled or younger physically disabled person is seen to require before his or her quality of life is acceptable.

Conclusion

It is quite clear that use of the Human Rights Act will both lengthen and enrich negotiations and litigation between public authorities and service-users. Social services can expect to be one of the main targets for far-reaching claims. This will make an awareness of law and legal reasoning even more important.

Before the incorporation of European human rights into UK law, judicial reviews and complaints about adults' social services were often dealt with by way of a compromise in order to avoid a further loss of management time, as well as to keep the local authority out of the courts and dubious policies out of the law reports. Disputes in the public law sphere were not settled by payments of *money* because unreasonable or unlawful action did not normally lead to a financial compensation award from the courts. As from 2 October 2000, however, citizens have been able to add a challenge based on an alleged breach of human rights to almost any form of dispute with a local authority. Since a breach of human rights can lead to an award in damages, claims can now legitimately be *settled* by way of the payment of money. Thus lawyers serving the community will have a much greater incentive to know about public law and human rights law.

If, however, a social services department is abiding by its UK statutory duties and already exercising discretionary functions lawfully and reasonably, it need not particularly fear a great onslaught of litigation. The problem is more a strategic one for such authorities – how to galvanise staff sufficiently into changing their practice (in order to enable the authority to prove that it acted proportionately) without overly alarming care staff and turning social work into defensive damage limitation. The Human Rights Act provides an opportunity for social care professionals, as well as an extra layer of responsibility. The law can empower both clients and professionals and can provide a bulwark against the worst excesses of managerialism run wild.

9

Family Breakdown

Lesley-Anne Cull

Divorce and separation can be an emotionally overwhelming process, particularly when there are children and extended families involved. In this chapter, I look at some of the issues arising following family breakdown, in particular at the legislation that regulates arrangements for children when the parents are unable to agree these. Some of the possible reasons underlying the need for the courts to become involved in family matters are considered, as is the issue of whether children have a voice in decision-making within the context of legal proceedings. Finally, I consider what mediation might have to contribute to the process of helping families to resolve contested issues in relation to children.

Following the implementation of the Children Act 1989, courts have a limited power to oversee arrangements for the children of divorcing parents when there is no apparent dispute, for example over where the children should live and what contact they should have with the non-resident parent. Although district judges are still required to consider the arrangements for the children of divorcing parents (under s.41 of the Matrimonial Causes Act 1973) and can delay the making of a decree absolute where it appears that circumstances may require the exercise of powers under the Children Act, this rarely happens. 'Private agreement is embraced by the court where there is no apparent disagreement between the parents. It is consistent with the pursuit of settlement of course, but it also reflects district judges' appreciation of their limited capacity to intervene effectively in post-separation family relationships' (Davis and Pearce, 1999). Where parents are unmarried and are in agreement, the court does not have even this limited degree of supervision over the arrangements for the children.

Although many parents are able to agree the arrangements for children after separation or divorce, an increasing number of separated parents have in recent years been looking to the courts to resolve their conflict over the upbringing of their children (Pearce *et al.*, 1999). The Children Act provides the framework for specific legal outcomes where parents cannot agree the arrangements for their children post-separation/divorce.

There is a collection of orders available to the court under s.8 of the Act. The courts are able to use these to settle where a child will live and what contact the child is to have with the non-resident parent, as well as to make prohibited steps and specific issue orders to achieve a wide number of outcomes. The court has the power to make any or all of these orders in a family case, even where the specific application before it is for only one of them, for example a residence order.[1]

Orders for residence determine where the child is going to live. There are a number of principles that the court must take into account, the first of these being that the welfare of the child is paramount. The court must have regard in particular to the 'welfare checklist' set out in s.1(3) of the Act. This includes taking into account the wishes and feelings of the child(ren) involved, the probable effect of any change in their circumstances, their physical, emotional and educational needs, and how capable each of the child's parents is of meeting those needs. Before making an order, the court has to consider whether it would be better in the child's interests not to make an order at all. Any change in a child's residence should interfere as little as possible with his or her relationships with both parents.

Each parent is expected to continue to exercise parental responsibility in respect of the child, although each parent may act alone and will not require the other parent's permission in meeting that responsibility.[2] Exceptions to this are that, when a residence order is in force, the child's surname cannot be changed, nor can the child be removed from the UK without the written consent of every person with parental responsibility, although there is a provision that the person in whose favour the residence order is made may take the child out of the UK for up to one month. This is subject to any conditions that the court may impose (under s.11 of the Act), for example regarding the notice to be given to the other parent or the maximum number of journeys abroad that can be made annually.

The formal language of the legislation conceals a range of motivations behind applications to the court for a residence order. In one study, which monitored and reviewed cases in five courts between 1994 and 1997, many residence applications were withdrawn or some agreement had been reached between the parents before the case went to a final hearing. Many of these applications were 'tactical' and had been made in conjunction with applications for contact. Most of the applicants knew or had been advised by their lawyers that they had no hope of getting residence, but they used the application to put pressure on the other parent with respect to contact (Pearce *et al.*, 1999).

Applications for contact also reveal a complex array of parental disputes in which the courts are being asked to intervene in order to settle matters. Contact may be opposed in principle; this is usually on the basis of the children not wanting any contact with the non-resident parent. In some cases, although contact is not disputed in principle, there are difficulties in arrangements, such as last minute cancellations or a parent being alleged to be late in collecting the children or taking them home after contact. These cases can become extremely intractable, detailed conditions being placed on the contact arrangements by the resident parent that the non-resident parent finds impossible to accept (such as where the children may be taken, whom they can meet and so on) (Pearce *et al.*, 1999).

Whether the courts' engagement with those disputes is productive to some form of resolution, and therefore intrinsically worthwhile, is questionable: 'the quarrel is about children, but it is a quarrel between parents' (Davis and Pearce, 1999). Where contact is sustained only by virtue of an order, there is likely to be tension, which can in many cases undermine the supposed value to the child of the contact. It is quite possible for a court to make an order for contact in terms that satisfy neither parent, leading in some cases to repeated appearances at court as one or other of the parents tries to persuade the judge to vary or discharge the original order. When a parent refuses to comply with an order, the judge is often faced with an impossible task of deciding how the order should be enforced. The options to the court may be to fine or imprison the parent in breach of the order, either of which may cause greater hardship to the children and damage their relationship with the parent who brings the matter back to court.

Difficult cases may be helped by professionals who work with children and families in the Court Welfare Service (which will become part of the new Children and Families Courts Advisory Service). A court welfare officer will become involved at an early stage when an application has been made to the court for an order for contact and/or residence. He or she will meet with the parents (and sometimes the children) and attempt to help the parents to resolve their differences. In some cases, this can be achieved, and the parents are able to reach an agreement without a court hearing, although the judge will want to see the parents' proposals for contact or residence. Where it is in the interests of the child for an order to be made, this will typically be expressed as a 'consent order' to reflect the fact that the parents reached agreement on the terms of the order. In those cases where the parents are unable to reach an agreement, the court will usually ask the court welfare officer to prepare a report for the court. This addresses the issues raised by the parents and sets out the wishes and feelings of the children, plus any recommendations for the order that the court should consider making.

Case law in the 1990s clearly demonstrated that there is strong presumption of contact between the child and the non-resident parent following separation or divorce. Evidence that over half of fathers had no contact with their children within two years of divorce gave rise to a concern that children were being damaged by the loss of a parent. It was thought that the worst effects of family breakdown could be ameliorated if contact were maintained between the child and father (Neale, 2000). The child's welfare is therefore being interpreted as the child's right to see or know that parent, on the assumption that the child will invariably benefit from the continuing relationship (Cantwell *et al.*, 1998). This view has come under increasing challenge, particularly where there has been a history of domestic violence in the parents' relationship (see Smart and Neale, 1997; Humphreys, 1999; Radford *et al.*, 1999). The issue of post-separation contact and domestic violence is discussed in Chapter 10 of this book.

What has more recently come under greater scrutiny is whether the children themselves have a voice in the decisions and orders that are made concerning the contact they are to have with a non-resident parent (Neale, 1999). Does the present legal system enable children to express their views on post-separation contact, and if so, are those views listened to? 'Listening to children so that they can participate in decision making about their everyday lives has become an established principle of child law and policy within the UK.' Where the context of the decision-making is parental divorce or separation, however, there are constraints to putting this principle into practice (Neale, 2000).

Although the Children Act requires children's views and wishes to be taken into consideration, a qualitative study of the practices of court welfare officers revealed that, in disputed contact cases, children were rarely seen, and when they were, 'seeing' children did not necessarily entail listening (Sawyer, 2000). Neale (2000) argues that the presumption of contact 'assumes a commonality of children's experiences and glosses over the complexities and pluralities of their real lives'. By presuming to know what arrangements best meet children's needs, consulting with them becomes superfluous. One court welfare officer interviewed by Sawyer thought the only point of seeing a child was when the case would go before a judge, since if the child had not been interviewed, the judge would send the court welfare officer back for that purpose.

Even where children have the opportunity to express their wishes and feelings, the weight afforded to these is debatable. Adults decide whether a child is competent enough to have his or her views taken seriously, and in cases involving younger children (for example, under 10 years old), it is unlikely that their views will greatly influence a judge's final decision about contact. In many cases where children are adamant that they do not want any contact with a non-resident parent, their long-term needs are still considered to be best met by contact being ordered: 'the assertion that a child has "a right to contact" with a parent has become a standard part of legal rhetoric... the assertion that they have "a right to no contact" is simply absent' (Smart and Neale, 1999). In these situations, where there is opposition to contact taking place, the court will often order 'supervised contact' to take place at a contact centre.

Contact centres provide a neutral venue for post-separation contact. About half of the families attending centres do so under a court order. For example, where the trust between the parents has broken down so completely, or where there has been a considerable period of time since contact last took place, the court may try to 'get contact going' by starting it off in a contact centre for a few months. Other families may come to a contact centre having been referred by their solicitor or social services. Where there are more serious problems, such as a fear of abduction or allegations of sexual abuse or domestic violence, the contact centre can provide a safe place for contact to take place. Although centres usually see themselves as providing a short-term service, these kinds of case can involve a long-term use of the centres: the risk posed by a violent or abusive parent will not disappear in the space of a couple of months. Indeed, whether there should be contact at all in such cases is a source of ongoing debate, as was indicated earlier in this chapter.

Contact centres have been increasingly seen as vital in ensuring that contact continues between a non-resident parent and child where there are difficulties preventing it taking place elsewhere. The vast majority of contact centres offer supported contact, that is, contact that takes place under the general eye of centre staff (usually volunteers). A small proportion of centres are able to offer supervised contact, where contact is closely supervised on a one worker to one family basis. Another common service provided is for the centre to act as a handover point, contact then taking place elsewhere (Furness, 1998). Although centre staff are not there to provide conciliation or counselling services, there is inevitably some low-key parenting education and mediation taking place in the weekly sessions (Halliday, 1998). At the very least, the presence of centre staff can help to diffuse the conflict between the parents.

The 1980s and 90s saw the growth of mediation services to provide an alternative option for parents to negotiate their agreements concerning their children. With the help of a neutral third party, parents are encouraged to talk to each other to reach a mutually acceptable solution on some or all of the issues relating to or arising from the separation or divorce. The aims of mediation are to reduce conflict (in contrast to the legal system, which many parents would say increases conflict); it is seen as a 'primarily future-focused, practical, issue based activity aimed at… resolving issues and preserving reasonable relationships, especially where there are children involved' (Bishop *et al.*, 1996). There have been criticisms about the process of mediation, however, for example that the language of mediation and conciliation can mask the power imbalance within the parties' relationship (see further Bottomley, 1984; Davis, 1988). In particular, there are issues surrounding whether a safe environment can be created where there is a history of domestic violence. Some mediators (particularly in the USA) take the view that mediation is always inappropriate for such cases.

In addition to disputes over where a child should live and/or arrangements for contact, there may be issues concerned with the day-to-day care of the child that the parents cannot agree. The remaining s.8 orders provide the court with the power to make directions about a child's upbringing. Prohibited steps orders (PSO) and specific issue orders (SIO) – are directly related to parental responsibility. The former is an order that certain action(s) (specified in the order), which could be taken by a parent in meeting his or her parental responsibility for a child, may not be taken by any person without the consent of the court. The order is a way of enabling the court to regulate the behaviour of a single person, usually one of the child's parents (although the wording of the section allows for the order to be directed at 'any person'). A parent may, for example, be forbidden by the order to contact the child at home or at school, or to remove the child from the UK. The SIO gives directions for the purpose of determining a specific question arising out of the exercise of parental responsibility. An SIO order could, for example, be granted authorising a court welfare officer to see a child when the resident parent is refusing to allow the child to be interviewed for the purpose of preparing a welfare report.

For many parents, divorce or separation is a time of immense distress; it can inspire feelings of intense anger and a wish for revenge. Disputes over where a child should live and what contact he or she should have with the non-resident parent are frequently carried out in a context in which the parents are locked into blaming each other and find it hard to make rational decisions or place the needs of their children first. And while the welfare of children caught up in their parents' quarrel will be the paramount interest of the court, it is hard to place children at the centre of decision-making when the arguments are largely framed with reference to what the parents want to happen.

It could be argued that trying to resolve what are essentially private family issues within a legal framework is unlikely to achieve a satisfactory outcome for either parents or their children. It is important to remember, however, that there are many families who are independently coping with family breakdown and the subsequent changes in relationships, and are creating workable solutions to contact and residence arrangements in the aftermath of divorce or separation (Neale, 2000). Neale argues that opening up debates about post-divorce family life to include those who are finding their own solutions 'would allow for a greater understanding of the interiors of family relationships and for knowledge to be shared about what works effectively under a range of circumstances'.

The most effective process for supporting separating families is one in which the emotions as well as the practicalities of changing families can be taken into consideration. Adversarial court litigation has failed many families on this count; more positive ways need to be used in order to support families through the difficult process of separation and to meet the challenge to adapt to change.

Notes

1 The orders are in fact available in any family proceedings in which a question arises in relation to the welfare of a child, for example in financial proceedings, and anyone can apply for such an order, although some will require leave of court to do so.

2 A residence order that is granted to an unmarried father allocates parental responsibility to him if he has not already acquired this by agreement with the mother or by a previous order of the court.

10

Violence in the Home: Social Work Practice and the Law

Lesley-Anne Cull

Introduction

One woman in four is attacked at some point in her life by a male partner (Economic and Social Research Council, 1998), and every week in the UK two women are killed by a current or former partner (Alabhai-Brown, 1999). In many cases, children are frequently either a witness to or aware of the violence and abuse (Hester and Radford, 1996). In a third of cases, the violence (including murder) against these women occurs post-separation (Kelly, 1998). These disturbing statistics reveal 'a scale of violence and abuse [which] has many dreadful consequences for individuals, families and the whole community' (Jay, 1999). In this chapter, I will explore how far current law and social work practice can offer protection and support to the survivors of domestic violence (both adults and children) and in particular consider issues relating to child contact post-separation.

Defining domestic violence

The Association of Chief Officers of Probation defines domestic violence as 'any form of physical, sexual or emotional abuse which takes place within a close relationship. In most cases the relationship will be between partners (married, cohabiting or otherwise) or ex-partners… [and] research indicates that in the great majority of cases the abuser is male and the victim female' (Advisory Board on Family Law, 1999). Domestic violence does not have to be physical; it includes psychological intimidation and harassment, emotional abuse, persistent verbal abuse and behaviour that is used as a means of one partner dominating and controlling the other (Advisory Board on Family Law, 1999). It is recognised that people in same-sex relationships and men in heterosexual relationships also experience domestic violence; however, according to the British Crime Survey (Mirlees-Black *et al.*, 1998), men tend to be considerably less frightened by their experience and are less likely to be injured or to seek medical help. Domestic violence has been described as 'the most significant problem damaging the health and safety of women' (Stanko and Hobdall, 1993).

Women and domestic violence

Many women experience great difficulty in disclosing the domestic violence they have suffered. One reason may be located within the legal and popular discourse: women may not identify with prevailing images of 'battered women' and not define what is happening to them as 'violence'. It has also been argued that a culture of silence and shame surrounded the issue of domestic violence during much of the twentieth century and that women might have found it difficult to admit abuse and to acknowledge what was really happening (Radford, 1996). Another reason may be a fear of children being removed from their care and of losing their home. Of those questioned for the British Crime Survey 1998, over half the survivors of domestic violence had not told anyone about the last attack, and of the 47 per cent who had told someone, nearly all had told a relative or a friend.

For some women, pressure and intimidation may be brought to bear to prevent what has happened being reported to the police. Domestic violence often occurs within the home, and there are frequently no adult witnesses who can support the survivor of an attack. Other reasons why women do not report incidents of domestic violence may include a lack of awareness about or access to services available and a feeling that agencies will be unable to provide the help needed. Some women do approach services, for example to receive medical attention. If, however, they are not asked about the cause of their injuries, the opportunity for intervention is lost and the violence may continue.

Under the Crime and Disorder Act 1998, it is a requirement that local crime audits are undertaken to identify the nature and prevalence of local crime, including domestic violence that has not been formally reported. In most local authority areas, domestic violence has emerged as a significant problem (Neville, 1999) and, according to the British Crime Survey (Mirlees-Black *et al.*, 1988), accounts nationally for one quarter of all violent crime. It is increasingly being recognised that the effectiveness of preventative work, intervention and continuing support relies upon coordinated work on the basis of an inter-agency approach, indeed the importance of working in partnership and information sharing having been highlighted by the Crime and Disorder Act 1998. At present, the help women receive is entirely a matter of where they live. In some areas, the services available for them are extremely good and efficient; in others, services simply do not exist (Dominy and Radford, 1996). Women are in some cases sent to as many as 10 different places before they get the help that they need, this experience creating yet another barrier to effective support (Dominy and Radford, 1996).

The police response to domestic violence also varies from area to area. In some areas, the police have developed policies with local authorities, relevant voluntary agencies and refuges with the aim of working together to ensure that women receive prompt and appropriate help. In others, however, there needs to be a change in police practice if women are to receive the support and understanding they need when reporting domestic violence. Too often, the police see such violence as a private dispute and even serious assaults are treated as being minor. In some cases, women are told that the man cannot be arrested if there was no witness to the violence. Criminal prosecutions are rare, occurring in only a minority of cases (Radford *et al.*, 1999). The British Crime Survey (Mirlees-Black *et al.*, 1996) results showed that only 11 per cent of domestic assaults occurring in the previous year had been reported to the police, suggesting that calling the police is last resort for many women who are attacked in the home.

Social work practice and domestic violence

Domestic violence is rarely a 'one-off' event. Physical and sexual abuse tend to increase in frequency and severity over time, and other forms of abusive behaviour may be part of an ongoing pattern. A woman seeking help and support may be doing so after months or years of abuse and find the prospect of leaving the abusive relationship as frightening as the prospect of staying. Women are at particular risk just before or immediately after leaving a violent relationship, and are right to feel vulnerable at this point. Therefore the way in which a social worker responds when first approached by a woman who has experienced domestic violence is crucial.

Listening to the woman and believing her is the first step. The next step is to respond in a way that is appropriate to the situation. It is, for example, essential to consider her immediate safety and that of any children in the family as their safety and welfare is paramount. Women need to be given privacy so that they can feel able to discuss what has happened to them, and it is particularly important that this should be offered at a pace they feel comfortable with. As well as offering emotional support, social workers should be able to provide information about protection, access to voluntary agencies that support the survivors of domestic violence, relevant health services, police powers, housing and how to obtain legal advice from a solicitor experienced in family law. If a woman's situation has reached crisis point, she may need access to several of these agencies, for example the police, the emergency accommodation services and the courts, at one time.

After the immediate crisis has passed, she may need assistance with long-term arrangements for housing, advice on benefits or counselling. It is important to remember that many women who have experienced domestic violence assume that they are to blame for the violence. Social workers need to emphasise to women the appropriateness of seeking help and stress that violence in the home is a criminal offence, that expert help is available and that legal intervention is possible (South and East Belfast Trust, 1998).

The legislation and domestic violence

Whether or not the police use criminal law provisions (for example, common assault or grievous bodily harm under the Offences Against the Person Act 1861) against a violent person, individuals may still use civil law in order to obtain protection. The Family Law Act 1996 (Part IV) provides a comprehensive range of remedies to protect individuals and to regulate occupation of the home, the protection being afforded to a wide category of people rather than just spouses and cohabitants. A woman can, for example, apply for an order against someone she had been living with in the past, she has agreed to marry or with whom she shares parental responsibility for a child. A non-molestation order (an injunction) forbids the abuser (the 'respondent') from molesting the applicant or relevant child. The order may be granted either where the relationship has broken down or where the woman wants to remain with the respondent.

It is important for social workers to be sensitive to the complexity of balancing the need for intervention (for example, where there are child protection issues) with the need to allow women to take control of their lives. In most cases, where the court finds that the respondent has used or threatened violence against the applicant or relevant child, it must make a power of arrest, so that if the order is not obeyed, the respondent can be taken to court by the police. There is some doubt, however, concerning the effectiveness of these orders for some women. The survey carried out by Radford *et al.* (1999) indicated that just under half of the women interviewed had obtained an injunction but the majority of these (70 per cent) were breached, some more than three times. There is also the danger that when the order is served upon the respondent, he will react with further violence, thereby placing the woman at even greater risk to her safety.

The court can make two types of occupation order under Part IV of the Act: 'declaratory' and 'regulatory'. Declaratory orders state, for example, that the applicant is entitled to occupy the dwelling, and regulatory orders concern a range of options including regulating one of the parties' occupation of the home or excluding the respondent from the home and/or the area around the home. In reaching a decision about which kind of order to make (if any), the courts have regard to all the circumstances of the case. These include the housing needs of both parties and the children, the financial resources of the parties, the probable effect of the order on the health, safety and well-being of the parties or any relevant child and the conduct of the parties in relation to each other and otherwise. There is also a 'balance of harm' test applied in these cases. That is, where the court finds that the respondent's conduct is likely to cause significant harm to the applicant or any relevant child unless an order is made, the court must make an order unless the order would cause greater harm to the respondent and any relevant child.

Applications for an order under Part IV of the Family Law Act 1996 are usually made with both parties attending (or at least having notice of the hearing). Where there is an emergency, it may be possible for a woman to apply to the court for an order without the respondent being given notice. The court is, however, only likely to grant orders 'in exceptional circumstances, where the interests of justice or the protection of the applicant or child clearly demanded immediate intervention' (Standing Committee E, House of Commons, 1996).

The Family Law Act 1996 (s.52 and Schedule 6) also created amendments to the Children Act 1989 by providing for the inclusion of an 'exclusion requirement' in an interim care order or emergency protection order. It can only be included when the court is satisfied that there is a person living in the home who is able to look after the child adequately and is willing to consent to the inclusion of the requirement. This is intended to be a temporary measure as an exclusion requirement cannot be attached to a final care order. It gives the applicant (usually the local authority) the alternative of removing an abuser or suspected abuser from the home rather than removing the child (which can create the feeling for some children that they are being punished in some way for what has happened to them).

Where a person is not protected by the provisions of the Family Law Act 1996, he or she may be able to rely on the Protection from Harassment Act 1997 to combat conduct amounting to harassment or that causes the fear that violence will be used against him or her. Such conduct is a criminal offence, but the Act also creates a civil cause of action, for which a 'restraining harassment order' may be sought.

When women approach social services for advice about an abusive situation, they may feel extremely anxious about applying to the court for an order and want to look at other options. Taking time to listen to what they want and to respect their wishes is therefore important. Good practice is about being sensitive and enabling women to discuss their fears, as well as exploring with them ways to maximise their safety. Understanding the potential danger of further violence towards women living in abusive situations is essential. There is a large body of evidence that shows convincingly that women are at the greatest risk of harm when they are attempting to leave the relationship or seek outside help, particularly where there are children (Barnett, 1999). This becomes a particularly significant issue in the context of post-separation contact disputes, and it is this and, more generally, the impact on children of witnessing domestic violence that I will now consider.

Children and domestic violence

Violence in the home has a significant impact on children. Children are frequently a witness to, or are aware of, violence and abuse against their mother. Studies have indicated that up to 80 per cent of the children of domestic violence survivors have been in the same or a nearby room when the violence occurs and that exposure to domestic violence has a significant consequence for children's health, development, self-esteem and confidence in both the short and the long term (Humphreys, 1999). However, children's experience needs to be understood not only in terms of the effects of witnessing or being implicated in conflict and violence, but also in the context of their perception of the emotional climate of the family. In most (although not all) cases, they will have experienced a family atmosphere that is characterised by stress and conflict, and that can affect their development in a number of ways. Young children in particular are likely to experience feelings of self-blame and fear.

There must clearly be concerns for the welfare of the child where domestic violence has been identified as an issue. It is increasingly recognised that children are themselves being emotionally abused by being a witness to the abuse against their mothers and that this is an issue of concern for those professionals involved in child protection work (Neville, 1999). As the law stood for most of the 1990s, however, it appeared that, in private law proceedings at least, there was little or no consideration of violence towards a woman by her former partner when contact with children was an issue after separation.

Although there is no presumption in favour of contact contained within the Children Act 1989, case law has established a strong precedent that contact will almost always be granted to the non-resident parent. Statistics indicated that in 1997/8 contact was refused in only 1.8 per cent of cases (Court Services, quoted in Saunders, 1999). Unless there were 'cogent reasons' indicating that direct contact would be contrary to the welfare of the child, it was usually ordered (*Re M (Contact: Supervision)* [1998] 1 FLR 727). Where there had been domestic violence, women's accounts of abuse were treated as evidence of the mother being 'hostile' to negotiations over contact between the children and the father (Hester and Radford, 1996). There was an expectation that 'women should be able to put the experience of violence behind them and that, because the relationship has ended, the violence [had] also ended' (Hester *et al.*, 1994). Research also suggested that lawyers were advising mothers not to mention domestic violence to the courts as a reason for opposing contact; pressure from the lawyer for the mother to reach an agreement with the father was also not uncommon (Radford *et al.*, 1999).

In 1997 a Court of Appeal judgment offered a glimmer of hope for women who had experienced violence. In *Re D (Contact: Reasons for Refusal)* [1997] 2 FLR 48 the father's application for contact was rejected as it was found that he was violent and threatening, and that the mother had a genuine fear of harm to herself and/or the child. The court stated that the label 'implacable hostility' (a term often used by courts and lawyers to suggest that a mother is being unreasonably difficult in refusing to allow contact) is an umbrella term that can be applied misleadingly. It is sometimes applied wrongly to cases where there is a good reason for opposing contact, for example where the mother's fears for herself and her child are rationally held. The Court of Appeal in this case appeared to be drawing a distinction between an 'unreasonable' hostility and one in which the parent with residence had well-founded grounds for opposing contact.

In a later case, a father was appealing a decision of the magistrates to refuse to make an order for contact on the basis that he had been violent to the mother. The Court of Appeal stated that:

> Often in these cases, where domestic violence has been found, too little weight… is given to the need for the father to change. It is often said that, notwithstanding the violence, the mother must nonetheless bring up the children with full knowledge and a positive image of their father and arrange for the children to be available for contact. Too often… the courts neglect the other side of that equation which is that a father… must demonstrate that he is a fit person to exercise contact; that he is not going to destabilise the family; that he is not going to upset the children and harm them emotionally. (*Re M (Minor) (Contact)* [1999] 2 FCR 56)

These two cases provide a strong counterbalance to previous case law. The courts have, however, made it clear that they are prepared to enforce, using imprisonment if necessary, their view that it is both the right of the child and in his or her interests to have contact with the non-resident parent (see *A* v. *N (Committal: Refusal of Contact)* [1997] 1 FLR 533, in which the mother was committed to prison for breaching a contact order). It may be that further case law develops suggesting that in those instances where a mother's opposition to contact is found to be genuine and reasonable, the court will refuse the father's application for contact. Concerns still remain, however, that allegations of domestic violence may not be taken seriously enough and may be regarded as an excuse to avoid contact (Smart and Neale, 1997). Yet research indicates quite clearly that the fear of violence post-separation is not academic. One third of women killed by a former partner have already separated (Home Office Statistics), and one third of calls to the police to report incidents of domestic violence come from women who have left their partner (Kelly, 1998). Post-separation violence continues to be a factor impacting upon the safety of women and children, and contact orders can have the effect of establishing a means by which intimidation and abuse can continue to take place.

Against this background, the consultation paper published in June 1999 inviting professionals to consider the question of parental contact in cases of domestic violence (the Advisory Board on Family Law: Children Act Sub-committee) was welcomed as an opportunity to open up the debate. However, in relation to suggestions by some academics and professionals that amendments to the Children Act are required to create a presumption against contact in cases where there has been domestic violence, the paper stated that 'it does not seem to us… that domestic violence, of itself and as a concept, can be put forward as an automatic bar to contact'. Good practice guidelines proposed by the Sub-committee were, however, viewed as having the potential to 'bring significant change in practice [and]… make court professionals more aware of the dangers associated with child contact in cases of domestic violence'. Nonetheless it was argued that the recommendations are unlikely to override the overwhelming presumption of contact (Radford *et al.*, 1999).

The above discussion concerned cases brought in private proceedings. A social worker may become involved in private family proceedings where a court orders a welfare investigation under s.7 of the Children Act 1989. It is, however, more usually the case that court welfare officers prepare the welfare reports. Despite research findings indicating a much-increased awareness on the part of court welfare officers of the impact of domestic violence on children, and an increasing awareness of the need for safety in contact arrangements (Hester *et al.*, 1997), research has shown that they seem quite consciously to allow themselves to be guided on social work issues by the judiciary. Court welfare officers have found themselves influenced by the apparent policy of contact at all costs, a policy that they felt put inappropriate weight on the benefits of contact and ignored its detrimental aspects (Sawyer, 2000).

The involvement of social workers in private proceedings is more probable where the court considers that it may be appropriate for a care or supervision order to be made in respect of the child in the case. Under s.37 of the Children Act 1989, the court can direct the local authority to undertake an investigation into the child's circumstances. In addition to considering whether to apply for a care or supervision order, the local authority has to consider whether it should provide services or assistance for the child or his or her family. It is at this private–public law interface that a contradiction seems to be emerging. On the one hand, in child contact cases, a 'robust' stance is taken by the courts towards mothers who are seen to be 'implacably hostile' in their opposition to contact with a violent father. On the other hand, the welfare system 'is becoming increasingly concerned about the significant harm to children created by domestic violence... admonishing women for their "failure to protect" children if they do not leave and take their children to a "place of safety"' (Humphreys, 1999).

Providing women with a safe environment in which to explore the options – both legal and practical – available to them is a vital part of the social work service. Social workers should be able to offer advice about securing safe accommodation, whether that be in the woman's home or in a refuge, and on how to pursue criminal or civil proceedings (for example, for assault or to obtain a non-molestation order). Some women leave and return to violent partners many times before they feel able to make a final decision to leave. Their wishes and right to choose should be respected and protected on their behalf. Where child protection is an issue in domestic violence, it is important that social workers do not lose sight of the woman's needs but work in partnership with her. This does not imply that children's needs should be conflated with those of their mothers but instead that supporting women, rather than admonishing them for their 'failure to protect', is an important underlying principle (Humphreys *et al.*, 2000). It is also important to recognise the emotional, psychological and financial costs attached to escaping from violence and the effects of being in a relationship characterised by long-term violence.

Social work in relation to domestic violence is a skilled and demanding task. That task should be seen as part of a multi-agency commitment in all local authority areas to developing a framework of best practice and creating an effective response to domestic violence.

11

Child Protection: Lessons from Abroad

Rachael Hetherington and Andrew Cooper

Introduction

The Judge for Children in a small town in France works in the court building in a block on the town square. Her office is a light room with a desk, some filing cabinets and enough chairs for about eight people. It opens on to the waiting area, and it is in this office that she sees the children and parents who are referred to her. The next '*audience*' was for Madame Dupont, who had three children and a partner who drank and was often violent to her. The social services department knew Madame Dupont and had set up a contract of work for her with a voluntary organisation. The social worker from the voluntary agency was concerned about the family and was in the process of referring all three children to the Children's Judge, but now the youngest child (aged 9) had just been referred to the judge by the school because he hit one of the dinner ladies. The Judge fetched Madame Dupont and her son from the waiting room. They were accompanied by the social worker from the voluntary agency, who had the previous night had an emergency call from Madame Dupont, asking for a refuge for herself and the children because of her partner's violence.

The Judge was unable at that point to make an order for the whole family because the referral from the school was for only one of the children. She therefore decided to postpone making an order for three weeks, at which time she would see the whole family. The Judge told Madame Dupont that she was not protecting her children and that it was her duty to do so; she had not shown that she was preventing her partner being violent to the children. She needed to talk about her problems concerning the children with the social worker, and she should not deny or minimise the problems. The Judge told Madame Dupont that she would certainly make an order when she saw them in three weeks' time. It would depend on the report from the social worker whether the order was a supervision order or a care order. The next three weeks should be used by Madame Dupont to begin to make changes. Madame Dupont, her son and the social worker left together and walked away from the courts deep in conversation – or argument.

This story shows many differences between the French and English systems of child protection, most strikingly in the relationship between the family, the social workers and the law. It demonstrates a very much less formal and more flexible relationship between the legal system and other stakeholders, in which referral to the judge comes about very much more readily than it does here. The very direct relationship between the judge and the family puts the social worker in a different relationship to the family, one at once both less powerful and more powerful (Cooper *et al.*, 1995). It demonstrates a more open access to referral – in this case, the school being the agent of referral to the children's judge – and a greater readiness to use the law.

The French system of child protection is in many ways different from the English, but it is also different from other European approaches, the system of the Flemish Community in Belgium offering a striking contrast. There the emphasis is on mediation and on preventing entry to the legal system (Hetherington *et al.*, 1997). This is institutionalised through the Mediation Committee, which has to see all families before they can be referred to the Children's Judge, and attempts to arrive at an agreed, voluntary plan that will make legal intervention unnecessary (see Hetherington and Sprangers, 1994, for a description of this system). The agency that is the nearest equivalent to the English Children and Families team is the service of the Committee for Special Youth Assistance. This service works only on a voluntary basis, providing a social work service offering help to families in which there is a 'problematic up-bringing situation'. It is the conduit for referral from other agencies to the Mediation Committee. If a case goes before the Judge for Children, a different social work service comes into action.

We wondered how it would have worked out for Madame Dupont and her family in the Flemish community and therefore approached An Sprangers, chair of the Mediation Commission of Leuven. She told us that, in the first place, the school would probably contact the educational social work service. If they found that they could not get anywhere with this mother, they would refer her and her son to the Special Youth Assistance service. This service is the equivalent of that which was already in touch with Madame Dupont in France, so it would already be working with the family. The Special Youth Assistance service could then take the case to the Mediation Committee, who would try to reach an agreed way of working. If they could not, they would refer the matter to the Judge for

Children. If they could, the Special Youth Assistance service would continue to work with the family.

The Mediation Committee would therefore come into the situation at the same point as the Judge for Children in France. The Mediation Committee would, in effect, be trying to persuade the mother to accept something very like a supervision order, setting up a negotiated contract of work. There is no legal compulsion but a very clear threat that a legal order would be the next step, and it might be for a placement away from home. It would also be possible for the mother to come back to the Mediation Committee if she felt that the social worker was being unreasonable.

Thus, although the French and Belgian uses of the law are very different from each other, they seem to achieve a similar effect. In both countries, Madame Dupont is likely to end up with a supervision order or something very similar. She will have to demonstrate an ability to protect her children from her violent partner and is given an opportunity to do so.

In England, there would be no grounds on which an application for an order could be made, so a supervision order would not be a possibility. A child protection conference might be held, but on the one hand this does not have the same negotiative approach as the Mediation Committee, and on the other it does not have the power for direct referral to the legal system. The two continental systems demonstrate in different ways the use of semi-compulsion (Hetherington *et al.*, 1997). Semi-compulsion is the state in which compulsion is imminent but can still be avoided, and in which a change or modification of behaviour is encouraged by the possibility but not the actuality of compulsion. For a further explanation of semi-compulsion, see Cooper and Hetherington (1999).

Differences: practices and principles

What is it that makes our child welfare practice so different from that of other European countries? Would changing our legal system make any difference? Why have attempts to introduce more flexible, negotiative ways of working, such as family group conferences, had such difficulty in taking hold? Why, to summarise, do other countries approach their work with families so differently, constructing a dialogue with families that uses a mixture of argument, cajolery and threat to keep open negotiation? Why, to pick a concrete example, do other countries use supervision orders so much more than we do?

In both the French and the Belgian responses to Madame Dupont's situation, there is an expectation that change is possible and that the authority of the system should be used to work towards change. The systems in both countries initially use the threat of compulsion rather than an order. The protective role of the social worker is to argue, persuade, motivate, educate and enable, using the authority of the system and the threat of possible legal action. The use of authority presupposes a level of optimism related to change.

Since the Jasmine Beckford Inquiry (London Borough of Brent, 1985) it has hardly been allowable for English social workers to be optimistic about the likelihood of families achieving change. Dingwall *et al.* (1983) looked critically at the readiness of social workers and health visitors to accept a low standard of childcare from some families and labelled this 'the rule of optimism'; optimism has had a bad name in English child protection work. If there is little or no possibility of change, social workers and health visitors are right to be pessimistic, but they are then reduced to monitoring and crisis intervention.

After studying child protection practices and systems in a number of European countries, trying as far as possible to stay close to the everyday working experience of practitioners, we began to see a pattern of linked themes that appear to explain some of the features of continental child protection work and that mark it out so clearly from English practice (Hetherington *et al.* 1997). In any particular country, we would argue that the historical, political and cultural context combines with the interplay of these factors to produce a child protection system that is unique but also comparable to neighbouring ones, rather like family members resemble each other but are never identical (Cooper, 2000).

The key factors that combine in this way are: an emphasis on negotiation and flexibility in the conduct of child protection interventions; the presence within the systems of institutions that support and legitimate negotiation and flexibility; social trust and confidence in professionals' capacity to use their authority and judgment responsibly; the overall subordination of legal and forensic imperatives to welfare, therapeutic and social ones; and, linked to this point, the widespread use of a variety of forms of semi-compulsion (such as community supervision orders) in order to protect children while minimising the disruption and damage to family relationships.

Complexity

The interaction of these factors inevitably produces a culture of professional complexity in dealings with families where there is a risk to the children; complexity is also a fact of life in English child protection work, but there are powerful forces working to deny this and promote an either/or, or binary, way of thinking about children and child protection in which, for example, abuse has definitely either occurred or not occurred, children must be clearly placed either within or outside the family, and risks are either acceptable or unacceptable in any particular case at any point in time. Other systems are more ready to make more or less provisional decisions in the face of inevitable uncertainty and doubt arising from the multi-factorial and evolving character of child abuse and the contexts in which it occurs. Sometimes, therefore, continental ways of thinking and practising in child protection appear to be straightforwardly contradictory or paradoxical, but rather than thus reject them outright, it is helpful to try to understand them as a function of what we have termed 'complexity'.

For example, when a French children's judge imposes a supervision order on a child, he or she must by law attempt to obtain the parents' consent to this move. In the UK, particularly perhaps in England, this is on the face of it a puzzling contradiction, but the French way of doing things embodies a number of principles worth examining. In attempting to obtain the agreement of the parents to the use of his or her statutory authority, the children's judge is trying to maintain parents in an active relationship to the law and thereby to society itself, which makes and enacts laws concerning family relationships. The use in France of law in situations where children's welfare is compromised is thus simultaneously a formal institutional matter and a symbolic event at the social and psychological level. In England, this is much less obviously the case since compulsion is conceived as something external to family situations that have reached the point of breakdown rather than something integral to all family and social relationships, which can take many forms, institutional law being just one fairly extreme example.

Systemic authority

Nevertheless, at first sight, the actions of the French children's judge can appear alarmingly arbitrary and unaccountable to English eyes, but while the powers of the judge are considerable, they are much more circumscribed than those of a judge or family proceedings court in England. A children's judge cannot permanently separate a child from his or her parents, which means that French parents and children approach court proceedings with much less trepidation and fear of the consequences than do their English counterparts. This, allied to the fact that the French family court is a very informal and accessible arena, enables us to understand how it is that parents, children, professionals and judges may all seem to behave as though they in some way own the court and its proceedings, and why in some areas a high percentage of parents with children under supervision orders request their renewal on expiry because they have found them helpful. In summary, while in one way the French child protection system is much more legally interventionist than the

English one, its character arises from the presence of the factors outlined above: the use of law is subordinated to concerns about improving family relationships; legal intervention occurs in the context of a flexible and negotiative set of institutional arrangements; and a judge representing a benign State authority is interested in repairing and sustaining the family rather than punishing and fracturing it.

In contrast to the French system, child protection work in the Flemish community of Belgium is characterised by legal minimalism. For a child welfare case to reach the courts, it must first, as outlined above, be referred to the Mediation Committee, a public and statutory body staffed by experienced lay people, which acts as an alternative to institutional law when it successfully effects mediation, a filter between civil society and the law when it passes a case to the courts, and a buffer separating the two spheres when it refers a case back into the civil domain. The functions of the Mediation Committee reflect a socially and politically agreed principle that, if at all possible, complex and conflictual family situations can and should be handled by professionals working in alliance with family members in the civil sphere.

But in order for professionals to be able to protect children adequately without the use of legal compulsion, two further important conditions are required. First, professionals working in multi-disciplinary teams in confidential centres are granted but must also be capable of exercising a high degree of professional authority in their dealings with abusers and children, who frequently want the abuse to cease but are also very frightened of the consequences of it becoming known about outside the family. Second, therefore, children and abusers are granted a high degree of confidentiality in their dealings with professionals working in confidential centres. This does not mean that abuse is allowed simply to continue without intervention but that professionals negotiate authoritatively with children and adults over time in order to instigate protection for the former and an acceptance of responsibility by the latter to cease the abuse. This way of working does not always succeed, and cases will be referred directly to the courts; on other occasions, a decision may be made that, despite continuing abuse, a referral into the legal domain will prove more destructive than helpful to the children. Unless, however, the risk to the children is very severe and there is a complete impasse in the possibility of negotiated change, the driving principle used by professionals is that the child's wishes should be respected and should set the direction of intervention.

Therapeutic authority and the law

The French, Flemish and English cultures of child protection represent three very different ways of exercising authority in relation to the lives of children and their family relationships. Are the principles informing practice in France and Flanders completely alien to the English way of working, or can we point to situations in which authority and negotiation are brought to bear in comparable ways? One of us recently worked jointly with a colleague in a Child and Family Consultation Service on the case we now describe.

The GP referred the Marks family because of a seemingly complete breakdown in the relationship between Simon (aged 16) and his father and mother. The GP also reported that Mrs Marks was concerned about the impact of violent arguments at home upon their younger child Sean (aged 7). Mr and Mrs Marks and Simon came to a first appointment, at which Simon mostly sat in sulky silence, occasionally sneering at attempts by one of the two workers to engage him. Both his parents seemed strikingly passive in relation to him, unable to respond robustly to his evident, if rather silent, aggression towards them. It emerged that Simon was living in a squat part of the time, had dropped out of school and was smoking heroin on a regular basis.

Simon failed to attend the following appointment, at which further serious concerns came to light. It seemed likely that Simon had stolen large sums of money from his father, either through fraudulently cashing cheques taken from his cheque book or by passing these to a friend. It also seemed probable that he had stolen money directly from his mother. A story emerged about Simon having been a possible victim of sexual abuse by a cousin some years ago, but what most struck the two workers was how much difficulty his parents showed in really being clear about this and about taking effective action in the past to ensure that Simon received help.

At a subsequent meeting with the parents, they reported that Simon had told them he was now earning money through prostitution, and it seemed to the workers that he had become involved with a dangerous and exploitative set of people, but although they presented as distressed, neither of his parents seemed able to take charge of Simon and his situation, either emotionally or practically. Eventually, and with a fair degree of feeling and force, one of the workers said to Mr and Mrs Marks that it seemed that their son really was in very serious trouble and might die unless some way could be found to engage with him and reverse his downward spiral. It was necessary to reiterate this view with emotional clarity and directness on more than one occasion before Mr and Mrs Marks, who tended to fight between themselves about their view of Simon and what to do about him, started to be able to join together and tackle their son as deeply concerned but firm parents.

In this instance, the use of professional or therapeutic authority addresses the fact not only that the parents will not, or have not shown themselves able to, exercise care and control over their son, but also that they manifestly cannot do this for reasons to do with their own complex histories and relationship. They were subsequently able to re-engage with Simon and to some degree bring him back within the orbit of his family. That Simon wished to be confronted about the destructive spiral he had entered was confirmed to some degree in one session when he turned to his mother and said, 'When I stole that first £100 from you, you knew that I had done it, and I knew that you knew that I had done it, but you never said anything to me.'

This is a case that, in English terms, only just borders upon the realm of 'child protection' but that nevertheless shows how questions of authority are linked at the level of the psychological, the familial and the societal. The workers understand that they are intervening at all these levels, even if not simultaneously. Of course, not all parents or children are as readily engageable as Mr and Mrs Marks and Simon, but the point we would wish to emphasise is that even if such a case did end up in court, the meaning of the authority that is exercised there and the way in which it is exercised remain just as significant. It is this understanding which is embodied in many continental systems, in France the work of the children's judge sometimes being referred to as 'therapeutic justice'. Children in England, just as much as parents and social workers, are overtaken by the procedural juggernaut, and this creates further pressure on social workers and other professionals either not to intervene or to delay their intervention. Elsewhere, social workers use their authority more readily and intervene earlier. We can learn from other countries the value for children of a system in which social workers can use professional authority.

Conclusion

English social workers are very conscious of the primacy of the interests of the child and sometimes critical of other systems on this ground (Pringle, 1998), but what we have seen elsewhere are approaches that understand the 'interests of the child' differently and that in many European countries give more power to children over the process of interventions. The interests of the child are seen in some European countries in a less individualistic light as being closely bound up with the community and the family; in others, there is an emphasis on the importance and appropriateness of the child exercising some control over, or significantly influencing the outcome of, the process of being helped or protected. There is no single 'European' conceptualisation of the interests of the child. What other systems have in common is a greater flexibility that more readily accommodates complexity. We cannot transplant these principles and practices to England outright, but what we can do is use them to inform a critical and reforming perspective on our own way of working.

12

Whistleblowing: Public Concern at Work

Philip Ells and Guy Dehn

Public Concern at Work is an independent charity that has been recognised by the UK government, the European Commission and the Organization for Economic Co-operation and Development as a leading authority on public interest whistleblowing. It has three key activities:

1. It runs a free legal helpline for people concerned about serious malpractice in the workplace.
2. It offers professional and practical help to organisations on how to encourage responsibility and accountability in the workplace.
3. It conducts research and informs developments in public policy.

Since its launch in 1993, Public Concern at Work has helped over 2000 people who have been concerned about serious malpractice at work. Its charitable remit means that the charity cannot deal with private grievances or dispute but only with matters that affect the wider public interest. Examples of these are fraud, public danger and abuse in care.

The free, confidential advice service is most useful for people at work who are not sure whether or how to 'blow the whistle'. In these cases, the approach of the charity is that, wherever possible, the people in charge of the organisation should have a chance to investigate the matter. This is usually the quickest and most effective way to remove any danger of malpractice and also the way that avoids, removes or reduces any risk to a client. Inevitably, it is sometimes necessary for the matter to be raised outside.

Building on this approach to whistleblowing, the charity was closely involved in the scope and detail of the Public Interest Disclosure Act 1998. A summary of this important new legislation is provided in this article, examples being given of the different sorts of whistleblowing that the legislation is aimed to protect and the implications of the major public inquiries in the care sector.

Whistleblowing in the UK – the story behind the legislation

When the idea of an independent resource centre on whistleblowing was first discussed in 1990, the issue was seen almost invariably in a hostile light. The term was most frequently used to describe public officials who had paid a heavy penalty for leaking information, usually anonymously to the media. Whistleblowers were presented, if not as villains, then as loners and losers. For this reason, there was some initial scepticism about the need for or role of a charitable organisation in this area.

Events conspired to give the charity a receptive audience. The background to the legislation lies in the major disasters and scandals of the last decade of the twentieth century, such as the ferry disaster at Zeebrugge,[1] the rail crash at Clapham Junction,[2] the collapse of the Bank of Credit and Commerce International[3] and the Arms to Iraq scandal.[4] Almost every official inquiry has shown that workers had been aware of the danger but either had been too scared to sound the alarm or had raised the matter with the wrong person or in the wrong way. This communication breakdown cost hundreds of lives, damaged thousands of livelihoods, lost tens of thousands of jobs and undermined public confidence in the organisations on which we all depend. Lyme Bay,[5] Barings,[6] Bristol Royal Infirmary[7] and numerous incidents of abuse in care have reinforced our essential message that misconduct would not be deterred and accountability could not work in practice while people felt that they had little choice but to remain silent. At the same time, individual cases, such as those of Chris Chapman,[8] Graham Pink,[9] Andy Millar[10] and Paul van Buitenen,[11] highlighted the plight of those who did blow the whistle.

Soon after the charity's launch in 1993, the Audit Commission[12] was quick to understand the relevance of the message of the charity and to endorse its work in the context of probity in local government. Even before the launch, the European Commission and Parliament had asked it to report on the role of whistleblowers in controlling financial malpractice in Europe.[13] Within its first year, a number of leading employers also offered their support, some having learnt, from bitter experience, the cost of a culture in which their employees had minded their own business.

The media, while disappointed that the cases the legal helpline handled were confidential, proved invaluable in promoting the message and publicising the charity's work. Several editorial endorsements ensured that the issue received the attention of opinion-formers. Beyond this welcome support, the fact that *The Times* helped to fund the successful legal claim of the British Biotech whistleblower is an important development in the attitude of the media toward those who make public interest disclosures.[14]

The most significant endorsement of the charity's work came in 1995 from the Committee on Standards in Public Life,[15] which accepted Public

Concern at Work's view that unless staff thought it safe and acceptable to raise concerns about misconduct internally, the probable result was that they would stay silent or leak the information. It was this culture which had provided fertile grounds for the birth of sleaze, in which the perception of possible misconduct appeared to justify as much – if not more – attention as proven malpractice. The Committee recommended that public bodies:

> institute codes of practice on whistleblowing, appropriate to their circumstances, which would enable concerns to be raised confidentially inside, and if necessary, outside the organisation'.[16]

Key aspects of these procedures, endorsed by the Committee on Standards in Public Life, are:

- a clear statement that malpractice is taken seriously in the organisation
- respect, if they wish it, for the confidentiality of those staff raising concerns
- the opportunity to raise concerns outside the line management structure
- access to independent advice
- an indication of the proper way in which concerns may be raised outside the organisation if necessary
- penalties for maliciously making false allegations.

Public Interest Disclosure Act 1999

The Public Interest Disclosure Act came into force in Great Britain on 2 July 1999 and in Northern Ireland on 31 October 1999. The legislation has been described by American campaigners as the most far-reaching whistleblower protection law in the world. In the House of Lords, Lord Nolan, one of the most senior judges, praised it as 'skilfully achieving the essential but delicate balance between the public interest and the interests of employers'.

By setting out a clear and simple framework for raising genuine concerns about malpractice, and by guaranteeing full protection to workers who raise such issues, the Act addresses this issue in a constructive and effective way. While the legislation readily acknowledges that concerns about malpractice are best raised and addressed in the workplace, it also recognises the role that regulatory authorities and outside bodies – including the media – can and do play in deterring and detecting serious malpractice. The Act signals a break from a culture in which inertia, secrecy and silence have allowed crime, negligence and misconduct to go unchallenged, all too often with devastating consequences for the individuals and organisations involved. It means that ordinary, decent people will be less likely to turn a blind eye to wrongdoing and more likely to do the right thing. The legislation is now being used as a benchmark against which developments in Europe and elsewhere will be judged.

The Act sets out a clear and simple framework to promote responsible whistleblowing by:

- reassuring workers that silence is not the only safe option
- providing strong protection for workers who raise concerns internally
- reinforcing and protecting the right to report concerns to key regulators
- protecting more public disclosures provided that there is a valid reason for going wider and that the particular disclosure was reasonable
- helping to ensure that organisations respond by addressing the message rather than the messenger and resist the temptation to cover up serious malpractice.

Scheme of the Act

The provisions are inserted into the Employment Rights Act 1996. The scheme of the Act is to provide protection to workers who make a 'protected disclosure'. The Act enables employees who make a protected disclosure to disclose information, confidential or otherwise:

- internally
- to prescribed regulators
- to a wider audience, usually indicating the media.

Workers who are victimised or dismissed for making a protected disclosure will be able to make a claim in an employment tribunal.

Individuals covered

In addition to employees, the Act covers agency staff, contractors, homeworkers, trainees and everyone who works in the NHS. The usual employment law restrictions on the minimum length of service and age do not apply here. The Act does not currenly cover the genuinely self-employed, volunteers, the intelligence services, the army or police officers.

Malpractice

Under the Act, a protected disclosure is defined as 'any disclosure of information which, in the reasonable belief of the worker making the disclosure, tends to show one or more of the following:

(a) that a criminal offence has been committed, is being committed or is likely to be committed

(b) that a person has failed, is failing or is likely to fail to comply with any legal obligation to which he is subject

(c) that a miscarriage of justice has occurred, is occurring or is likely to occur

(d) that the health or safety of any individual has been, is being or is likely to be endangered

(e) that the environment has been, is being or is likely to be damaged, or

(f) that information tending to show any matter falling within any one of the preceding paragraphs has been, is being or is likely to be deliberately concealed. (s.43B (1))

The range of information capable of constituting a protected disclosure is extremely wide, applying to most malpractice.

Reasonable belief

The requirement that the worker has a 'reasonable belief' means that the belief need not be correct but only that the worker held the belief and it was reasonable for him or her to do so. Accordingly, it would still be a protected disclosure if the worker reasonably but mistakenly believed that a specified malpractice was occurring. The Act confirms that workers may safely seek legal advice on any concerns that they have with regard to malpractice.

The Act protects disclosures made in *good faith* to bodies such as the Health and Safety Executive,[17] the Inland Revenue,[18] Customs and Excise[19] (for sanctions controls) and the Financial Services Authority,[20] where the whistleblower *reasonably believes that the information and any allegation in it are substantially true*. At the time of writing, in the care field, the SSI is **not** a prescribed regulator.

Wider disclosures: (1) good faith, (2) reasonable belief, (3) the trigger to go wider, and (4) reasonable in all the circumstances

Wider disclosures (for example to the police, the media, MPs, pressure groups and non-prescribed regulators) are protected if, in addition to the tests for regulatory disclosures (good faith, reasonable belief and reasonable belief that the allegation is substantially true), there is a specific trigger for the whistleblower to go wider *and* the disclosures are reasonable in all the circumstances. The whistleblower is not protected if the wider disclosure is made for personal gain.

For wider disclosures only, whistleblowers must satisfy one of the following tests. They must have:

(a) reasonably believed they would be victimised if they raised the matter internally or with a prescribed regulator
(b) reasonably believed that a cover-up was likely and there was no prescribed regulator;
(c) already raised the matter internally or with a prescribed regulator.

When considering the category of 'reasonable in the circumstances', the employment tribunal is, in deciding the reasonableness of the disclosure, directed under the provisions of the Act to consider, among other factors:

- the identity of the person to whom it was made
- the seriousness of the concern
- whether the risk or danger remains
- whether the disclosure breached a duty of confidence that the employer owed a third party
- where the concern had first been raised with the employer or a prescribed regulator, the reasonableness of his or her response (which will be particularly relevant)
- if the concern had first been raised with the employer, whether any whistleblowing policy in the organisation was or should have been used. (This means that it is not enough just to have a whistleblowing policy. Concerns that are reported must be investigated and action taken as appropriate.)

Where the concern is exceptionally serious, the Act provides a further safety valve for workers who make a wider disclosure without having satisfied the normal conditions of raising the matter internally or with a prescribed regulator. This is in practice likely to apply only when, for example, a worker is genuinely concerned that a child is being sexually abused and that there is no time to waste, thus immediately reporting the matter to the police.

Full protection

Where whistleblowers are victimised in breach of the Act, they can bring a claim to an employment tribunal for compensation. If they are dismissed, the award is uncapped and based on the losses suffered. When the whistleblower is victimised in some other way but not dismissed, the award will be what is just and equitable. Losses may include expenses reasonably incurred by the whistleblower in bringing the claim to an employment tribunal and the loss of any benefit (such as bonus or pension rights) that he or she might otherwise have expected. Workers are under a duty to mitigate their loss, which, if their contract is terminated, includes obtaining or seriously seeking another job.

Whistleblowing and childcare

All organisations working with children, young people and families now need to consider whether they have the appropriate culture, procedures and review systems to ensure the well-being and safeguarding of the children and young people in their care. Whistleblowing is increasingly being recognised as a key tool in achieving this.

In the report *People Like Us,* Utting observed:

> Numerous reports of inquiries into abuse in residential settings since Court Lees refer to other staff suspecting or knowing what was going on, but not reporting it or being frustrated by management's unwillingness to act. (DoH, 1997b)

After considering recent developments in whistleblowing, Utting made a number of important recommendations, set out below:

> Shifts are needed in three cultures:
>
> - that of directors, trustees and councillors, who for reasons of money, prestige or politics find good reasons for keeping quiet about problems in organisations for which they are responsible,
> - that of salaried managers for whom the failures of subordinates may be represented as an indictment of their own performance,
> - that of staff themselves who – from a sense of worker or professional solidarity – are reluctant to rock the boat they are all in together. (DoH, 1997b)

The report also referred to the recommendation of Sir Ralph Gibson, the Chairman of Public Concern at Work, who stated:

> There should be set up within all public, private or voluntary bodies which have responsibilities for the care of others, procedures whereby those who work within organisations will be effectively encouraged and helped to raise issues of concern and conscience so that abuse of those in care and damage to the organisations themselves may be prevented or revealed. (Gibson, quoted in DoH, 1997b)

The Utting Report continues:

> All organisations which accommodate children should instruct staff that they have both a duty to their employer and a professional obligation to raise legitimate concerns about the conduct of colleagues or managers, and guarantee that this can be discharged in ways which ensure thorough investigation without prejudice to their own position and prospects.
>
> In addition:
>
> - Cultural change must be led and supported from the top.
> - Boards of management should adopt and promulgate policies of openness and promptness in dealing with complaints which affect the safety of children, and designate a board member with special responsibility at board level.
> - Executive management should be instructed to investigate and report on all complaints about staff conduct which is likely to affect children.
> - A senior official should be nominated to institute investigations where the complainant feels unable to act through line management.
> - A duty should be included in codes of conduct for staff to report behaviour by staff, managers, volunteers or other people which may cause or result in harm to the children accommodated.
> - Such reports should normally be made to a member of line management or to a nominated officer outside of line management or to a nominated member of the board of management.
> - The code should offer confidentiality for initial reports and protect a complainant in good faith against any subsequent disadvantage.
>
> These measures would substantially improve the protection of children in all residential settings. Members of staff are the adults most likely to suspect that children are being abused physically, emotionally or sexually. (DoH, 1997b)

The publication in February 2000 of *Lost in Care*, the Waterhouse Report into Child Abuse in North Wales (DoH/Welsh Office, 2000), reinforces this point. The investigation was initiated by Alison Taylor, a care worker who had sought repeatedly but unsuccessfully to blow the whistle internally and to the appropriate authorities. The report was a vindication of Mrs Taylor and led to recommendations that:

> (8) Every local authority should establish and implement conscientiously clear whistleblowing procedures enabling members of staff to make complaints and

raise matters of concern affecting the treatment or welfare of looked after children without threats or fear of reprisals in any form. (DoH/Welsh Office, 2000)

Whistleblowing policies assisted by the new legislation are therefore now recognised as an important tool in combating abuse.

Practical implications for health and care sectors

In the light of these developments, health and care providers would be well advised to consider the following:

- Employers should make it clear that it is both safe and acceptable for workers to raise any concern that they may have about misconduct or malpractice in the organisation.
- When a worker raises a concern about a specified malpractice, every effort should be made to ensure that the employer responds to the message rather than shoots the messenger.
- Employers ought to recognise that it is in their own interests to introduce effective whistleblowing procedures. This will help both parties to separate the message from the messenger.
- Employers should decide upon a person in the organisation to whom confidential disclosure can be made. This person must have the authority and determination to act if concerns are not raised with – or properly dealt with – by immediate line management.
- When a protected disclosure has been made, employers should take all reasonable steps to try to ensure that no colleague, manager or other person under its control victimises the whistleblower.
- In-house legal advisers should be directed to review confidentiality clauses in contracts of employment and in severance agreements when the working relationship has terminated.
- Although requiring a higher level of proof than internal whistleblowing, disclosure to a prescribed regulator is protected, whether or not the concern had first been raised internally. When workers reasonably believe that they will be victimised if they go to a prescribed regulator, they will be entitled to protection under the Act if they make a wider, public disclosure. Accordingly, employers should make it clear that reporting concerns to a prescribed regulator is acceptable.
- Anything that might be construed as an attempt to suppress evidence of malpractice is now particularly inadvisable since (a) reasonable suspi-

cion of a 'cover-up' would itself provide a basis for a protected disclosure; (b) a disclosure to the media is more likely to be protected; and (c) there is a much reduced scope for containing any damage by a private settlement with a confidentiality clause.

- Anonymous whistleblowing may not afford any protection because an employment tribunal must be satisfied that the employer believed that the whistleblower made the disclosure and victimised him or her because of it.

The future

There is growing recognition that whistleblowing needs to be encouraged as best practice not only to comply with the provisions of the Act, but also as a means of establishing a change in the culture of organisations. For this change to occur, it is essential that a lead is given from the top, that responsible whistleblowing is promoted and that management genuinely appears to address the issue. In England and Wales, all NHS trusts have purchased Public Concern at Work's toolkit on whistleblowing. The toolkit provides a means of devising and implementing a whistleblowing policy.

The existence of legislation protecting whistleblowers is a radical shift away from the old perceptions of whistleblowers being labelled sneaks or telltales. It is early days in terms of the legislation, but the imperative must now be for employers generally to encourage and promote whistleblowing. The existence of an interim remedy (which is already available in other circumstances under the Employment Rights Act 1996) means that a worker who is dismissed may apply for an interim order to keep his or her job as long as the application is made within seven days of the termination of employment. The employment tribunal may, at a preliminary hearing of such an application, order the employer to continue paying the worker his or her salary until the matter is finally determined.

The consideration by an employment tribunal of whether an existing policy was used when asked to determine the reasonableness of a wider disclosure, and that real compensation without statutory limits may be awarded to workers, should provide workers with sufficient protection to require organisations in the public, private and voluntary sectors to deal quickly and effectively with the message rather than the messenger. The effectiveness of the Act should not be judged solely by whether more claims are successfully made against employers. Instead, the design of the legislation, and the purpose behind the introduction of whistleblowing policies, is for responsible organisations to react and deal immediately with the problems to which they are alerted. Judged by these criteria, success will mean fewer financial scandals affecting the public purse and fewer losses of life that could and should have been avoided.

Raising it internally – defusing the situation

Where workers reasonably suspect malpractice (including physical abuse), they will be protected from victimisation if they raise the matter with their employer in good faith.

Case Study

Jane worked as a day care assistant at a private rest home. She had been there for eight months and worked happily with 20 other staff looking after the elderly residents. The only downside to the job was one of her colleagues, Mary, who was abusive to the residents and bullied the staff.

Mary was particularly unpleasant to two residents: she would startle them from behind and push them around. On one occasion, Jane saw Mary bend one of their thumbs back. When Jane asked Mary what she was doing, Mary said that she had been given permission to do this. Jane raised the matter with the home's owner; he said he would sort it out and told Jane to keep on smiling.

A few weeks later, some of Jane's colleagues told her that they had seen Mary hit one of the residents and that they had reported the matter to the owner. Mary nevertheless carried on working normally, and nothing seemed to happen. Thus, while Jane liked the owner of the home, she thought that it would be futile to raise the matter with him again. Jane knew that the local authority inspectors would be visiting the home soon and decided to mention her concerns directly to them.

When the inspector came, Jane mentioned the matter. The inspector asked whether the colleagues who had seen Mary hit the resident would give a statement. Jane discussed this with them, and the colleagues contacted the inspector. When the inspector had all the evidence, he wrote to the home and said that the matter was so serious that he was referring the incident to the police.

Mary was suspended, but Jane was suspended too in case her presence at work hindered the investigation. Jane was told she should not talk to anyone about the suspected misconduct or about her suspension. She was very upset because she thought she had done nothing wrong. Two weeks later, she got a letter at home telling her she was to return to work the following week. The letter also said that she was to receive a written warning: she had disclosed

Case Study (cont'd)

confidential information and had damaged the reputation of the home. Jane thought this was a prelude to her being sacked, and contacted Public Concern at Work.

A legal adviser discussed the matter with Jane over the telephone and assured her she had done nothing wrong. As it was clear that she liked the home and did not want to lose her job, she was advised to try to defuse the situation rather than assert her legal rights or have the charity write a lawyer's letter. With the assistance of a legal adviser, Jane drafted a letter to send to the owner in which she apologised for any inconvenience she had caused. Jane also explained that she had tried to do the right thing and hoped that the owner would in time recognise that Jane had been protecting rather than undermining the reputation of the home. She also pointed out that she herself had not called in the police and stressed how much she liked working at the home. The letter worked. The written warning was withdrawn, and the owner, residents and colleagues welcomed Jane back into the home.

An exceptionally serious concern

Where a worker reasonably suspects malpractice of an exceptionally serious nature, a wider disclosure will be protected if he or she reasonably believes that the information and any allegation relating to it are substantially true, provided the disclosure is reasonable and made in good faith.

Case Study

Judy was the deputy matron at a private nursing home for the elderly, run by Mr and Mrs T. Some of the residents were blind, and some suffered from senile dementia. While Judy had been worried about the behaviour of Mr T for a couple of years, things came to a head when a care assistant told her she had entered one of the resident's rooms and found him behaving strangely next to one of the female residents. When Judy returned with the care assistant, Mr T had left the room and they discovered what seemed to be semen on the lady's cardigan and hair. Judy immediately tended to the

Case Study (cont'd)

resident and washed her and her cardigan – thinking first of the resident rather than of the value of the evidence.

A few weeks later, Judy read about Action on Elder Abuse, who referred her to Public Concern at Work. As her concerns were about the manager of the home, Judy did not feel confident that she could safely raise the matter with him or its owner, who was his wife. Equally, if she went to the health authority inspectors or to the police, there was a risk that, as she had removed the evidence, it would simply be a matter of her word against Mr T's. As Mr T had a long career in the caring sector – during which he had received a prestigious award for medical proficiency – Judy's word alone might well not have been enough.

The charity advised Judy to keep a vigilant eye on Mr T and to try to ensure that he was not left alone with the female residents. If some other incident occurred, she was advised to contact Public Concern at Work immediately, and if there was any supporting evidence, she should take care to keep it. A legal adviser from the charity contacted the SSI at the DoH to check that the advice given to Judy was sensible and was told that if Judy came back with more evidence, she should contact the specialist police who dealt with abuse cases.

Several months later, Judy rang. The previous night she had entered a room in which three ladies were sitting. Two were blind and one was suffering from senile dementia. Mr T appeared to have his groin in the face of the lady with senile dementia, and Judy thought he might be forcing oral sex on the resident. She left the room and fetched a colleague. Once Mr T had gone, they entered the room, opened a clean cotton swab, swabbed the lady's mouth and sealed the specimen. Once Judy was home, she contacted Public Concern at Work.

The charity went back to the SSI, but they were unable to offer any practical advice. The charity then contacted the local police, who said it was a matter for a special division at police headquarters. There the legal adviser handling the case on behalf of Public Concern at Work was told that the special division dealt only with child and not elder abuse, which was a matter for the local CID. He explained that all that was wanted at this stage was a forensic test of the swab – if the specimen were positive, the police would need to be called in. The police headquarters explained that, because of financial constraints, the police could not spend any money on forensic tests until there was a formal complaint. The legal adviser pointed out that this put Judy in an unfortunate situation as the matter would have to be put to Mr T even if the forensic evidence cleared him.

The charity then contacted the Home Office Forensic Laboratory, explained the situation and agreed to pay the costs of the tests. They collected the swab from Judy's home and, within 24 hours, the sample had been analysed and had been found to contain semen. The evidence was immediately forwarded to the

Case Study (cont'd)

local CID, who then interviewed Judy before arresting Mr T the next day. He initially denied the incident but, when confronted with the forensic evidence, he changed his stance. Other incidents were put to him, including one in which his victim died the day after his assault.

Mr T pleaded guilty to three charges of indecent assault between 1987 and 1996 and was sentenced to four years in prison. The judge told him, 'Your behaviour was disgusting. It is almost beyond belief someone running a nursing home could abuse patients in such a grotesque manner. It is completely out of my experience of the law.'

The home was taken over by new owners shortly after Mr T's arrest. Judy's job was secure, and the residents are now being well cared for. As for Judy's actions, one relative said, 'All of us owe a great deal of thanks and debt of gratitude to Judy, without whom this scandal would never have been exposed.' Another commented 'If it hadn't been for her, it could still be going on and no one would ever have known. Judy really deserves a medal.'

Notes

1 The ferry sank, and 194 people died, because it had been sailing with its bow doors open. The inquiry found that staff had on five previous occasions reported that this was happening, but their concerns had got lost at the level of middle management.

2 The inquiry found that a supervisor had noticed the loose wiring in the junction box a couple of months earlier but said nothing as 'he did not want to rock the boat'; 35 passengers died.

3 The inquiry into the £2 billion collapse found there had been an autocratic environment at The Bank of Credit and Commerce International in which no one was prepared to speak up. The only employee who had was an internal auditor who was made redundant.

4 An employee at Matrix Churchill had written to the Foreign Secretary warning that munitions equipment was being exported to Iraq. Although this letter was ignored by civil servants for a number of years, it was a fear that the whistleblower would contact the press during the prosecution of the company for breaching the arms embargo that caused the Deputy Prime Minister to refuse to suppress evidence that the government had been aware of the suspect exports.

5 Four schoolchildren drowned when a school canoeing trip went badly wrong. One of the instructors at the centre had written to the managing director weeks before the tragedy warning that 'You should have a careful look at your standards of safety. Otherwise you might find yourself trying to explain why someone's son or daughter will not be coming home.' Because he had ignored this graphic warning, the Managing Director was jailed for two years for corporate manslaughter.

6 The official regulator banned one of the senior managers at Barings Bank from future work as he had been aware of the risk inherent in Nick Leeson's activities. Although the manager said that he had expressed his fears, the regulator found that he had failed to blow the whistle either loudly or clearly.

7 A consultant anaesthetist, Steven Bolsin, was victimised after raising concerns about the techniques of surgeons working on children with heart complaints. An inquiry into the deaths of 29 children found that the standard of care at the hospital was inadequate.

8 Chris Chapman was a biochemist who was made redundant shortly after raising his concern about misconduct in the area of medical research.

9 Graham Pink was a nurse who challenged understaffing in geriatric wards, leading to the neglect of and danger to the patients. On going to the media, he was suspended and later dismissed.

10 Dr Millar was sacked as head of clinical trials for British Biotech after he raised his concerns about the efficacy of key drug developments.

11 The European Commission internal auditor whose disclosure of financial irregularities led to the resignation of the European Commission in March 1999.

12 Appoints auditors to all local authorities and NHS bodies in England and Wales, as well as addressing issues of financial conduct and value for money in these services.

13 First published in 1996 by Public Concern at Work as an analysis of the laws and practices in Europe that affect attitudes toward whistleblowing, fraud and the European Union.

14 Times Newspapers and the British Medical Association helped to finance the cost of Dr Millar's successful legal defence in an action for breach of confidence.

15 Cm 3270-1 (May 1996). The Committee was set up to examine current concerns about the standards of conduct of all holders of public office, including arrangements relating to financial and commercial activities, and to make recommendations on any change in present arrangements that might be required to ensure the highest standards of propriety in public life.

16 ibid, Recommendation 2.

17 Aims to ensure that risks to people's health and safety from work activities are properly controlled.

18 Responsible, under the overall direction of Treasury Ministers, for the efficient administration of taxes.

19 Deals with VAT (Sales tax). Enforces export sanctions, including arms embargoes.

20 Responsible for the supervision of banks and the wholesale money market regime.

13

Social Work Practice in the Criminal Justice System

Anne Worrall and Anna Souhami

Introduction

The relationship between the social work profession and the criminal justice system has been one of tension and ambivalence since the demise of the rehabilitative ideal in the latter decades of the twentieth century. This has been particularly evident in the changing nature of the Probation Service – once the embodiment of the presence of social work in the criminal courts – culminating in the detachment of its training from the training of social workers in 1996 and the government's proposal to change its name to the Community Punishment and Rehabilitation Service in 2001. It might be argued that the Probation Service has ultimately resolved the tension by compromising (some would say, abandoning) its social work roots (Harris, 1996).

Local authority social workers, who have traditionally worked in juvenile courts (and, to a lesser extent, with mentally disordered offenders) have had a different experience. For them, the criminal justice system has been hostile territory ever since the failure of the Children and Young Person Act 1969, which had promised them so much power in the treatment of juvenile delinquents but which, instead, saw them villified and ignored by magistrates and judges, who sent an unprecedented number of juveniles to borstals and detention centres in the 1970s. Magistrates frequently compared social workers unfavourably with probation officers (Carlen and Powell, 1979; Parker, 1989; Brown, 1990). Social workers were perceived to be unfamiliar with court 'culture', too idealistic and lacking 'common sense.'

The struggle of juvenile justice (later youth justice) workers to recover their credibility while retaining their commitment to the welfare of young offenders throughout the 1980s can be seen, in retrospect, as an heroic enterprise, but one which was all but overturned by developments in the 1990s, culminating in the Crime and Disorder Act 1998 and the Youth

Justice and Criminal Evidence Act 1999. During the 1990s, youth justice workers were required to distance themselves somewhat from traditional social work skills and values, creating a legacy of ambivalence that has re-surfaced with the creation of Youth Offending Teams (YOTs). Youth justice workers have come to view themselves as 'officers of the court', accountable more to the courts than to social services and having less and less in common with other social workers. They have also adopted what some perceive to be a male-dominated, working-class 'culture' in their relationships with young (predominantly male) offenders:

> not like social workers at all, the youth justice team aren't. Social work teams tend to be, generally speaking, female oriented, more women workers than men and... sometimes the culture is white, middle class and suffocatingly so in my view, but maybe I'm wrong there... there's a bit more in youth justice teams of the male working class attitude, and you could argue that that's better for the young people we're working with, you know. We can approach them more directly, without trying to patronise them... I feel more comfortable in a youth justice team for that reason really. (Male social worker, reflecting on establishing a YOT in 1999)

This chapter will examine the historical fortunes of the continuous conflict between 'care' and 'control' in the role of youth justice workers before outlining the major developments that led to the Crime and Disorder Act 1998. It will then discuss the principles and key provisions of that Act and the Youth Justice and Criminal Evidence Act 1999 before concluding with a discussion of the implications of these Acts for the future of social work practice in youth justice, using material from recent research on the formation of a YOT.

For the sake of coherence, this chapter will focus on the role of social workers in relation to youth justice, but it should be remembered that social workers working both for the local authority and in voluntary organisations come into contact with the criminal justice system in several other ways:

- In *child protection* work, they are involved with the victims of child abuse and neglect, and frequently find themselves working alongside other criminal justice personnel dealing with the perpetrators of crimes against children (see, for example, Otway, 1996).
- Social workers have always had a role in caring for *mentally ill* people. With the shift from institutional to community care, that role now includes protecting the public from the nuisance and danger of mentally disturbed people whose behaviour is criminal or criminalised. In so doing, they are expected to provide a diversion from, or an alternative to, the criminal justice system. In both of these roles, social workers are increasingly required to adopt a multi-agency approach, working with

the police, the Probation Service, the courts and the prison service to protect the public from dangerous offenders (Nash, 1999).

- Under the Children Act 1989, social workers have a responsibility to ensure that juveniles living away from home are protected from harm. The Utting Report (DoH, 1997b) highlighted the needs of *juveniles in custody* and recommended that Young Offender Institutions should be represented on Area Child Protection Committees.
- Social workers are involved with the *families of prisoners*, especially female prisoners. Increasingly called upon to convey children to prisons to visit their mothers, they also have to make decisions about the short- and long-term care of those children. The increase in the number of women being sent to prison, as well as in our existing knowledge that their children are less likely to be cared for by a partner than are the children of men in prison, makes the role of social workers increasingly significant (Shaw, 1992; Caddle and Crisp, 1997).
- Social workers are designated *'appropriate adults'* under the Police and Criminal Evidence Act 1984. They are called upon to accompany 'vulnerable' people (typically young people or people experiencing mental illness or learning difficulties) who are interviewed by the police. Their role is to ensure that the interviewee understands what is happening and that his or her welfare needs are attended to. The Audit Commission (1998) update on *Misspent Youth* suggested that such a role is very expensive and that volunteers should be trained to do this work.
- Residential social workers in children's homes and secure accommodation are involved in caring and controlling particularly difficult young people who may be engaged in criminal activity. For example, there has been concern in recent years about the involvement of looked-after teenage girls in prostitution (Barnardo's, 1998; Children's Society, 1999).

In the best interests of the child – from maximum intervention to minimum intervention to early intervention

Ever since the Children and Young Person Act 1933, juvenile courts have been required to give paramount regard to the welfare of any child or young person appearing before them. This legislation has never been repealed, but many would argue that it fell into disuse in the latter decades of the twentieth century, for a variety of reasons. Acting in the best interests of a child's welfare often meant, in practice, the removal of the child from his or her family to an institution – a children's home, approved school, detention centre or borstal. During the 1960s, concern about the institutionalisation of naughty children was high on the political agenda and resulted in a series of reports (Gelsthorpe and Morris, 1994) culminating in the Children and Young Person Act 1969. The aim of this legislation was to decriminalise and depoliticise juvenile justice. The philosophy of treatment was intended to remove the stigma of criminal proceedings from young offenders. The distinction between the delinquent and the non-delinquent child in trouble was blurred (crime being viewed as just one of many possible manifestations of underlying disturbance), the most appropriate people to deal with both being the trained experts – namely, local authority social workers in the newly created social services departments (Worrall, 1997)

But the political tide had already turned, and the Act was never fully implemented or resourced. Instead of diverting young people from the criminal justice system, newly introduced police cautioning drew more young people into its net. Magistrates refused to entrust them to the care of social workers, and custodial sentences increased, contrary to the intentions of the 1969 Act. Notions of rehabilitation came under increasing attack from a number of directions, and this had implications for work with young offenders. Magistrates seeking a greater control of young offenders found themselves in uneasy alliance with radical lawyers who believed that social workers had too much power to infringe the civil liberties of youngsters, and a return to principles of 'justice' and 'due process' emerged in the 1980s (Pitts, 1988, 1990; Muncie, 1999).

Although a small number of juvenile offenders were still sent to custody, this figure dropped dramatically, a policy of 'bifurcation' meaning that the majority of less serious offenders were dealt with in the community by social workers specialising as juvenile justice workers. Throughout this period, juvenile justice workers developed a clear philosophy of maximum intervention in the courts and minimal intervention with young people, persuading decision-makers of the need to allow young people to 'grow out of crime' in line with the developmental theory of adolescence. According to this theory, based on the sociological theory of symbolic interaction (or 'labelling'), many young people committed minor crime as part of growing up (Rutherford, 1986, 1992). The more formal intervention they experienced (however benignly meant), the more likely they were to become embedded in a criminal subculture and to continue their criminal behaviour. In contrast, they would be assisted to desist from crime by being supported in their own communities with resources that encouraged their sense of 'belonging' and developed their repertoire of skills and problem-solving choices.

In retrospect, the 1980s can now be seen as the 'successful decade' for work with young offenders – known crime by young people fell by 26 per cent, and the number of custodial sentences fell from a peak of 12,000 in 1984 to 3,600 in 1994. The government White Paper *Crime, Justice and*

Protecting the Public argued that 'there is no evidence that the reduction in the use of custodial sentences has resulted in increases in juvenile crime' (Home Office, 1990).

Much, however, changed in the early 1990s and, as we shall see in the next section, the philosophy of minimal intervention has now given way to a return not only to maximum intervention, but also to the early identification of potential offenders and early intervention, involving electronic monitoring and secure training centres (run by the prison service), for children as young as 10 years of age, as well as formal supervision orders for troublesome children even younger.

The demise of the child in criminal law

The abolition of 'criminal care orders' by the 1989 Children Act meant that there was, by the 1990s, no non-secure institutional provision for juvenile offenders under the age of 14 years. The creation of the Youth Court by the 1991 Criminal Justice Act was more concerned with bringing proceedings into line with the age of majority than with dealing with very young offenders – it being assumed that fewer and fewer delinquents aged under 14 years would be brought to court. However, two moral panics in the early 1990s led to a reversal of this trend.

The first moral panic related to persistent young offenders – a small number of children who were thought to be responsible for a disproportionate amount of not-so-trivial crime, especially burglary and criminal damage. In response, in 1992, Michael Howard announced his intention to introduce secure training units for 12–14-year-old persistent offenders who were unable or unwilling to be subject to supervision in the community. This provision was included in the 1994 Criminal Justice and Public Order Act, the first secure training unit being opened in 1998.

The second moral panic was triggered by the killing of Jamie Bulger by two ten-year-old boys in 1993. There has always been an equivalent to a life sentence for juveniles who commit extremely serious offences such as murder, manslaughter and rape. This provision is to be found in s.53 of the 1933 Children and Young Person Act, which allows courts to hold juveniles in secure accommodation 'at Her Majesty's Pleasure' and to transfer them to prison when they are old enough. The number of young people, most of them very disturbed youngsters, who have been detained in this way for murder or manslaughter has fluctuated between 20 and 40 a year for the past 20 years, and of these, only 12 in the whole 20 years have been under 14 years of age (Boswell, 1996; Cavadino, 1996). Despite this, the Jamie Bulger murder became symbolic of a perceived increase of 'pure evil' among very young children and a growing public belief that children who commit 'adult' crimes should be treated as adults.

Misspent youth and 'no excuses'

In 1996, the Audit Commission produced a report on the youth justice system entitled *Misspent Youth* (Audit Commission, 1996). The Commission's priority was to establish whether the youth justice system was working efficiently, effectively and economically – whether it was providing 'value for money'. The report criticised the delay in processing young offenders through the courts, the insufficient emphasis on addressing offending behaviour, the uncoordinated work between concerned agencies and the lack of preventative work with potential offenders. Unsurprisingly, it argued that performance was not related to resources and that, although there were examples of good practice by social services departments, there was a lack of consistency across the country. It recommended greater inter-agency cooperation, a clearer focus on work intended to address offending behaviour and a greater investment in preventative measures.

This agenda was taken up by the new Labour government in 1997, which declared itself 'tough on crime and tough on the causes of crime'. In an attempt to create an ethos of 'no more excuses', it produced a number of consultation papers, including an update of *Misspent Youth* (Audit Commission, 1998), which paved the way for the Crime and Disorder Act 1998.

Curfews, tags and group conferencing – in the name of restorative justice?

The government has ensured earlier formal intervention in the lives of naughty children in three ways through the provisions of the Crime and Disorder Act 1998. First, it has abolished the concept of *doli incapax* which provided a transitional zone between the age of criminal responsibility (10 years) and the age at which a young person was deemed fully to understand the difference between 'serious wrong' and 'simple naughtiness' (14 years). Between the ages of 10 and 14 years, there existed a rebuttable presumption that the child did not have that understanding. That presumption no longer exists.

Second, the Act makes major changes to the lower end of the youth justice system, changes that will almost certainly increase the number of young teenagers drawn into the purview of the system. Police cautions are to be replaced with a system of reprimands and warnings, the latter involving referral to the new multi-agency YOTs (consisting of police, social workers, probation officers and education and health representatives) for possible further intervention in the form of a rehabilitation programme. The courts are also being given additional powers to sentence young offenders to reparation orders and action plans, both of which are to be imposed at an early stage of a criminal career. At what is supposed to be a later stage, the new detention and training order provides a new single custodial sentence for 10–17-year-olds. Half the term of such orders will be served in custody and half in the community.

Third, the Act introduces a number of civil orders (backed with criminal sanctions) to control sub-criminal antisocial behaviour – or incivility. Antisocial orders can be issued against families who harass or intimidate their neighbours. Although the Act envisages that these orders will be used only to control serious criminal or sub-criminal behaviour rather than minor neighbour disputes, it remains to be seen how this will be used in practice. Parenting orders can be made against parents deemed to be in need of counselling or guidance in good parenting, requiring them to attend classes or sessions. Child safety orders (which have nothing to do with child protection, child abuse or child neglect) are designed to control children under the age of 10 years who appear to be unsupervised or causing a nuisance.

Local child curfews allow the police to impose a temporary curfew in a particular area, and the police are also given the power to remove any child in a public place whom they suspect to be truanting from school. A child who breaches a curfew order is returned home, but if there is no-one at home to receive them, they may be taken into police protection under childcare legislation. Presumably, they may also be made the subject of a child safety order and their parents the subjects of a parenting order. Goldson (1999) argues that these new orders 'distort and corrupt the language of child protection to legitimise expanded forms of child confinement'.

In addition to the specific provisions of the Crime and Disorder Act, legislation already exists to enable courts to impose curfew orders on young people from the age of 10 years upwards and for those curfews to be electronically monitored. Since December 1999, this provision has been available to all courts, raising the interesting spectacle of children in school sporting tags.

One final twist in the 'no excuses' agenda is provided by the 1999 Youth Justice and Criminal Evidence Act. Rather belatedly adopting the now fashionable concept of 'restorative justice' (which the Act interprets as involving 'responsibility, reparation and reintegration'), this new Act makes provision for a form of group conferencing called a Youth Offending Panel, to which courts may refer a first offender after a guilty plea in court. The panel will consist of predominantly lay people from the local community who will engage in conflict-resolution processes, following the now celebrated 'family group conferencing' innovations in New Zealand, Australia and Canada.

All at sea? YOTs and (partner)ships

The Crime and Disorder Act 1998 has established a national Youth Justice Board and local multi-agency YOT. YOTs are to be set up by every local authority with social service and education responsibilities, and they are required to provide the following youth justice services (Home Office *et al.*, 1998):

- Appropriate adult services (under PACE 1984)
- Assessment and intervention work in support of a final warning
- Bail support for young people remanded from court
- The placement in local authority accommodation of children and young people remanded or committed to such accommodation
- Writing reports (such as pre-sentence reports) and other information by the courts
- Providing responsible officers in relation to parenting orders, child safety orders, reparation orders and action plan orders
- Supervision of children and young people under supervision orders and detention and training orders
- Post-release supervision of children and young people released from custody.

A key issue for YOTs is how the roles of different practitioners are developed. How far do members retain their identity as practitioners from different agencies? The Crime and Disorder Act does not prescribe a role for particular members, and the official guidance, *Establishing Youth Offending Teams* (Home Office *et al.*, 1998), allows 'in principle' any team member to undertake any function, such as writing pre-sentence reports and supervising offenders.

The emphasis is on the 'flexibility' of working practice: YOT members should expect work to be allocated 'in the light of their personal skills and experience, not solely because of their professional background' (Home Office *et al.*, 1998). Some degree of specialism could, however, be maintained. Job outlines for members from different agencies are suggested. For example, the duties of the health staff could include identifying and addressing the physical and mental health needs of young offenders, liaising with other health professionals who are working with the young offender and providing advice on 'healthy lifestyles' as part of an offending behaviour programme.

So in developing practitioners' roles and creating the 'cultural change' in practice required by the Crime and Disorder Act (Universities of Sheffield and Hull, 1999), YOTs have to decide how to balance this flexibility in working practice with specialist input. The bulk of the work of the YOT encompasses the administration and supervision of court orders, and it is in this context that the questions concerning the roles of practitioners can most clearly be observed. There appear to be two ways in which the roles of practitioners from partner agencies can be developed. Will these practitioners provide specialist input into cases held by social workers? Or will they become caseholders themselves? In short, on what basis are professionals other than social workers appointed to YOTs? Are they there to represent the interests and policies of their 'home' agency, or do they bring a range of experiences, skills and knowledge to contribute to a newly conceptualised generic service to young offenders? If the latter is the case, how will their home agency support and respond to their new role (Hunter, 1999; McCurry, 1999)? These roles have different implications for the identity of YOT practitioners:

> I've done a pre-sentence report. I don't want to do another one. Well, it detracts from what I'm here for, doesn't it? If I'd wanted to be a social worker on the YOT, I would have trained as one, wouldn't I? (Health worker, newly appointed to a YOT in 1999)

The formation of multi-agency teams may also bring about a 'cultural change' in the approach to work with young offenders. As well as bringing different skills and expertise to the YOTs, practitioners from partner agencies also bring different occupational cultures. Will the introduction of police officers to the teams, for example, produce a change in ethos in work with young offenders?:

> It is my feeling that the bringing together of the different organisations was to certainly bring a hardening of the shell. The police officer's general attitude is one of having a stricter guideline towards offenders. (Police officer in newly formed YOT in 1999)

> The police have always seen social workers as in league with the service user; social workers have always seen the police as b****s who are locking them up. (Social worker in newly formed YOT in 1999)

The qualifications of YOT members may be an important determinant of their role. If their roles are clearly differentiated according to their agency, the problem of equivalence in qualification might not be as acute: they would be performing duties in which they were likely to be experienced. It may, for example, seem quite appropriate for police officers on teams to oversee curfew orders, liaise with attendance centres and so on. But are they qualified to write pre-sentence reports? And, perhaps more importantly, will they bring a different ethos to the writing of these?

The development of new processes and procedures poses another major set of problems. The establishment of YOTs provides an opportunity to review and revise procedures to ensure 'ownership' by all partner agencies. But which agency will dominate? How are the differences in the processes understood by practitioners in different agencies? Are there processes that cannot be standardised, and what does this indicate about the extent to which practitioners can lose their identity into the common role of a YOT member? Of most significance are the procedures and protocols for information exchange. The issue of confidentiality inevitably causes tension between workers from different agencies. Health workers, in particular, have difficulty in sharing what they perceive to be confidential information about a service-user. For the police, however, 'intelligence' gathering is now one of the most important aspects of their role:

> If I know about his [class A] drug use I can minimize it and change his pattern of offending. Now I'll have to tell him to shut his mouth. The whole philosophy has changed. (Social worker in newly formed YOT)

In addition to these team-building concerns, the YOTs will also be required to develop different ways of working with young offenders. In particular, they are required to develop programmes for violent and sex offenders, most of whom will already have served time in custody as part of their detention and training orders. At the other end of the spectrum, preventative group work with younger and younger offenders may involve very different skills and activities:

> The population of young offenders isn't going to change, but work with them is. And we're getting them younger. (Team leader of newly formed YOT)

Conclusion

This chapter has attempted to outline some of the traditional dilemmas facing social workers when they enter the world of criminal justice, as well as identifying probable future directions in the light of recent legislation. One message is clear: we are moving into a phase of greater, rather than less, formal intervention in the lives of naughty children. Advocates of the 'growing out of crime' school of juvenile delinquency will predict an unprecedented number of criminalised and stigmatised young people as a result, while those who believe that it is indeed possible to identify potential offenders before they reach the age of criminal responsibility will welcome the present government's commitment to early intervention.

14

Special Educational Needs

Tanya Callman

The Education Act 1996 defines a child as having special educational needs if he or she has a learning difficulty which calls for special educational provision to be made.[1] The same Act then defines 'learning difficulty' with reference to the child (a) having a significantly greater difficulty in learning than the majority of children his age (b) having a disability which prevents or hinders the child from making use of educational facilities of a kind generally provided for children of his age in schools within the area of the local education authority.

Essentially, therefore, a duty arises on the local education authority if the child has a learning difficulty which calls for special educational provision to be made. The Statementing process, referred to in the Education Act and the Education (Special Educational Needs) Regulations 1994,[2] enables the child's parents, the school or the local authority itself to commence a process whereby the child's needs are assessed with a view to determining whether the local education authority should issue a Statement of Special Educational Needs (the Statement), a formal document recording the child's special educational needs and then setting out the special educational provision required to meet those needs. The Statement has been likened in the case law to a medical prescription,[3] which first diagnoses the needs and then prescribes the provision to meet those needs. The Court of Appeal has specified that there should be provision (in Part III of the child's Statement of Special Educational Needs) to meet each and every educational need set out in (Part II) of the child's Statement.[4]

Not all children with special educational needs receive a Statement. There is a Code of Practice *(Code of Practice on the Identification and Assessment of Special Educational Needs)*[5] that sets out the school-based stages for identifying children with special educational needs and providing them with support. These stages must have been gone through before the local education authority can commence the assessment of special educational needs with a view to the local authority deciding whether to issue a Statement.

If, following an assessment of the child's needs, the local authority determines that it is necessary to provide the special educational provision to meet them, it issues a Statement. This is a significant document that provides the child and his or her parents with a valuable tool, since the requirement to provide the special educational provision specified on the Statement is legally enforceable. The courts are frequently being approached about issues relating to the Statementing process and recently set down criteria, for example that the child's Statement should be sufficiently specific to enable anyone looking at it to know exactly what was to be provided.[6]

The backdrop to the legislative framework is a policy of 'inclusion', whereby the child with special educational needs should normally be educated in mainstream schools, as long as this is compatible with:

(a) his receiving the special educational provision which his learning difficulty calls for

(b) the provision of efficient education for the children with whom he will be educated and

(c) the efficient use of resources.[7]

There is a general principle, derived from s.9 of the Education Act 1996, that pupils are to be educated in accordance with their parents' wishes, as far as this is compatible with the provision of efficient instruction and training, and the avoidance of unreasonable public expenditure. In the context of special educational needs, the legislation and the case law[8] also make provision for parental preference regarding choice of school to be taken into account, subject to similar exceptions. The House of Lords has recently clarified how the question of prejudice towards the efficient use of resources is to be approached in the context of parental choice of school. It is the responsible local authority's resources, rather than the cost to the public purse as a whole, that have to be considered.[9] Unsurprisingly, the law also requires that the school that is named in a child's Statement must be capable of making the special educational provision set out in the Statement.

A social worker can be involved in the statutory assessment process as one of the professionals who assists in providing reports on the child. The local education authority will request these reports. The reports are attached (in a series of appendices) either to the initial assessment documentation or to the child's formal Statement. The Code of Practice provides guidance to professionals about the detailed way in which special educational needs should be addressed, with useful flowcharts regarding the strict timetable that must be adhered to in the statutory process. Practitioners need to ensure that they keep up to date with any changes in this field – at the time of writing, for example, a new Code of Practice has just been issued by the Department for Education and Employment (DFEE).[10]

Children with special educational needs have a range of difficulties, ranging from specific learning difficulties to physical disabilities, sensory impairments and emotional and behavioural difficulties. This latter category can often involve social workers, who have to liaise closely with the education and health professionals in providing multi-disciplinary input for a child with a Statement. The child's school will provide an individual education plan for the child that identifies in detail targets and objectives for that child. All children with a Statement have their statements reviewed annually, and the school will arrange a meeting that the child's social worker may be invited to attend. Once again, further reports are required, and the review meeting recommends whether the child's Statement should be amended. Children ready to leave school have separate transition reviews in which the emphasis is on looking at their options on leaving school.

In an ideal world, all professionals dealing with children with special educational needs would regularly liaise and would ensure that all the special educational provision was being provided. Reality is, however, in stark contrast to the idyll. Resources – casting their ever-familiar shadow – play a key role in the ability of the service providers to meet needs. Consequently, the local education authority and health authority often engage in unseemly brawls as each seeks to 'pass the buck' to the other to provide certain forms of special educational provision.

The courts have ruled that if some form of special educational provision is set out in a child's Statement, the local education authority is under a duty to supply this and cannot be relieved of its duty to arrange the special educational provision by arguing that the people who were to supply it were employed within the NHS and were not in their direct employment.[11] In one case, a local education authority sought to argue that it was relieved of the necessity of complying with a child's Statement because of a failure by the district health authority to provide adequate resources to comply with the local education authority's request for help. The judge held that, under the education legislation, it was the duty of the local education authority itself to arrange that the special educational provision specified in a child's Statement was made. That duty was owed personally to the child and was not delegable. Moreover, if the local education authority requested help from the health authority and no help was forthcoming, there was no 'let out' under the legislation for the local education authority.[12] The dispute regarding whether a particular form of provision is the responsibility of the local education authority or the health authority has also loomed large in the context of therapy provision for children with special educational needs.[13]

If a parent of a child with special educational needs is unhappy with the contents of his or her child's Statement, the parent can bring an appeal to an independent special educational needs tribunal. The right of appeal is vested in the parent rather than the child,[14] although the impact of the Human Rights Act 1998 may mean that new cases are brought to challenge this. The special educational needs tribunal process is set out in the Education Act and in the recent Special Educational Needs Tribunal Regulations 1999.[15] The special educational needs tribunal comprises a panel of three members with a legally qualified chairperson. The tribunal process enables parties to air their case orally and to call witnesses. The tribunal is governed by strict procedural rules, such as those regarding the submission of late evidence. A decision of the special educational needs tribunal can in some cases be appealed to the High Court.[16] Although social workers may attend hearings of the special educational needs tribunal, this rarely happens, social work input being more likely in the preparation of reports for the tribunal to read or the provision of costings for the social services that a family might need, for example respite care, which may be available to the family of a child with special educational needs. Issues relating to special educational needs may often overlap with the duties of social workers in relation to children's welfare and safety.

It is important for any social worker to be alert to the prospect of litigation for negligence. The courts have recently been considerably exercised by attempts to bring negligence actions against local authorities for failing to provide adequately, or at all, for children with special educational needs. A high-profile negligence action was brought against a local authority by Pamela Phelps. She asserted that the local authority had been negligent in failing to have diagnosed or adequately provided for her dyslexia, with the result that she had left school at the age of 16 with a spelling age of 7 years 8 months.[17] There had been a significant discrepancy between her chronological age and her performance level. Many professionals, including social workers, had been involved in her case, and the educational psychologist had taken the (incorrect) view that Pamela's difficulties arose out of emotional and behavioural difficulties rather than specific learning difficulties. The Court of Appeal held that no such claim could lie in law and that Pamela Phelps was therefore not entitled to damages; however her case was appealed to the House of Lords.[18] The House of Lords issued a landmark judgment finding the local authority, the London Borough of Hillingdon, liable for the acts or omissions of its employees, in failing to have diagnosed or adequately provided for Pamela's dyslexia. The judgment, in holding that persons providing educational services owe a direct duty of care to the children with whom they are engaged, is very significant. There is no blanket immunity for such professionals from liability. The local education authority can therefore be vicariously liable for any negligent acts or omissions by such professionals.

Social workers can also become involved in broader issues than just the content or delivery of a child's Statement. The legislation enables the local education authority in certain circumstances to provide education otherwise than in a school for children with special educational needs.[19] Pupils who have been excluded from school or are being educated in pupil referral units are another key group who require support and assistance not only from the local education authority, but also from social services departments. There is an entire raft of legislation and guidance regarding pupils who are excluded from school, the emphasis once again being on inclusion wherever possible. The recent circular produced by the DFEE, Circular 10/99, entitled *Social Inclusion: Pupil Support*, addresses issues relating to pupil behaviour and discipline, school attendance, exclusion from school and the re-integration of excluded pupils. It places an emphasis on early intervention and prevention through multi-agency working and partnership with parents.

As this chapter has hopefully demonstrated, there are numerous issues relating to children with special educational needs of which social workers need to be aware. There is a discernible and alarming trend of those in different departments failing to cooperate fully, each asserting that a matter is an 'education' issue rather than a 'social services' one. Good practice, however, clearly demands a multi-disciplinary approach. This is essential to provide fully and responsibly for all children with special educational needs.

Notes

1 Education Act 1996 s.312.

2 S.I. 1994 No 1047.

3 *R* v. *Secretary of State for Education and Science ex parte E* [1992] 1 FLR 377.

4 See note 3 above.

5 ISBN 0 855224444, 1994. See also note 10 for new draft Code of Practice.

6 *L* v. *Clarke and Somerset County Council* [1998] ELR 129.

7 S.316 Education Act 1996.

8 See *C* v. *Buckinghamshire County Council and the Special Educational Needs Tribunal* [1999] ELR 179, Court of Appeal.

9 See *B* v. *London Borough of Harrow and the Special Educational Needs Tribunal* [2000] 1 WLR 223, House of Lords. See also a discussion of the issues in Special Educational Needs and Prejudice to the Efficient Use of Resources by Richard McManus QC in *Education, Public Law and the Individual* Volume 5 Issue 1 2000 (Hart Publishing).

10 See DFEE website at http://www.dfee.gov.uk/sen/standard.htm.

11 *R* v. *Lancashire County Council ex parte M* [1989] 2 FLR, Court of Appeal.

12 *R* v. *London Borough of Harrow ex parte M* [1997] ELR 62.

13 See, for example, *London Borough of Bromley* v. *Special Educational Needs Tribunal and others* [1999] ELR 260, Court of Appeal and *R* v. *Wakefield MBC ex parte G* [1998] 2 FCR.

14 See *S* v. *Special Educational Needs Tribunal and the City of Westminster* [1996] ELR 228, Court of Appeal.

15 In draft at the time of writing.

16 In accordance with the provisions of the Rules of the Supreme Court Order 55.

17 *Phelps* v. *London Borough of Hillingdon* [1998] ELR 587, Court of Appeal.

18 *Phelps* v. *London Borough of Hillingdon*; *Anderton* v. *Clywd County Council*; *Jarvis* v. *Hampshire County Council*; *G* v. *London Borough of Bromley* – decisions of the House of Lords given in a joined judgment on 27 July 2000 (*The Times*, 28 July 2000).

19 S.319 Education Act 1996.

15

The Disability Discrimination Act 1995

Jeremy Cooper

Introduction

Social workers may be the first point of help and assistance to disabled clients who believe that they have suffered discrimination by virtue of their disability. Clients may, for example, be threatened with losing their job because a developing disability is making it more difficult for them to carry out the tasks for which they were originally employed. Alternatively, their disability may be proving an insurmountable barrier to obtaining a job interview, notwithstanding their capacity to perform that job. They may be finding it difficult to enjoy the same range of social amenities and services enjoyed by their able-bodied acquaintances simply because of their physical inaccessibility. Or they may be afraid to visit certain places because they know they will be treated differently because of their disability. In all these circumstances, a good working knowledge of the broad principles of the Disability Discrimination Act 1995 (DDA) is an important aid to a social worker as part of an essential 'toolkit' for helping clients to use the law to overcome discrimination based upon their disability.

The DDA applies in England, Wales, Scotland and (in a slightly modified form) Northern Ireland. It provides protection to disabled people from discrimination in a range of defined situations. It is generally considered to represent a major advance in the way in which society treats disabled people (Meager and Doyle, 1999). The Act is divided into a number of discrete parts, which cover discrimination in connection with employment (including access to employment) and discrimination in the provision of access to goods, facilities and services. In the future, it will extend to other areas, including discrimination in relation to education and transport services. In many ways, the Act follows the parallel provisions of the Sex Discrimination Act 1975 and the Race Relations Act 1976 with regard to discrimination on the grounds of gender or race. Although there was originally to be no equivalent central Commission to oversee the enforcement of the DDA, a Disability Rights Commission (DRC) was established in April 2000. The brief of the DRC is to assist disabled people by providing a central source of information and advice, via research, conciliation, investigation and a range of advisory powers.

The meaning of 'disability' and 'disabled person' under the Act

The status protected by the Act is that of 'a disabled person', defined as 'a person who has a physical or mental impairment which has a substantial and long-term adverse effect on their ability to carry out normal day-to-day activities'.[1] According to the minister responsible for the legislation, the word 'substantial' means 'more than minor'.[2] The 'adverse effect' must also be *long term*, that is, have lasted for at least 12 months, *or* the period that it can reasonably be expected to last is at least 12 months *or* the rest of the person's life (whichever is the shorter).

'Normal day-to-day activities' include mobility, manual dexterity, physical coordination, continence, the ability to lift, carry or otherwise move everyday objects, speech, hearing or eyesight, memory or the ability to concentrate, learn or understand, and the perception of the risk of danger. So far, cases involving acute vertigo, chronic pain in the legs and feet induced by fallen arches, transient epileptic fits, a sight loss in one eye, back strain with a continuing ability to carry out light duties and rheumatoid arthritis in the absence of independent medical evidence have all failed the test of having 'a substantial adverse effect upon normal day-to-day activities' (Meager and Doyle, 1999). In contrast, conditions causing pain from kidney stones and 'an undiagnosed cause', and sciatica in conjunction with a club foot, have passed the test. Each case is ultimately decided on its particular facts, and social workers should be cautious to offer definitive advice on whether a client's disability is covered by the Act. Expert advice is available from specialist employment lawyers and advice centres, as well as from disability action groups.

Although mental impairment is not defined by the Act, it does state that if the mental impairment emanates from mental illness, disability will only be established if it is 'from or consisting of a mental illness that is clinically well recognised'. This restriction is thus likely to exclude not only 'controversial' mental disorders such as kleptomania, psychopathy, or pyromania, but also 'recognised' mental disorders that are still not fully established in the patient.

In addition to the above situations, the Act covers a number of special situations, as follows:

- *Progressive conditions*: This aspect of the Act is one of some controversy, and social workers advising clients on this issue should be aware of the importance of applying strict legal logic rather than relying upon sentiment or emotion. According to the DDA, a person with a progressive condition causing an impairment that has 'some but not yet substantial' adverse effect on normal day-to-day activities is deemed to be a 'disabled person' for the purposes of this Act if his or her condition is expected to produce *at a later stage* a substantial adverse effect. Sufferers from multiple sclerosis, some forms of cancer and HIV may come into this category. Not included in this definition are those with asymptomatic conditions, those who are not yet experiencing any impairment, and those who are genetically predisposed to such conditions but who have not yet acquired them (see Meager and Doyle, 1999).
- *Controlled or corrected conditions*: A condition that is controlled or corrected, for example by medication or the use of a prosthesis or other aid, is still deemed to be a disability for the purposes of the Act if, but for the control or correction, there would be a disability meeting the general definition of disability. The Act does, however, exclude sight impairment correctable by spectacles or contact lenses.
- *Severe disfigurement*: A person with a severe disfigurement (for example, scars, birthmarks, a skin disease or a limb or postural deformation) is to be treated as falling within the definition of a disabled person for the purposes of this Act, although disfigurement caused by self-mutilation, for example tattoos and body piercing, is excluded from this provision.[3]
- *Persons already registered as disabled*: As a general rule, a person who meets a generic definition under one piece of legislation will not automatically satisfy that definition for other purposes. For example a person deemed to be self-employed for the purposes of tax law will not automatically be deemed self-employed in employment law. Thus a person who is on the local authority disabled person's register under the Chronically Sick and Disabled Persons Act 1970 (Darnbrough and Kinrade, 1995) will not automatically be deemed to be 'disabled' for the purposes of the DDA. The exception to this general rule is a person registered as a 'disabled person' for employment purposes on 12 January 1995, who will in certain defined circumstances be deemed to be covered by the Act.

Discrimination in connection with employment

Part II of the DDA deals with discrimination in connection with employment. This covers recruitment, selection, treatment while in employment and dismissal. There were 301 applications under these provisions in the first six months after the enactment of the DDA, rising to 5,841 by the end of 1999.

The general purpose of Part II is to render unlawful certain types of discrimination against actual or potential employees or 'service providers' where that discrimination is based upon their disability. It applies only to employment within Great Britain or Northern Ireland. It does not cover discrimination in partnerships, although it does cover discrimination by partners with regard to the employees of that partnership. Much of the detail on the interpretation of the DDA is to be found in regulations and the Codes of Practice and Guidance.

The following groups are exempted from the provisions of the Act:

- small businesses with fewer than 15 employees[4]
- statutory office-holders, for example the police force, prison officers, the armed forces and fire fighters, although not non-statutory employers carrying out any of these tasks, for example security firm employees acting as custody officers.

If employers are providing special supported employment to disabled people under the Disabled Persons (Employment) Act 1944,[5] or some other charitable authority, they will not be bound by the Act if, for example, they discriminate on behalf of one disabled group against another disabled group.

Discrimination in employment will be unlawful, and therefore actionable through an application by the client to an employment tribunal, if it can be shown:

- that the employer has for a reason related to the person's disability treated that person less favourably than the employer treats, or would treat, others to whom that reason does not apply, and
- that the employer cannot show that the treatment in question is justified.

An employer cannot be said to discriminate for a reason related to a person's disability unless he or she knows of the disability.

To establish 'less favourable treatment', the employment tribunal will apply the 'comparator test'. This means that the applicant must produce an example (real or hypothetical) of another individual *without* their disability being treated *more* favourably than themselves in the employment-related situation. They must be able to relate their less favourable treatment to their disability (for example, a refusal to employ a wheelchair user because of the inconvenience of a wheelchair in the office, or a blind person because of a dislike of guide dogs).

This provision has to be read alongside the very important further provision placing a statutory duty on employers (unless exempted) to make *reasonable adjustments* to work arrangements[6] and the working environment in order to accommodate disabled employees. The duty to make reasonable adjustments arises whenever any physical feature of the premises, or any arrangements made by or on behalf of an employer, place the disabled person concerned at a substantial disadvantage in comparison with those who are not disabled. In these circumstances, the employer (or potential employer when related to a job application) must take such steps as can be considered *reasonable in all the circumstances* in order to prevent those features or arrangements having that effect.

In many cases, the adjustments necessary to allow a disabled employee to continue working require more imagination than expense, and a social worker can play an important intermediary role, negotiating with an employer on the question of reasonable adjustments. One employer was, for example, found to have discriminated against an employee who suffered from pain and discomfort associated with a clubfoot by failing to provide her with a suitable chair, which would have been a simple adjustment to the workplace.[7] Modifications to equipment, seating, lighting, rest places, hours of work and work locations are often all that is needed to allow the employee to continue, and the role of the social worker in helping the parties to achieve such a compromise arrangement can be crucial.

But employers do not have a duty to make reasonable adjustments if they do not know that they are necessary for the employee and could not reasonably be expected to know, so it is important that employees realise that they must declare their disability in order to give the employer a chance to make adjustments, before they can establish any discrimination. This can be a sensitive issue and is again an area in which social workers can play an important role, helping the client to decide whether or not he or she wishes to declare the disability.

Detailed advice on what sorts of steps employers might be expected to take by way of reasonable adjustments in order to avoid charges of discrimination has emerged through the code of practice and case law. The DDA provides some illustrations of typical 'adjustments' as follows: making physical adjustments to premises; allocating some duties to another employee; being flexible with regard to working hours; being flexible in terms of place of work; being flexible as to absence from work for rehabilitation, treatment and assessment; giving or arranging special training; acquiring or modifying equipment; modifying procedures or reference manuals; modifying procedures for testing or assessment; providing a reader or interpreter; and providing supervision.

The Act provides guidance on what factors should be taken into account in deciding whether a particular proposed adjustment is or is not reasonable in all the circumstances. The factors it lists are the following:

1 Consider the preventative effect of the action (that is, will it achieve its goal?).
2 Is the proposed adjustment practicable?
3 Weigh up the financial and other costs that it would incur.
4 Consider any disruption to the employer's activities.
5 Consider the employer's financial and other resources.
6 Consider the availability of financial or other assistance.

Note, however, that employers faced with expensive adaptation bills to carry out reasonable adjustments may well have access to the government sponsored Access to Work Scheme whereby they can receive an unlimited grant towards the cost of reasonable adjustments to premises over a five-year period.[8]

Was the discriminatory treatment justified?

Once a discriminatory act has been shown to exist, the employer can only avoid a finding of unlawful discrimination if it can be established that the discriminatory act was *justified*. Although this provision appears to undermine the fundamental principles of the Act, the employer has to show that the reason for the less favourable treatment of the disabled employee was both *material* to the circumstances of the particular case and *substantial*.

The Code of Practice stresses that substantial means 'not just trivial or minor' and goes on to provide a series of examples to explain the scope of the defence. Thus a general assumption that blind people cannot use computers is not a material reason unless it is related to the particular individual in question; dismissing a clerical worker with a learning disability who cannot sort papers as fast as other colleagues, but with relatively little overall difference in productivity, would not be justifiable as a substantial reason; but rejecting a person with psoriasis for a job modelling cosmetics on a part of their body severely disfigured by the condition would probably be justified as the reason is material to the circumstances of the particular requirement, and is substantial. This is another key area in which the intervention of a social worker as a third party negotiator can provide an invaluable means of avoiding dismissal or unwanted litigation.

Enforcement provisions

Under Part II of the DDA, any individual experiencing discrimination under the above provisions can apply to an employment tribunal, alleging discrimination, as long as they do so within three months of the alleged discriminatory act. As legal aid is not available for representation at employment tribunals (although free or subsidised legal advice and assistance short of representation is), disabled people's action groups have an important role to play in this activity.[9] Applicants will be assisted by a requirement in the Act that employees can insist that the defendant employer fill out a detailed 'statutory questionnaire,' similar to those used in sex and race discrimination cases, in response to the allegation.

If the matter is not resolved informally, it will proceed to an employment tribunal hearing. Applicants should be aware of a number of procedural problems they will have to face. Employment tribunals are rather formal, intimidating settings, overburdened with procedures and often the need to argue complex points of law. Surprisingly, tribunal members are not currently required to have any expertise, or even training, in disability issues, and many of the early case applicants have reported negatively on tribunal members' ability to understand or relate to the challenges of disability.[10]

The employment tribunal has *all* the following options in the event of a finding in favour of the applicant:

- a declaration that discrimination occurred
- recommendations to ensure that there is no future recurrence of such discrimination
- the power to award to the applicant 'unlimited compensation', plus interest, such compensation to include, where appropriate, a category of compensation for 'injury to feelings'.

A major study of the first 2,500 cases registered in employment tribunals up to July 1998 showed that 90 per cent related to dismissal and 10 per cent to failure to recruit. The great majority of cases settled, or were withdrawn, before coming to a tribunal. Citizens' Advice Bureaux were the most common source of advice for applicants. Thirty-four per cent of applicants attending a tribunal were legally represented. In only 16 per cent of cases heard was the applicant successful, and in these cases the applicants were normally legally represented. Although the median compensation award was about £2,000, awards ranged widely from £700 to, in one case, around £167,000.[11]

Discrimination in relation to access to goods, facilities and services

A second goal of the DDA is to provide protection from unlawful discrimination in relation to access to goods (that is, any personal or moveable property), services and facilities, and in relation to the management and disposal of premises. The Act, supported by a detailed Code of Practice,[12] provides an illustrative list of what services are caught by the legislation, including:

- access to, and the use of, any place that the public are permitted to enter
- access to, and the use of, means of communication or information services
- accommodation in hotels, boarding houses and so on
- banking and insurance facilities, grants, loans, credit or finance
- facilities for entertainment, recreation or refreshment
- the services of a profession, a trade and a local or public authority.

These provisions are largely contained in Part III of the DDA.

The DDA makes it unlawful for service providers 'to treat disabled people less favourably than they would treat other people, for a reason related to their disability, when offering or providing goods, facilities or services'. These parts of the Act are being introduced over a phased period.

At the time of writing, the following provisions have become law:

1 It is unlawful for service providers to refuse to provide, or deliberately not provide, to a disabled person a service that is offered to other people, or to offer a lower standard or worse manner of service, or to offer less favourable terms.

2 Service providers must make reasonable adjustments to policies, procedures or practices that exclude disabled people or make it unreasonably difficult for disabled people to use the service.

3 Service providers must provide auxiliary aids and services (for example, portable hearing loops and information on cassettes) to enable disabled people to make use of the service.

4 Where a physical feature is a barrier to receiving or accessing the service, the service provider must find a reasonable alternative method of delivering the service (a shop owner, for example, could relocate certain goods to a part of the shop that is accessible to disabled customers).

The 'justification' defence also applies to these provisions.

Some services are excluded from the Act, of which the most significant currently are education and related services such as youth and other recreational and sports clubs, the use of any means of transport, and services not available to the public, such as private clubs.

From 2004, where a physical feature is a barrier to receiving or accessing the service, service providers will have either to take reasonable steps to remove, alter or avoid it (for example, by installing a ramp to enable wheelchair users to access premises hitherto inaccessible), or to provide their service by a reasonable alternative method that enables disabled people to make use of it.

Finally, it should be noted that, in addition to the burdens and responsibilities contained in the DDA, *Part M of the Building Regulations: Access and Facilities for Disabled People* requires the needs of disabled people to be taken into account in the construction of buildings in England and Wales. Parallel provisions apply in Scotland and Northern Ireland.[13] The government has issued guidance on how these regulations should be interpreted, although this is not mandatory.[14] It is ultimately a matter for local authority building control officers or approved inspectors, who have the responsibility to certify that building work complies with the building regulations.

Summary of key points for social work practitioners

- The DDA is an important piece of legislation that for the first time provides a positive protection to disabled people from discrimination, and which can lead to substantial financial compensation in the employment tribunal.
- The DDA applies both to the clients of social workers and to social workers themselves as employers, employees and service providers.
- In addition to bringing the DDA to the attention of clients in relevant situations, and referring them on to expert legal advice, social workers can play a key mediating role, in particular in relation to the making of 'reasonable adjustments' in the workplace, and to opposing the reasonableness of the 'justification' defence.
- In their role as facilitators of a wider range of services to clients, social workers can play an important role in ensuring that service providers bring their standards in line with the DDA.

Notes

1 DDA s.l(1). The definition in the Act is further supplemented by Schedule 1 of the Act; *The Code of Practice for the Elimination of Discrimination in the Field of*

Employment against Disabled Persons or Persons who Have Had a Disability 1996; Guidance on Matters to be Taken into Account in Determining Questions Relating to the Definition of Disability (HMSO, 1996); The Disability Discrimination (Employment) Regulations 1996; The Disability Discrimination (Meaning of Disability) Regulations 1996; and case law. Social workers should note that the definition of disability under this Act differs slightly from the definition of disability contained in the National Assistance Act 1948 s.29(1).

2 Alistair Burt MP, Minister for Social Security and Disabled People, Consideration of Lords Amendment, Official Report, 31 October 1995, Co. 174.

3 Disability Discrimination (Meaning of Disability) Regulations 1996.

4 Disability Discrimination (Exemption for Small Employers) Order 1998 SI No. 2618.

5 This is separate from the employment of disabled people under the quota system, which ended in 1997.

6 DDA s.6(2) (a) (b) defines 'arrangements' in this context as arrangements for determining to whom employment should be offered and any term, condition or other arrangements on which employment, promotion, transfer, training or any other benefit is offered or afforded.

7 *Tarling* v. *Wisdom Toothbrushes*, Note, however, that in another case, *Kenny* v. *Hampshire Constabulary, 1999, IRLR 76, EAT*, the tribunal ruled that this duty is restricted to 'job-related' matters and did not therefore extend to the provision of a carer to attend to the worker's personal needs. See also *Ridout* v. *T C Group, 1998, 82 EOR 46, EAT*.

8 The Disablement Employment Advisors (DEAs) based in job centres will provide advice and assistance in relation to this scheme.

9 The DDA Representation and Advice Project (DDARAP), for example, provides a nationwide *pro bono* network of volunteer lawyers willing to advise or take on cases under the DDA; similarly, the Disability Access Rights Advice Service (DARAS) provides free, independent advice on the DDA, as a second-tier agency, to both consumer groups and service providers. The Placing, Assessment and Counselling Teams (PACTS) run by the employment service through job centres, are another source of general advice. The Disability Rights Commission may also take up a case.

10 See Meager and Doyle, 1999, pp.193–7.

11 EOR Discrimination Law Digest No. 41, Autumn 1999.

12 DDA Code of Practice Rights of Access. Goods, Facilities, Services and Premises (DFEE, 1999).

13 Scotland: *Part T of the Scottish Building Standard Regulations;* Northern Ireland: *Part R of the Northern Ireland Building Regulations*.

14 *The Approved Document for Part M, Part T and Technical Booklet R*.

16

Care in the Community

Ann McDonald

Applying the law in community care involves working with a wide range of statutory powers and duties. There is no unifying statute like the Children Act that applies. The National Health Service and Community Care Act of 1990 (NHSCCA) did not replace the existing statute law relating to the provision of services in the community for adults. What it did was to introduce a new duty to assess the need for those services and make arrangements for their provision. Eligibility for the services themselves, such as day care, residential care and home care, still depends upon the interpretation of pre-existing legislation. Those who thought that the 1990 Act would herald the introduction of a whole range of innovative services were therefore disappointed. The law has been added to piecemeal since 1990 with new legislation on carers' rights, direct payments and disability discrimination. The practitioner in the area of community care law therefore has to have a knowledge of a wide range of different types of legislation, going back as far as 1948.

The National Assistance Act of 1948 is still one of the major pieces of legislation in this field; social circumstances, social work practice and the balance between State and private provision have obviously moved on greatly since 1948, but the archaic language remains. Finding a unifying value base within the legislation itself is impossible. The enabling power of the local authority to make direct payments instead of services given by the Community Care (Direct Payments) Act of 1996 sits alongside the power in s.47 of the National Assistance Act 1948 compulsorily to remove from home persons who are 'aged, infirm and suffering from grave chronic disease'. Unlike the Children Act 1989, there is no welfare checklist to provide guidance when difficult decisions have to be made, no 'no order' principle to support working in partnership and no explicit mention of racial and cultural needs. This absence of a legislative mandate means that social work practice within community care must be especially sensitive to the application of sound professional values.

There is also no unity within community care practice of the user groups that it serves. The NHSCCA applies to the provision of services to older people, to people with learning disabilities and physical disabilities, to people with mental health problems and to users of the drug and alcohol services. Many of these groups will also be in receipt of other services, such as health care services and housing, but there is again no unifying statute bringing together these different sources of service provision. Although there may be statutory duties to cooperate imposed upon the different services, each service can, in situations of unresolved conflict, retreat behind its own statutory boundaries. This is most apparent in the areas of homelessness (many people with a need for community care services having a housing situation that is precarious) and continuing care (where the provision of health care does not attract a financial assessment of the individual service-user, but the provision of social care does).

The application of any legal regime involves the consideration of rights, duties, powers and remedies. What rights does an individual have to any particular type of service? Is this or that organisation under a legal duty to provide this service, or does it simply have a power to do so if it sees fit? What about the person who fails to get what he feels he is entitled to? What remedies does he have? Rights, duties, powers and remedies all interconnect in this way.

Knowing what to ask for is a crucial first step. The idea (commendable though it is) of needs-led assessment is meaningless unless one knows what sort of services might be available and what sort of needs the body doing the assessment has a duty or a power to respond to. *The Policy Guidance, Community Care in the Next Decade and Beyond* (DoH, 1990) recognises the priority to be given to information by making 'publishing information' the first stage of care management. Section 46 of the NHSCCA also requires local authorities to publish as public documents community care plans, which are to list the available services and means of accessing them. Section 9 of the Disabled Persons Act 1986 also places a duty upon the local authority to inform service-users of any other services that they or *any other organisation* provide for people with disabilities. Yet despite this legislative mandate, consumer surveys show that service-users are often ill informed and not kept up to date about services that may be available.

Where resources are limited, so that not everyone can receive that for which they ask, procedural rights become more important. In order to have an equal opportunity of being considered for a scarce service, individuals must be reassured that they will be assessed by a fair procedure with all relevant circumstances being taken into account. If refused a service, they should be told why and given an opportunity to challenge that decision.

Section 47 of the NHSCCA 1990 tries to introduce such a procedure. It imposes upon the local authority a duty to assess anyone who may appear to be in need of a community care service, and requires the local authority to take that assessment into account when making a decision on what service to provide. It should be noted that it is the appearance of need that triggers the duty to assess, so there is no requirement that a specific request for an assessment should be made. This is just as well as most people, not having a full knowledge of the system, would not request 'an assessment' but would probably ask for a single resource such as day care or home care. Similarly, many social workers would talk about 'doing an assessment for day care' or home care. But s.47 imposes a much broader and less conventional duty than this: it speaks of a general assessment of a person's need for community care services. This opens up access to the list of community care services set out in s.46(3) of the Act, which are the services that the local authority has either a duty or a power to provide under the pre-1990 legislation. These are services provided under:

- Part III of the National Assistance Act 1948
- s.45 of the Health Services and Public Health Act 1968
- s.21 and Schedule 8 of the National Health Service Act 1977
- s.117 of the Mental Health Act 1983.

These services include social work support, residential care, laundry services, meals on wheels and mental health aftercare services among others, although they also include day care and home care. A proper assessment under s.47 therefore involves looking at the whole potential range of services for one individual. Although the format for such an assessment is not statutorily prescribed, the factors that such an assessment should take into account are set out in the Practice Guidance. These include the person's mental and physical health, the social history, sources of support, risk factors and carers' needs. A needs-led assessment of this sort is thus fundamentally different from a resource-led assessment, which simply checks a person's eligibility against what is available. It also opens up the potential for an exchange model of assessment as opposed to a professional checklist, and facilitates feedback on the expression of unmet needs.

The inclusion of carers' needs within a comprehensive assessment means that the interests of family, friends and neighbours who provide some essential support is not overlooked. Those who provide a substantial amount of care on a regular basis are further entitled to a statutory assessment under the Carers (Recognition and Services) Act 1995 of their ability to provide or continue to provide care. The Act also applies to those who intend to take on a caring role; it therefore enables people who, for example, are contemplating having an older relative to live with them to anticipate what support services might be available to them before they make the commitment. The definition of 'carers' in the Act also includes young carers (a welcome policy development) and the carers of disabled children.

Although service-users are proactive in the assessment process, the service provision decision under s.47 of the NHSCCA (how much of what sort of service this person will receive) remains the prerogative of the local authority to decide. Thus 'a need for 24 hour care' may be met either by the provision of an intensive home care package or by the offer of a place in a residential or nursing home. The local authority will determine the resource, and financial constraints may appear to make residential care inevitable. Although the Gloucestershire case ([1997] 2 WLR 459) legitimised the application of resource constraints, it also emphasised the individual nature of assessments. Applying a single solution to each individual case would therefore be unlawful; in particular, emotional as well as physical needs should be taken into account. Again, the key is good-quality assessment.

Freedom from local authority conventions on service delivery may be obtained through the use of direct payments. The choice of personal assistants lies with the user as employer, although still subject to the local authority's assessment of need. In order that direct payments may be extended to all those potentially eligible, restrictive interpretations of who is 'willing' and 'able' to receive such payments need to be overcome; this is particularly important for people with learning difficulties. Policy and practice guidance on direct payments (DoH, 2000c) makes it clear that such schemes should be inclusive and not unduly restrictive. A statutory limitation on payments to close relatives, however, restricts the potential of direct payment as a means of financial support for informal carers.

A range of case scenarios may illustrate the use of community care legislation in practice and highlight some of the dilemmas that those who work under the legislation may face. One such situation is hospital discharge. Seventy-five per cent of the hospital admissions of older people are unplanned, and there is a clear link between admission to hospital and entering residential care. Older people are therefore particularly vulnerable in the hospital setting, the most vulnerable being those who live alone and those who have few or no visitors during their stay in hospital. This most vulnerable group is the one most in need of referral for social work intervention, and ward staff should be alert to their particular needs. Good practice in hospital discharge arrangements involves multi-disciplinary teamwork to facilitate planning for discharge soon after admission and certainly when the patient's medical condition has stabilised. Health authorities and social services departments will have protocols on hospital discharge that specify targets for the time taken to respond to a referral and for the assessment to be completed. This may lead to a tension between the need to free up beds and avoid 'bed-blocking' and the need for a comprehensive and sensitively paced assessment.

So what has been the impact of the NHSCCA 1990 on hospital social work? One consequence of the implementation of the Act is that hospital social workers have become more keenly aware that they are doing 'statutory work' and that this should, by its very nature, be given priority over the other tasks that social workers may perform, such as counselling.

Other professionals may also look to social workers as representatives of the 'lead authority' from whom they may prescribe the provision of community care services. Social worker intervention at this time may provide an opportunity for people who have been experiencing difficulties in the community for some time to bring these to the fore. The difficulty inherent in hospital social work is that the social worker is assessing people's ability to live in one place (their own home) when they are temporarily in a completely different place (the hospital). The best way round this is to arrange a home visit (perhaps with an occupational therapist) to experience at first hand what daily life back at home might be like. An admission to hospital can lower a person's self-confidence, and pain and discomfort can be both physically and mentally debilitating. Any assessment will need to bear this in mind.

Some hospital social work teams have access to specialist resources that target people newly discharged from the hospital. Adequate support at this stage can have a positive effect on people's sense of well-being and fitness even six months after discharge. This is a justification for making additional resources available at the point of discharge. Attention to transport arrangements, a warm house to return to and an adequate stock of food all contribute to a 'good' discharge. The good discharge for the patient is of course the discharge that the patient wants and in the planning of which he or she has been fully involved. Hospital patients may easily become the focus of other people's concerns rather than active participants in their own treatment and assessment. Many surveys of the recipients of community care services have shown that people like to be informed that they are being formally assessed and of the format that this assessment will take.

Issues of rights versus risks are often attenuated in the hospital setting, particularly in relation to discharge. The patient's perception of a 'good' discharge back to the home environment may be seen by hospital staff as a barrier to the patient's 'safe' discharge to a physically more secure and better resourced environment – perhaps residential or nursing home care. The social worker's potential role as advocate for the patient is put to the test here, as may be his or her professional autonomy. In the community too the social worker needs to have an adequate legal as well as professional response to the question 'Why can't this older person be made to go into residential care?' Those who have the mental capacity to make decisions about their own care cannot be compelled to accept services that they do not want, or give up their home to move into institutional care. The only legally prescribed exceptions to this are compulsory admission to hospital under the Mental Health Act 1983 and, for those who are not mentally disordered, compulsory removal from home under s.47 of the National Assistance Act. The former is unlikely to lead to a permanent situation: the emphasis on care in the community has meant that hospitalisation is likely to be a temporary, albeit possibly repeated episode, in the life of an individual.

The use of s.47 is fortunately rare, amounting to barely 200 cases per annum. Removal under s.47 is a judicial process, by application to the local magistrates' court on the recommendation of the community physician, or 'proper officer' as he is called in the Act. Environmental health officers are usually involved to clean up the premises, and it is vital that this momentum is kept up in order to ensure that the premises are made suitable for a future return home. Although removal for a period of up to three months is allowed, the return home should take place as soon as possible because institutionalisation can happen very quickly. Section 47 is more talked about than actually employed; most local authorities prescribe a case conference process before deciding upon an application to court, and this can be used to underscore the seriousness to a range of different professionals of a deteriorating situation involving an older person living alone in insanitary conditions. Arguably, s.47 can also be used in cases of abuse, where care is being provided but that care is inadequate.

There are many ethical issues surrounding the use of s.47, which is a clear deprivation of liberty. It is important to know the person's social history and usual ways of living. The person who has always lived surrounded by piles of possessions in insanitary conditions will have a strong attachment to that place, and a precipitate removal to hygienic surroundings will break both a physical and an emotional attachment. In the converse situation, where there has been a fairly rapid deterioration in the situation of a person who had placed a premium on comfort and good order, intervention in the role of 'rescuer' may be thought to be more justifiable. Pressure from family and neighbours may be intense in such situations, hence the value of sharing information and assessment through a multidisciplinary approach. Where there is a choice of legislation, the Mental Health Act is to be preferred for its greater procedural safeguards, including a right of appeal. Both the Mental Health Act and the National Assistance Act are examples of professional law with a limited field of application whose interpretation and use are a matter of professional discretion.

The application of the Mental Health Act and s.47 of the National Assistance Act is replete with professional dilemmas concerning rights and risks. The right of the individual to freedom from intervention is to be balanced against the risk to that person from his own behaviour or environment and the risk to others from those same things. Anti-oppressive practice would guide decision-making towards the least restrictive alternative consistent with acting in the best interests of the individual whose wishes are being overriden. However, it is not only in these most extreme of circumstances that anti-oppressive practice should guide professional action. The individual worker is often caught up in the tension between needs, rights and resources. Workers need to be able to challenge their own agency if it is remiss in meeting its legal obligations or in adhering to principles of good administration.

Everyday examples of this may be found in the process of arranging community care services. Although local authorities have a power rather than a duty to charge for community care services other than residential care, charging is almost universal. Indeed, standard spending assessments for local authorities are based on the assumption that a charge will be made. There are a variety of formulae in existence for charging for services ranging from home care to meals on wheels to day care, all essential services for people with disabilities or older people. The social worker organising such services will also be initially responsible for the financial assessment. This may have to be done, as a formal commercial process, within the context of a therapeutic relationship or, in a minority of cases, a compulsory relationship. Individuals who could certainly benefit from the provision of services may be tempted to refuse them because of the cost. The assessor may then be faced with the dilemma of allowing such a withdrawal to happen or emphasising the duty of the local authority to continue to provide services where there is a legal obligation to do so. Ever tighter eligibility criteria may exclude people from services if their needs are deemed to be insufficient to reach even tighter threshold criteria.

Yet the Gloucestershire judgment ([1997] 2 WLR 459) did not say that resources were to be the only criteria against which the targeting of services should take place. Other relevant criteria are an acceptable standard of living, the degree of disability and the relative gain to be made from intervention by way of services. The judgment also emphasised that services (at least those provided as a duty under s.2 of the Chronically Sick and Disabled Persons Act 1970) could not be withdrawn without re-assessment, giving service-users an opportunity to advocate for their individual needs against new eligibility criteria.

One weakness in the assessment of people with disabilities is the non-implementation of ss.1–3 of the Disabled Persons (Services, Consultation and Representation) Act 1986. These sections of the Act would have provided for the appointment of representatives (or advocates) to speak alongside disabled people through the assessment process. The legislation was designed to facilitate a transition from a rather stereotypical view of what services might be needed by disabled people as a group to a system of services constructed around the needs of individual disabled people who might otherwise have lacked a voice. There has been no growth in voluntary advocacy schemes commensurate with such a system.

Choice in the provision of services may also be more apparent than real in the mixed economy of care that the NHSCCA was intended to facilitate. Local authorities need no longer be direct providers of care, whether residential or domiciliary care; they can in effect fulfil their statutory obligations to provide services through contracts with independent sector providers. This has in turn led to concerns about the variable quality of care where there is a multiplicity of providers. Consumer protection will therefore lie in increasingly refined quality assurance mechanisms.

Paradoxically, challenges to local authority practice in this mixed economy of care have often been based on a failure by the local authority to exercise choice. There is still a tendency for local authorities to fail to look outside their own boundaries when making placements or commissioning services. The choice of placement in residential care may be particularly contentious, local authorities emphasising the availability of third party top-ups when making placements in expensive accommodation or in a different part of the country rather than analysing the appropriateness of any particular placement in being uniquely able to meet the individual's needs. The argument is again brought back to the importance of comprehensive and individualised assessments rather than the fitting of individuals into resources.

Local authorities may also be criticised for failing to take a long-term view of service provision. This is particularly important with younger disabled people, where 'planning for life' is an important concept. In terms of methods of intervention, this necessitates a move away from short-term, task-centred solutions to longer-term involvement, planning for important transitions. One important transition for young people is leaving school. The legal framework for consultation and forward planning between education, social services and health is already there in ss.5 and 6 of the Disabled Persons Act, but the research evidence is that, without specialist workers, little focused planning takes place.

Another important transition is leaving home, cooperation between the same combination of agencies, with the addition of housing, being necessary to ensure that 'community presence' is an effective and sustained reality. Emphasising that assessment includes re-assessment and that the whole process of care management cannot reach fruition without the proper monitoring, review and re-evaluation of services is an important administrative support to the legal process of securing necessary services.

The legal status of the policy guidance *Community Care in the Next Decade and Beyond* (DoH, 1990) and the practice guidance in the *Managers' Guide* (DoH, 1991b) and the *Practitioners' Guide* (DoH, 1991a) to the 1990 Act should not be overlooked. The policy guidance says *what* should be done; the practice guidance says *how* it should be done. Policy guidance *must* be followed unless there is good reason not to do so; practice guidance *should* be followed although there is scope to depart from the guidance provided that agencies do not take a substantially different course. The emphasis within the policy guidance on partnership and the clarity of the process is thus a fundamental requirement; the practical expression of such principles in the practice guidance, through the use of consultation and written care plans, is a blueprint for good practice. Both will take precedence over departmental procedures manuals when a legal challenge to decision-making is made.

Using law in the practice of community care is therefore broader than simply having a knowledge of the major statutory provisions. Their active translation into practice through such guidance is what makes community care practice so dynamic. This is the difference between law in books and law in action worked out through real-life dilemmas and professional values. The social worker as an agency representative should not lose sight of these wider perspectives.

17

Children Looked After

Isabelle Brodie

Introduction

Children looked after by local authorities ('in care') are among the most vulnerable in our society. This will often involve children living away from home. In situations where the usual supports of parents and other family members cannot be relied upon, it is clearly essential that the legislative framework offers sufficient protection for the safety and well-being of these children.

This chapter will conduct a broad-brush examination of the legal principles that currently inform the care of children looked after by local authorities. Throughout the discussion, account will be taken of research evidence concerning the policy and practice implementation of these principles. The chapter will consider the background to the Children Act 1989 and the way in which this approaches the care of all children in need of services. It will then focus on some more specific issues, including the rights of children in care and young people leaving care.

The Children Act 1989

The main piece of legislation informing the care of children looked after in England and Wales is the Children Act 1989. It is important to note that other legislation – for example relating to education and criminal justice – is also very important in relation to children looked after.

The Children Act 1989 was implemented in 1991, against a background of a series of scandals concerning the care and protection of children during the 1970s and 80s involving cases of serious physical and sexual abuse. A substantial body of research had also demonstrated shortcomings in State care for children (DHSS, 1985). In this context, it was widely agreed that a rather drastic change was needed, and in the light of this, it is notable that the Act achieved cross-party support in its passage through Parliament.

The changes wrought by the Children Act 1989 were wide ranging. Crucially, it brought together public and private law concerning children (that is, all those under 18 years of age). The legislation was also accompanied by nine detailed volumes of guidance examining the implications of the new legislation in different areas of child welfare, including those of disabled children, family support and family placements.

While the significance of the Children Act 1989 should in no way be diminished, the fact that it has now been implemented for 10 years means that we are in a position to evaluate some of its effects. The passage of time has inevitably resulted in the identification of certain gaps in or difficulties with the legislation, and research has continued to play an important role in the development of policy relating to looked-after children. It is important to point out that this chapter is being written against the backdrop of a rapidly changing policy context. While not all the policies being generated will be translated into law, they nevertheless have the potential to influence professional practice greatly with respect to looked-after children. Professionals who are involved in the care of looked-after children need to be alert to changes in policy and statute.

Children in need and children looked after

The main purpose of the legislation is described as promoting and safeguarding the welfare of children. The Act also takes the view that children are generally best looked after within the family, and that even when there are problems, parents should continue to have an active role in the upbringing of children. This is supported by the concept of 'parental responsibility'. Parental responsibility refers to the collection of duties, rights and authority that a parent has in respect of his or her child. Consequently, when there is a breakdown in family life, parents should continue to play a full part in bringing up their children, and local authorities also have a duty to work in partnership with parents in promoting the welfare of their children.

While there is at times likely to be some tension between the principle of welfare and that of family involvement, the Act seeks to provide a framework of services ensuring that the best interests of the child are protected. Central to this framework is the concept of 'children in need'. Section 17(10) of the Act defines this group as all children whose health or development will be impaired, or further impaired, without the provision of services by the local authority, or if the child is disabled.

Research has shown that the groups of children defined as being 'in need' by local authorities varies somewhat and can include, for example, children who are delinquent or at risk of becoming so, children at risk of abuse and neglect, young carers and children living in poverty (see, for example, Colton *et al.*, 1995). It is important to emphasise that children looked after by local authorities and those leaving care are also children in need. The Act therefore provides a more integrated framework for understanding children's needs. Overall, it is estimated that there are 600,000 children in need at any one time. Of these, some 350,000 will receive services. A significantly smaller proportion – about 30,000 in all – will become looked after (DoH, 1998c). The Act envisages that services to children in need should operate on a continuum, of which provision for children looked after should be a part. Thus family support services should be provided so that, where possible, children can continue to live within their own families.

In some circumstances, however, it will be necessary for a child to become looked after by the local authority. The term 'looked after' refers to all children who are the subject of a care order or who are provided with accommodation on a voluntary basis for more than 24 hours (s.22(1)). Children may also be looked after by way of a planned series of short-term placements. This tends to be thought of as a way in which local authorities support disabled children and their families – traditionally termed 'respite care' – but available statistics in fact show that other reasons, including other forms of family stress and relationship difficulties, are equally important.

On any day, some 53,000 children are likely to be looked after by the local authority, although in the course of a year, many more children will move in and out of the care system. Although discussions of the care system often focus on children living in children's homes, the reality of the pattern of placements is actually very different. The majority of looked-after children – some 35,000 (66 per cent) – will live with foster carers in a family setting. A much smaller group of around 6,500 (12 per cent) will live in residential accommodation. Interestingly, a similar proportion (5,600 or 11 per cent) of children looked after will be 'placed' with parents and be receiving support from social services and other agencies (DoH, 1999).

In keeping with the emphasis on the continued involvement of parents in the upbringing of looked-after children, the Children Act 1989 states that children should, where possible, be looked after via voluntary arrangements with their parents. Court orders should only be used when no other route is open to the local authority. Recently, however, statistical evidence shows that the use of care orders is increasing for looked-after children. At 31 March 1998, 60 per cent of this group were looked after under care orders, 1,800 more than a year previously. The reasons for this are as yet unclear.

When a child becomes looked after, a number of issues must be considered. The Children Act 1989 requires local authorities to give due consideration to the child's religion, racial origin and cultural and linguistic background (s.22(5)). Account must also be taken of the child's own views, according to his or her age and understanding. When the child becomes looked after, local authorities have an ongoing duty to work in partnership with parents. Thus, for example, parents should be given information about what is happening, and planning should take place with the involvement of the parents. Arrangements should where possible be made for looked-after children to live near their home, and siblings should be accommodated together. Accommodation for disabled children should be provided according to their needs.

Local authorities also have a duty to promote contact between the child and the parents. Again, the nature of this contact will vary according to the child's circumstances. In addition to face-to-face contact, telephone calls, letters and emails will be important. Research during the 1980s showed that there were often barriers to such contact when a child was looked after, and that the failure to sustain relationships had damaging consequences when the child returned home (DHSS, 1985). Current evidence shows that, overall, policy and practice in this area have become more 'family friendly' (Hill, 2000): for example, carers have a more positive attitude towards ensuring that children see their parents and other family members who are important to them (DoH, 1998c).

There is, however, no room for complacency. Research shows that planning for placements is often poor and that partnership is, in practice, difficult, especially where the parents are hostile to service intervention. A significant proportion of children continue to lose contact with a parent or other significant person (Masson *et al.*, 1997). It should also be cautioned that, for some young people, contact with at least some family members will be detrimental to their welfare and is undesirable.

The voice of the child

Article 12(1) of the UNCRC states that children capable of forming their own views should be assured of the right to express those views freely in all matters affecting them. The Children Act 1989 requires that children, taking account of their age and level of understanding, should be consulted about decisions concerning them (s.22(4)). These decisions might cover a wide range of issues, including placement arrangements, educational issues and young people's views about the care they are receiving.

The recognition that children should be listened to is not only a matter of principle, but also essential to ensuring the safety of children looked after. Enquiries into the maltreatment of children in the care system have regularly highlighted the fact that children who tried to make complaints and expose the abuse being experienced were regularly ignored (DoH, 1997b).

Putting this principle into practice has, however, proved far from easy. This is in part due to the status of children in society more generally. Research suggests that children are often excluded from decision-making. Some groups of children, such as disabled children, may be especially vulnerable to marginalisation. It is therefore essential that effective ways are found of communicating with children in order to maximise their participation.

More encouragingly, it seems that children's voices are increasingly heard within the policy-making process. Evidence was, for example, taken from young people by the House of Commons Committee examining the experiences of young people looked after. The SSI, which inspects different aspects of the care system, routinely consults with young people. Additionally, there are a number of voluntary organisations – such as The Who Cares? Trust and the National Children's Bureau – through which young people who are looked after can share their experiences, obtain information about their rights and lobby on specific issues. The government has also recently announced measures intended to promote children's rights, including the extension of the role of independent visitors.

Promoting welfare

As noted above, the 'cornerstone' duty of local authorities to looked-after children is to safeguard and promote their welfare (DoH, 1989a). This must inform practice relating to children looked after, and the courts must treat the welfare of the child as the paramount consideration when reaching any decision about his or her upbringing.

However, while legislation emphasises that being looked after should promote the child's welfare, research evidence tells us that the care system is often unsuccessful in improving children's life chances and even in providing a basic level of care and protection. Indeed, the safety of looked-after children has been a major issue following a succession of public inquiries that have uncovered numerous instances on which children have been mistreated physically, sexually and emotionally while living in public care. Most recently, an enquiry undertaken by Sir Ronald Waterhouse revealed extensive abuse of children living in residential accommodation in North Wales during the 1970s and 80s (DoH/Welsh Office, 2000). It is also evident that the longer-term outcome for children who have been looked after is frequently poor. For example, the level of attainment of looked-after children is considerably lower than that of their peers (SSI/OFSTED, 1995). A disproportionate number of young people looked after become unemployed and are represented in the prison population.

Promoting the welfare of looked-after children is far from easy, not least given the complex problems that children entering public care present. In addition to the fact that children from poor and disadvantaged backgrounds are more likely to become looked after, a very high proportion will have experienced extremely difficult family relationships, as well as problems at school and in the community. In a study of children entering residential and foster care in two local authorities, for example, it was found that two out of five had been sexually abused or had abused another child (Farmer and Pollock, 1998). Another study of residential care in three local authorities found that, in comparison with the resident population in the 1980s, recognised behavioural problems had more than doubled, and previous abuse and neglect were identified as 'major' stress factors in almost two-thirds of the cases studied (Berridge and Brodie, 1998).

The wide-ranging and often complex needs presented by children looked after and children in need means that it is likely they will need the services of more than one agency. The Children Act 1989 is clear that, while social services will usually have lead responsibility, other services – such as local education authorities and district health authorities – must comply with a request from a social services department for assistance in providing services for children in need, as long as this is compatible with their duties (s.27). Unfortunately, however, evidence suggests that inter-agency working has in practice proved highly problematic (see, for example, Audit Commission, 1994; House of Commons Health Committee, 1998) and that this has been detrimental to the welfare of children and young people.

The unsatisfactory nature of the outcome for children looked after has attracted an increasing level of concern. Initiatives such as the Looking After Children Assessment and Action records seek to improve processes of planning and follow-up action in key areas of children's development. More recently, the government has introduced a wide-ranging programme of reform. Central to this is the Quality Protects initiative, a three-year programme that sets new objectives for children's services (DoH, 1998d). The programme is backed by a special grant for social services of £375 million over three years. The six priority areas for which the grant is to be used are: increasing the choice of adoptive, foster and residential placements for looked-after children; improving aftercare services; enhancing management information systems; improving assessment, care-planning and record-keeping; strengthening quality assurance systems; and consultation with young people. Local authorities are required to provide regular information to government on how services are being developed in each of these areas and how the money is being spent.

More specific objectives, with associated targets, have also been set that match the priority areas. One objective, for example, is to:

> ensure that children looked after gain maximum life chance benefits from educational opportunities, health care and social care. (DoH, 1998b)

The associated target for education is to:

> improve the educational attainment of children looked after, by increasing to at least 50 per cent by 2001 the proportion of children leaving care at 16 with a GCSE or GNVQ qualification: and to 75 per cent by 2003. (DoH, 1998b)

It is still too soon to evaluate the effects of the Quality Protects initiative, but it should be recognised that, in addition to the specific provisions of the programme, it also indicates an ambitious attempt to change the culture and focus of social work with looked-after children. The programme is to be welcomed in that it seeks to address areas in which, as the above discussion illustrates, there are serious deficits in the services provided. It also promotes a better planning of services in accordance with local contexts, and has the added carrot of additional resources. At the same time, questions have been raised concerning, for example, whether target-setting is the best way to measure children's progress, and whether the specific targets set are too ambitious or too limited.

Leaving care

Given that looked-after children often come from extremely disadvantaged backgrounds and have usually suffered various stressful experiences, it might be anticipated that young people would require additional support in making the transition to adulthood. Research findings have demonstrated that this group is indeed vulnerable: for example, the majority leave care with no educational qualifications, and up to one in four young women leaving care is already pregnant (DoH, 1998c).

Young people also tend to leave care at an earlier stage in their lives than their peers who are not looked after. Indeed, during 1997–98, there was a marked increase in the proportion of young people leaving care on their sixteenth birthday. The irony is, therefore, that young people leaving care are most vulnerable but lack the resources that might ease the route into education, training or employment and to living on their own.

Section 24 of the Children Act requires local authorities to advise, assist and befriend looked-after young people with a view to protecting their welfare after they cease to be looked after. They also have a duty to advise and befriend the young people they have looked after until the age of 21. It should, however, be noted that they have only a power, and not a duty, to assist them in kind or, exceptionally, in cash. Research evidence shows that there has been considerable variation in the amount of help that young people have received on leaving care. It is important to stress that this should not be a matter only for the social services, as the needs of young people leaving care will require input from a range of agencies, including education, the careers service and housing and benefits agencies.

While there are some very effective projects within individual local authorities that support young people leaving care, the provision is uneven (DoH, 1996). As part of their attempt to remedy some of these problems, the government introduced the Children (Leaving Care) Bill. This proposes a number of important changes, including a new duty on local authorities to assess and meet the care needs of eligible and relevant children and young people, and improvements in the planning and support systems.

Conclusion

The legal framework for the care of looked-after children has many unique ingredients. Informed by research findings, the Children Act 1989 offers a philosophy of care that seeks to balance parental responsibility for the upbringing of children with the need for State intervention when the child's safety or welfare is endangered. Nevertheless, evidence continues to reveal shortcomings in the care provided for children looked after by local authorities and indicates that this group often continue to be disadvantaged into adult life.

While there are numerous examples of good practice in this area, the fact remains that the quality of care is often uneven. Current policy initiatives such as Quality Protects require local authorities to reassess policy and practice relating to looked-after children, and in time to produce evidence of a better outcome in key areas such as health and education. Such policies are, however, unlikely to succeed unless the wider factors of socio-economic disadvantage that contribute to children becoming looked after are also addressed.

18

The Law, Social Work Practice and Elder Abuse

Alison Brammer

Introduction

In the 1960s, child abuse emerged as a social phenomenon arousing concern among social care agencies. In the 1970s, domestic violence was similarly recognised. The 1990s saw the emergence of elder abuse as a complex social problem that is high on the agenda at central and policy level. Reference had been made in the 1970s to 'granny-bashing' (Baker, 1975), this being followed by Eastman's graphic account of cases of abuse in 1983. For a variety of well-documented reasons, however, it received little attention until the late 1980s and early 1990s (Biggs *et al.*, 1995). A variety of terms have since been used to describe the phenomenon, including elder mistreatment, old age abuse, inadequate care and mis-care.

Many local authorities, through their protection policies, now focus on adult protection as a generic category that encompasses elder abuse, and it is certainly helpful to place any discussion of elder abuse in the context of vulnerable adults. There are issues of similarity to be drawn with the position of adults with learning disabilities and mental health problems, as well as with the experience of domestic violence. It has also been argued that it is appropriate to address a continuum of 'family violence,' ranging from child abuse to elder abuse, as the best way of understanding abuse (Kingston and Penhale, 1995). There are, however, many areas of difference between the categories, and it remains legitimate, for a variety of reasons, to consider elder abuse separately. This in part follows the position in the USA, where elder abuse has legitimate status as a social problem. In addition, demographic changes leading to an increased proportion of elderly people within the population are relevant, as are the changes introduced by 'community care', which have placed a greater emphasis on the role of voluntary carers for older people. Structurally, increasing specialism in work with older people is evident across various professions. A powerful counterargument to a separate consideration is that this reinforces ageist stereotypes.

This chapter will consider definitions of elder abuse, the extent of abuse, its nature and its indicators. The discussion leads into a consideration of the legal context and possible interventions where there is abuse, concluding with a look at some practice issues and current debates pertinent to an understanding of elder abuse.

What is elder abuse?

In contrast to the situation in the USA, there is no specific offence of elder abuse in the UK. Abuse may nevertheless encompass behaviour that constitutes a criminal offence under common law and statute, such as assault, actual or grievous bodily harm, indecent assault and rape and theft. Reservations have been expressed questioning the appropriateness of criminal law to elder abuse cases, particularly where family members are included. Williams (1993) argues that use of the word 'abuse' can undermine the impact of the act, which in other circumstances would clearly be seen as a crime. Hugman (1994) suggests that, given the complexity and sensitivity of some abuse situations in which it may not be clear who the 'victim' is, criminalising all abusive acts is inappropriate.

Our knowledge base has drawn heavily on a north American, largely academic, debate concerning the nature of abuse. There is much to be learnt from the US experience while acknowledging intrinsic social and structural differences. Much of the UK debate has centred on definitions of elder abuse. While the search for a definition may be problematic, the value of a clear working definition has been well established:

> Definitions are important not least because they help construct a field of legitimate action and thereby include some and exclude other phenomena as worthy of concern. They also influence the structural arrangements and flow of resources which determine responses made by statutory authorities and research agencies. (Brammer and Biggs, 1998)

The first formal definition appeared in official practice guidelines in 1993:

> Abuse may be described as physical, sexual, psychological or financial. It may be intentional or the result of neglect. It causes harm to the older person, either temporarily or over a period of time. (SSI, 1993c)

The SSI subsequently commissioned a newly formed pressure group, Action on Elder Abuse, to develop a definition that reflected working practices and the experience of the organisation's membership (SSI, 1994). The group adopted the following definition:

> Elder abuse is a single or repeated act or lack of appropriate action occurring within any relationship where there is an expectation of trust, which causes harm or distress to an older person.

Each of these definitions illustrates the difficulties inherent in attempting to define an emerging social problem in the absence of comprehensive research, professional consensus or significant grass-roots pressure. Although not obvious from the definition, it is apparent from the full title that the SSI definition focuses on abuse within domestic settings, that is, the family or victim's home, to the exclusion of institutional care settings. The Action on Elder Abuse definition does not locate abuse within a physical setting, instead making reference to it occurring within a relationship in which there is an 'expectation of trust'. This is a highly subjective term that does little to clarify abusive situations other than to appear to exclude those situations in which elderly people are targeted by strangers because of their perceived vulnerability and become the victims of, for example, fraud or theft, often referred to as 'stranger abuse'. Such an approach has not been taken regarding the stranger abuse of children or adults with learning disabilities.

Both definitions identify the possibility of abuse occurring by positive, intentional action or unintentional or neglectful behaviour. The complexity of the legal consequences of acts or omissions is familiar to lawyers and has a bearing on the type of legal action available. The subject of abuse in both definitions is an 'older person'. Even this element can be a source of confusion as there is no agreed legal definition of old age.

The language used in the latest official definition is in marked contrast to those recited above. *No Secrets* (DoH, 2000d) offers the following phrase as a basis on which to proceed:

> Abuse is a violation of an individual's human and civil rights by any other person or persons.

No Secrets goes on to note that, beyond that definition, there are certain categories of abuse over which some consensus has emerged. These are physical, sexual, psychological, financial and neglect, although abusive acts may embrace more than one category. In an area in which our knowledge base is rapidly developing, the importance of keeping an open mind to 'new' categories cannot be overstated. In some areas, institutional and professional abuse have separate category status.

Each category includes a variety of types of behaviour. Physical abuse includes hitting, slapping, pushing, unreasonable restraint, hair-pulling and forced or over-medication. Sexual abuse may involve physical contact such as touching of the genitals or breasts, masturbation or penetration. Equally, activities that do not involve contact, such as photography, indecent exposure, sexual harassment or forced exposure to pornography, may be considered abusive. Psychological abuse includes verbal assault, threats and humiliation, isolating the elder person, ignoring or being overprotective of the person, racial abuse and intimidation. The most common form of abuse is thought to be financial abuse, which includes theft, the use of money or property without consent, the forced transfer of assets, the misuse of power of attorney or appointeeship and denial of access to funds or property. Neglect includes a failure to provide medical care, food, clothing, shelter or stimulation and a failure to attend to the personal hygiene needs of, for example, an adult who is incontinent.

For each category, possible indicators of abuse have been established. While the existence of any of these indicators would not by themselves be conclusive proof of abuse, they should arouse suspicion or concern. Injuries incompatible with the history given, uncared for, untreated pressure sores, bruises in the shape of fingers, belts or other objects, poor skin condition, weight loss and an absence of hair are all possible indicators of physical abuse. Sexual abuse may be indicated where an individual has difficulty walking or sitting, suffers pain in or bruising to the genitals, or exhibits withdrawn, depressive, sexually overt or self-destructive behaviour. Concern regarding possible financial abuse might be aroused by a sudden inability to pay the bills, a lack of available cash despite a regular pension, the unexplained disappearance of financial documents or personal belongings or a change to the will of an individual who is incapable of making such a decision. Possible indicators of neglect include a general deterioration of health, inadequate clothing, malnutrition or dehydration, a poor home environment, ulcers and sores.

Certain injuries or medical conditions, for example bruising or bed sores, can occur very easily in older people. Where such a condition did not arise out of abusive behaviour, it would nevertheless be a prompt for action to ensure appropriate attention or assessment by a relevant professional, such as a district nurse.

The understanding of the causation of abuse is largely based on anecdotal accounts and is an area in which further research is required. It is clear that family members, neighbours or friends, paid staff or volunteers, other service-users or strangers may all perpetrate abuse. A number of 'risk factors' that may suggest a predisposition to abuse are the subject of current debate; these are stress, dependency, graduated domestic violence, psychopathology in the abuser and social isolation

(Bennett *et al.*, 1997). Again, caution must be exercised. While 'carer stress' may be a factor in some cases, it is clear that not all stressed carers abuse.

There has been one published UK study on the prevalence of elder abuse in the community (Ogg and Bennett, 1992). This was carried out using an Office of Population and Census Survey to interview adults over pensionable age in the general population about physical, verbal and financial abuse. The method used excluded adults in residential settings or adults who were disabled or ill. This is an important limitation, particularly when related to the risk factor social isolation and would suggest that the results are an underestimation. The result showed that 1 in 20 older people had suffered verbal or financial abuse, and 1 in 50 reported physical abuse. When the same definitions were used to ask adults under the age of 60 whether they had abused an older person, the survey produced a rate of 1 in 10 for verbal abuse. The Ogg and Bennett study replicated prevalence figures from Pillemer and Wolf's 1986 Boston study (Pillemer and Finkelhor, 1988).

Legal context

It is necessary for social care professionals to have an understanding of the legal context of elder abuse. On one level, there are a number of relevant responsibilities of agencies in terms of the provision of support and formal intervention. As important is the role of providing support and information to older people who may wish to utilise the law themselves.

The legal framework for dealing with elder abuse lacks cohesion. Elder abuse has not been conceptualised in legal terms, and lawyers are more likely to associate elderly client work with issues of probate or property rather than complaints of abuse. There is no statutory duty to investigate elder abuse. *No Secrets* (DoH, 2000d) provides guidance on the development of policy for the protection of vulnerable adults at risk with reference to social services' responsibility towards vulnerable adults. Proposals from the Law Commission (1995) for the introduction of public powers of protection for vulnerable adults, including a duty to investigate (closely modelled on the Children Act 1989), seem unlikely to be implemented at this stage (LCD, 1999). Criticisms were made of certain details of the proposed scheme, but there was widespread support for a unified framework clarifying the responsibilities of the agencies (Brammer, 1996). In the absence of such a scheme, it is necessary to draw widely upon a range of existing legislation. Relevant provision will depend on the type of abuse and the desired outcome.

Table 18.1 summarises the relevant legal provisions by the category of abuse to which they are most likely to be applicable.

Table 18.1 Legal provision for different catgeories of abuse

Type of abuse	Legal remedies
Physical	Criminal prosecution – Offences Against the Person Act 1861
	Civil action – assault, battery or false imprisonment (restraint)
	Family Law Act 1996 non-molestation and occupation orders
	Criminal Injuries Compensation claim
	Mental Health Act 1983 ss.115,135, 127, 117 (aftercare)
	Police and Criminal Evidence Act 1984 s.17 (power to enter to save life and limb)
	Registered Homes Act 1984 – regulation of residential and nursing homes: s.10 (cancellation of registration), s.11 (emergency cancellation, breach of regulations)
	NHS and Community Care Act 1990 s.47 (support)
Sexual	Criminal prosecution – Sexual Offences Act 1956 and 1968
	N.B. specific offences against people with severe learning disabilities
	Civil action
	Family Law Act 1996 non-molestation order
	Mental Health Act 1983
	Registered Homes Act 1984
	Community Care support
Psychological	Protection from Harassment Act 1997
	Registered Homes Act 1984
	Anti-discrimination legislation
	Community Care Support
Neglect	National Assistance Act 1948 s.47
	Mental Health Act 1983 s.127
	Criminal law *R* v. *Stone* 1971
Financial	Enduring Power of Attorney
	Court of Protection
	Criminal prosecution – Theft Act 1968

Certain legal provisions will be more or less appropriate for particular types of abuse, and some, for example the Sexual Offences Act 1956 and the Theft Act 1968, will be applicable only to specific categories. It is clear, however, that, for most cases, there will be a range of legal options. The selected option will depend on a number of factors, including the evidence available and the seriousness of the case. A major predisposing factor will be the desired outcome in tackling the abuse. Table 18.2 offers a further classification of legal provision by outcome or objective.

Table 18.2 Legal provision by outcome or objective

Objective	**Legal provision**
Support	NHS and Community Care Act 1990 s.47 Domiciliary services Duty to promote welfare Mental Health Act 1983 s.7 (guardianship) Carers (Recognition and Services) Act 1995 Provision of accommodation – National Assistance Act 1948, regulated by the Registered Homes Act 1984
Prosecution	Criminal law – statute and common law Investigation by the police and Crown Prosecution Service
Remove perpetrator	Family Law Act 1996 occupation order Civil (law of tort) injunction Mental Health Act 1983
Remove subject	National Assistance Act 1948 s.47 Mental Health Act 1983 (Provision of accommodation)
Compensation	Civil law Criminal Injuries Compensation Scheme Order of criminal court

Social services are expected to be the lead agency dealing with cases of elder abuse (DoH, 2000d) and have a number of existing powers, collectively known as community care services, to provide services to older people. In terms of intervention, except in the most serious cases, the provision of an appropriate care package will often be the first step. The link between the assessment of need, the provision of services and local authority resources was unsuccessfully challenged in *R* v. *Gloucestershire County Council and Another, Ex Parte Barry* [1997] HL 2All ER 1 and remains a contentious issue in times of finite resources. In attempting to provide a solution to abusive situations, it is crucial that workers have confidence in any services being offered to minimise the possibility of an already abused person being subject to further abuse. In this context, a concern remains that domiciliary or day care services, often included in care packages, are presently not subject to any formal regulation. The Care Standards Bill offers some protection by providing for the voluntary registration of agencies and by imposing a requirement that authorities contract only with registered agencies.

As a matter of good practice, an anti-oppressive approach should guide service delivery. Limited statutory provision to outlaw discrimination exists in the form of the Race Relations Act 1976, the Sex Discrimination Act 1975 and more recently the DDA 1995, offering some recourse to individuals who feel that they have suffered discrimination, whether as part of abuse or in the response to abuse.

In limited circumstances, the Mental Health Act 1983 may be utilised in respect of the older person or the perpetrator of the abuse. An ASW has the power to enter the premises in which a mentally disordered patient is living if there is reasonable cause to believe that the patient is not under proper care (s.115). Furthermore, under s.135, where a person suffering from a mental disorder is being ill treated, neglected or kept otherwise than under proper control, or is living alone and is unable to care for him- or herself, a magistrate may issue a warrant authorising a police officer to enter (by force if need be) the premises and remove the person to a place of safety for up to 72 hours. This short-term power, as part of an investigation, may provide for an assessment of a situation causing concern, particularly if access is being denied. It must be stressed that the definitions of mental disorder under the Act will restrict the application of these powers to a limited proportion of elderly people. There may also be circumstances in which the provisions of the Act will apply to the abuser.

Numerous reports of scandals in institutions clearly establish the existence of abuse within the residential sector (Glendenning and Kingston, 1999). In addressing this area, the framework for regulation and inspection, currently provided by the Registered Homes Act 1984, must be examined. Residential and nursing homes must be registered with the registration authority, the local or health authority respectively. The registration authority must visit all homes in its area twice annually and has the power to refuse or cancel registration, as well as enforce regulations. An emergency procedure may be invoked where there is a serious risk to the life, health or well-being of residents. Reported decisions of the registered homes tribunal provide documented evidence of abuse. Cases often turn on the interpretation of whether the home-owner is a 'fit person' and include an analysis of personal traits and the way in which the home is run. A number of shortcomings in the current system have been identified (Brammer, 1999), and a formal review of the inspection process (DoH, 1998a; DoH/Welsh Office, 1996) has led to the Care Standards Bill. This introduces measures for setting national quality guidelines and new inspection arrangements for care services, also establishing a register of people unsuitable to work with vulnerable adults.

Inter-agency guidelines will increasingly involve the police and provide for some level of joint investigation of elder abuse by the police and social services. The decision of whether to bring a criminal prosecution ultimately rests with the Crown Prosecution Service, who must be satisfied that to do so is in the public interest and that there is a good prospect of conviction. Evidential difficulties, including the high standard of proof required, the fact there will often be no witnesses to abuse and the perceived inability of older individuals who may be mentally or physically frail, to give evidence may influence the decision not to proceed. Encouragingly, the Youth Justice and Criminal Evidence Act 1999 introduces provisions to assist 'vulnerable witnesses', including use of video-recorded evidence and the presence of a 'supporter' when a vulnerable witness is interviewed. It is important not to deny this route to older people if they are willing to become involved in the criminal process, which serves to position acts of abuse as unacceptable criminal behaviour.

It may be effective and empowering for an individual to take private law action to counter the abuse. Potentially useful areas of law are contract, tort and family law. Individual contracts between residents and home owners are not routinely used but can offer some basis for a challenge to bad practice. Local authorities can set standards in homes with which they contract higher than those specified under legislation (*R* v. *Cleveland Care Homes Association and Others* (1993); *Independent*, 30 December). More relevant to financial or property abuse, the law of contract offers protection whereby an individual who entered into a contract under duress or undue influence will not be bound by its terms. Where an individual lacks the capacity to bring legal proceedings, a 'litigation friend' may be appointed to do so on their behalf (as for example in *R* v. *Bournewood Community and Mental Health NHS Trust, ex parte L* [1998] 3 All ER 289).

Under the law of tort, civil action may be instigated for assault (reasonable cause to fear direct harm), battery (actual direct and intentional application of force) and false imprisonment (the infliction of physical restraint not authorised by law). Negligence may also be relevant (particularly regarding 'professional' care) where a duty of care has been established, there is a breach of that duty and harm is suffered as a consequence. The principal remedy is compensatory damages, but there are examples of the use of an injunction to prevent further abusive acts (*Egan* v. *Egan* [1975] 1 CH 218).

The Family Law Act 1996 provides for an injunction to remove an individual from a property (occupation order) or prevent abusive acts (non-molestation order). This area of law may be particularly relevant in those cases of elder abuse which can be described as graduated domestic violence. The Act considerably extends the availability of domestic violence injunctions beyond spouses and cohabitees to 'associated persons'. This term includes ex-spouses, relatives and people who share the house (with certain exceptions), which would include homosexual couples. Unfortunately, the limited availability of Legal Aid may, in practice, restrict access of some people to these remedies.

Practice issues

Elder abuse cases present complex practice and ethical issues for professionals. Central to these is the debate about 'protection versus autonomy'. This is perhaps the crucial defining difference between work with children and work with adults. Adults are, for the most part, assumed to be autonomous and entitled to make their own decisions, however eccentric and risky these may appear.

Concerns for such an individual translate into a dilemma for professionals set against a context in which social workers in particular will be criticised by the media if they 'overreact' and take protective measures, but will equally be damned for a lack of action in respect to an individual's right to self-determination. The policy aim of the Law Commission provides a helpful statement on the principle of intervention:

> that people are enabled and encouraged to take for themselves those decisions which they are able to take; that where it is necessary in their own interests or for the protection of others that someone else should take decisions on their behalf, the intervention should be as limited as possible and concerned to achieve what the person himself would have wanted; and that proper safeguards be provided against exploitation, neglect and physical, sexual or psychological abuse. (Law Commission, 1995)

Issues of capacity and consent are often crucial to the determination of whether an act is abusive and whether protective steps can be justified. Actions are more likely to be classified as abusive where an individual has not consented, or cannot consent because he or she lacks the capacity to understand the issue and make an informed decision, or consent may be invalid as a result of undue influence or duress.

In other cases, an act may be perceived as abusive, but if the victim has the full capacity to make decisions, his or her right to refuse help or intervention must be respected. It is crucial that support networks are in place in the workplace for professionals involved with difficult non-intervention cases. It is also clear that, in some cases, an immediate refusal of help will not be conclusive, and there is a need to keep open offers of support in the context of ongoing monitoring. Advocacy can play a crucial role here in ensuring that an individual's wishes are voiced and listened to.

Abuse can take place in a variety of settings perpetrated by a variety of individuals. There has been a tendency to look separately at domestic and institutional settings, a tendency reinforced by official documents (DoH, 2000d; SSI, 1993c). Intrinsic differences exist between the settings, not least the legitimate expectation of a certain standard of care in a residential setting. It is important, however, that a two-tier system of responding and investigating abuse, which differentiates between abuse in domestic and residential settings, is not rigidly adopted. Abusive regimes in a care home, such as the routine use of restraint or over-medication, may well be areas for the registration authority to deal with. An increasing emphasis on national standards should lead to a greater consistency in care standards in future. An entirely different situation is where, for example, a resident is being sexually abused by a relative on private visits to a home that otherwise provides good care. Powers of the registration authority will be of little use in the latter scenario. Clearly, social services, as the lead agency with responsibility for adult protection, and inspection teams must work closely together, complementing each other's roles and not restricting their operation to either the domestic or the residential sector.

Conclusion

If elder abuse as a phenomenon follows the models of other forms of family violence, we can expect to see many developments over the next 10 years. As a professional group, social workers will be at the cutting edge of these. The level of awareness should increase, and new categories of abuse may be discovered. As views differ between professionals, carers and older people, all need to be involved in further conceptualising the problem. Equally different professionals have different approaches to intervention and need to work together to develop good practice.

The need to distinguish this area of practice from work with children has been noted. Nevertheless, there may be useful lessons to be learnt from child protection (Stevenson, 1996). This is particularly so at an operational level as practice in this area must develop to produce an appropriate response to abuse in the absence of a clear statutory framework for investigation. A range of interventions, some more therapeutic in nature, such as family therapy, mediation and anger management, will need to be considered alongside legal options.

As with childcare, the key to effective future work relating to elder abuse will be a development of policy and inter-agency procedures to provide for work in partnership. As a minimum, guidelines need to address the following areas: the identification of relevant agencies and their respective roles; recognising the differing responsibilities of operational and managerial staff; incorporating values and principles; guidance on the identification of abuse; principles for sharing information and confidentiality; the prescription of procedures for investigation, including record-keeping, the emergency response, how to respond to disclosures and preserving evidence; the availability of legal advice; data collection; and monitoring and review.

The emergence of elder abuse as a social problem presents an obvious challenge for social workers. The emphasis on the social services as the lead agency for investigating potentially abusive situations will inevitably lead to a change in working practice, which should be supported by appropriate training. A greater emphasis on following agency guidelines closely may appear restrictive to some workers and at times unnecessary bureaucracy, but such procedures may offer security and protection to workers who may, in the absence of a clear statutory framework, flounder when faced with a possible referral.

There is, compared with other forms of family violence, a limited knowledge base for the issues surrounding elder abuse from which professionals can draw to inform their practice. A stated objective of *No Secrets* (DoH, 2000d) is to encourage local and national data collection and promote research. Even sophisticated research is unlikely to reveal the true extent of abuse as there are many reasons why people might not report it.

The existing legal framework is fragmented and was not designed specifically to deal with elder abuse. In an area in which social care professionals are more focused on therapeutic intervention, the use of the law may be considered to be a last resort (Stevenson, 1995). Where it is appropriate to have recourse to legal intervention, that action must be informed by values with an appropriate emphasis on empowerment and self-determination, and seek to achieve an outcome that improves the older person's situation. It is also clear that if legal action is contemplated, appropriate legal advice should be sought, especially regarding the extent of evidence required. With these qualifications, and an imaginative use of the existing framework, it is possible for the law to have a positive and empowering impact on practice relating to elder abuse cases.

19

An Introduction to Family Group Conferences

Paul Nixon

> Every family has a secret and that secret is they are not the same as other families. (Alan Bennett, *Writing Home*)

Introduction

This chapter examines some of the strengths and limitations of the family group conference (FGC) approach and its potential impact on social work practice. It will argue that the development of FGCs in the UK conflicts with, rather than complements, the prevailing procedural and organisational professional culture but may paradoxically re-assert original social work values. The chapter will also consider the themes of responsibility, participation and cultural sensitivity, as well as the balance between protection and support services for children in the context of FGC practice.

The underpinning assumption of the Children Act is that children are generally best cared for by their families, the legislation intending 'family' to be interpreted broadly (Ryan, 1994). Affirming that there is no one ideal way to bring up children and that family life varies according to culture, class, religion and community (DoH, 1989b), the Act identified ethnicity, culture and language as significant factors in shaping decisions affecting children. It envisaged that children's welfare would be promoted through providing services and helping their families, and kin and community were seen as having a fundamental role to play (Hill and Aldgate, 1996). The State now has a legal duty to support and strengthen the families of children 'in need', this positive approach being designed to encourage the provision of a range of services to meet diverse needs.

FGCs, first conceptualised and practised in New Zealand, have attracted interest in the UK because they appear to provide a practical approach emphasising family responsibility, offering a format for partnership and culturally sensitive practice and utilising family and community strengths in a way that appears to fit with the aspirations of the Children Act.

Partnership in practice

The Children Act sought changes not just in policy and practice, but also in attitudes about children and families. It was hoped that the new law would produce fundamental changes in thinking about partnership, participation, choice, openness, parental responsibility and every child's need for both security and family links.

Ten years on from the arrival of the Children Act, there is compelling evidence, both in policy and in practice, that the aims of partnership and family support have remained substantially unrealised (Audit Commission, 1994; DoH, 1995b; Gibbons *et al.*, 1995; Thoburn *et al.*, 1995; Bell, 1999).

Research has highlighted the difficulties that social workers encounter attempting to operate within two different and sometimes competing systems that do not easily mesh (Bell, 1999) – the professional system, with its own organisational, political and procedural requirements, and each family system, with its own unique aspirations, priorities and different cultural ways of running *that* family. Studies of 'families' caught in social work systems show that they have little influence on the nature, quality or quantity of services delivered or on defining their preferred outcome for the interventions (Kelly, 1990; Thoburn *et al.*, 1995; Freeman and Hunt, 1999). 'Partnership' with families has remained 'an idea in search of practice' (Ryburn and Atherton, 1996) and is often reduced to parent(s) observing a meeting of professionals. As Marsh describes:

> The current model of partnership in child welfare is, in general, one of limited family participation. It is concerned predominately with the ways that the family, primarily parents, can help the professionals do their job. (Marsh, 1994)

With an increasing emphasis in social work on gate-keeping, risk assessment and procedurally driven practice, partnership with families has not been a priority (Howe, 1992) when it should in fact be at the very heart of the social work task. Agencies set the criteria of 'need', and, through assessment, social workers are required to establish who is 'eligibile' for help. This is rarely a shared activity, families and communities being subject to organisational interpretations of their 'need'. The power that professionals have to define problems and prescribe solutions is inversely related to families' determining their own needs (Ryburn, 1991). Service-users' voices are routinely marginalised, which means that the terms and conditions of 'partnerships' between families and professionals are often pre-set by the professional agenda (Braye and Preston-Shoot, 1995; Cleaver and Freeman, 1995).

If families are excluded from the decision-making processes affecting them, a lack of commitment to plans made by professionals is likely. This is often misinterpreted by the professionals as lack of family commitment to their children (Rowe *et al.*, 1984; Millham *et al.*, 1986). The net effect is to create a cycle of mistrust and misunderstanding that has a corrosive effect on the relationships between families and professionals. UK research into child protection practice has shown how partnership and a good outcome are linked (DoH, 1995b; Thoburn *et al.*, 1995). Improving partnership work is likely to require some move away from procedure-bound and defensive practice. Social workers will need greater autonomy and flexibility if they are to be given the space that is needed for negotiating the common ground for collaboration with families to develop.

Family group conferences

The FGC is a family-centered decision-making process involving a wide network of family and friends. It is predicated on the principles of inclusion and partnership, and adopts a strengths-based perspective. The FGC approach attempts to capitalise on the knowledge, skills and resources of both the formal (professional/agency) and the informal (family/community) systems within the child's ecological network. Through the work of an independent coordinator, these two systems are brought together, families being encouraged to take up decision-making responsibilities. The role of the State and other service providers is to facilitate and resource plans and decisions.

Referral and preparation phase

Referrals come from a variety of sources, most commonly from social workers. They are usually made when a crisis has emerged, such as a breakdown in a child's placement or an incident of child abuse, and decisions have to be made about the child's future.

Referrals are given to an independent coordinator who has the task of finding out who is in the child's ecological network and of 'mapping out' the 'family', which includes the extended family and friends and any professionals who are relevant to the decision-making. A significant period of time (3–5 weeks) is spent preparing the family and professionals for the FGC, helping them to focus on the child's needs, put aside family conflicts and think about how they will get what they want out of the meeting. The family leads the decision-making on arrangements for the meeting, the time and the venue, as well as negotiating with the coordinator, who will attend. The coordinator may exclude certain people from the FGC, but exclusions are rare and should be especially justified.

Stage one (information-sharing)

The professionals and family meet, usually with more family than professionals present, to share information offering their analysis of the problem and to discuss the needs of the child. The coordinator chairs the meeting and ensures that clear information is provided by professionals, who set out what the basis for referral was, what concerns they have and what services and resources could be called upon. Information is presented in the chosen language of the family, and they are encouraged to ask questions and clarify points. The professionals then leave the meeting.

Stage two (private time)

A defining moment in the FGC is when the family group are left in private to discuss the problems and create their own solutions based on the information they have been given. They will draw on their knowledge, experience and problem-solving abilities. They have as much time as they need, food often being provided to emphasise this and help to encourage informality. No record is made of private discussions.

Stage three (agreeing plans)

The family ask the coordinator back into their meeting and write up their plan. This is presented to the referrer and the professionals for their agreement, which they should give unless the plan places the child at risk. The resources and plans for monitoring and review are negotiated. If a plan is not safe for the child, the family group are asked to re-think, but if the professionals still cannot agree, the matter goes to another decision-making forum, such as a child protection conference or the court, for resolution.

Initial FGCs are usually followed by reviews or 'follow-up meetings', the FGC reconvening to look at how plans are working and make any necessary changes or adjustments. For a further discussion of the key practice stages of FGCs, see Nixon (1992); Morris (1995); and Marsh and Crow (1998).

Practice issues and dilemmas

Responsibilities and rights

An enduring theme of the Children Act and the practice of FGCs has been balancing the sometimes conflicting rights and responsibilities of children, their families and the State. FGCs attempt to build a consensual approach to decision-making, encouraging a focus on the *shared responsibilities* that can exist within family groups and between professionals and families, rather than on adversarial processes.

Concern has been expressed about whether the balance of responsibility with FGCs is tipped too heavily in favour of the family group so that the child's interests may sit in the shadow of the needs of the family. Moreover, practitioners adopting an undifferentiated approach to partnership may reinforce the power of an abusive parent. As Biss argues:

> Power relationships within the family can be allowed to operate unquestioned. Non-abusive parents and children who are already in a powerless position can have this reinforced. (Biss, 1995)

The FGC attempts to counteract this by widening the parameters of 'family', bringing in family members and support people outside the nuclear family, so that the wider family group can act with collective responsibility for the child. The involvement of extended family has served either to increase support for the child and parents or to provide a placement in the extended family when the parents cannot care for their children (Hassall and Maxwell, 1991).

Participation and inclusion

A central aim of the FGC is to improve family participation, and those involved have been mainly positive about a meeting including the extended family, feeling that it was good to get family problems out in the open and identify any possible sources of help and support. Practice has, however, been hampered by professional concerns about the perceived weakness of kin networks, while research has highlighted that coordinators had more difficulty getting professionals to FGCs than family members (Lupton *et al.*, 1995).

There are no pre-set limits to family attendance. In one study, an average of seven family members had been invited to the FGC and an average of six had attended (Marsh and Crow, 1998). FGC practice starts from the assumption that the 'family' has something of value to contribute, the empirical evidence demonstrating that families are more extensively involved than in other types of social work meetings and that there is a high level of satisfaction with the FGC process (Thomas, 1994; Barker and Barker, 1995; Lupton *et al.*, 1995; Lupton and Stevens, 1997; Marsh and Crow, 1998; Smith and Hennessey, 1998).

Enhancing children's participation in decision-making is a central challenge for social workers. 'Traditional' meetings (for example, case conferences and statutory reviews) still tend to be adult and professional orientated, often containing strangers and modes of communication that are conducted 'over the child's head', children frequently seeming to be passive observers (Mittler, 1992; Farnfield, 1997). In contrast, children are more likely to attend FGCs than other more orthodox meetings and, once present, to participate more effectively (Crow and Marsh, 1997; Lupton and Stevens, 1997). The coordinator may identify an advocate or support person for the child, most commonly from within the family group, to ensure that his or her voice is heard. Support people from the family network can also be involved in helping more vulnerable adult family members to adopt a substantive role in the conference. FGCs are less formal and more flexible, perhaps providing a more accessible environment for the child to take part. Children may understand more about how decisions are reached in their family and how they can influence the outcome.

The use of information in FGCs is a central practice issue. Active participation relies on good-quality information provided in a respectful, jargon-free manner. Assessments need to be open to challenge and discussion, as well as directly relevant to the decision-making task facing the family. Professionals have to be aware, however, that providing information can soon spill over into prescribing a solution (Lupton *et al.*, 1995).

Cultural sensitivity

The Children Act requires race, culture, language and religion to be taken into account in decisions made about children looked after by local authorities (Children Act 1989 s.22(5)(c)). Despite this, however, there remain significant problems in the provision of culturally sensitive services for black and ethnic minority groups. Services are generally still predicated on white European norms and assumptions. Barn (1993b), for example, found black children to be over-represented in admissions to public care and found significant problems with the engagement between professionals and families. Sinclair *et al.* (1995) identified some progress in services for African-Caribbean families but still noted considerable barriers in working with the Asian community which is the biggest ethnic minority population of England and Wales.

The FGC is designed to enable each family to set the method of decision-making in line with their own culture and traditions. Practice should, however, guard against presenting FGCs to families as a professional 'idea' or 'way forward' when it may be their usual way of decision-making. The coordinators have to avoid assumptions about the family's traditions and culture, being guided by the family in setting up the FGC. The practice of matching coordinators to the family by language and culture may help, and the family should be consulted on this matter.

Protection and support

The Children Act was constructed to provide a balance between child protection and family support (Parton, 1991). Research has shown that most children coming into public care have experienced disrupted family relationships and poverty, implying that their needs relate at least as much to material deprivation and lack of support as to the consequences of abuse and neglect (DHSS, 1985; Packman *et al.*, 1986).

FGC practice and research shows that families ask for a range of services frequently relating to material help or support (Thornton, 1993; Lupton *et al.*, 1995) They are also far more likely to be involved in offering support, and producing plans that tend to be more creative than those designed by the professionals with traditional approaches. This was evident in a study that looked at 80 FGCs in UK in which 94 per cent of FGC families offered some level of support, in 31 per cent of cases offering to look after the children for at least some period of time (Crow and Marsh, 1997).

Private family discussions are the most distinctive and contentious characteristic of FGCs. They are considered to be an important part of the FGC process as the continued presence of a professional presence may either dominate or inhibit the discussions. Families occasionally decline private time, sometimes because there is only a small family present and it is seen as being unnecessary (Paterson and Harvey, 1991), or because they have had doubts about their own ability to plan (Lupton *et al.*, 1995).

There is concern, however, that private discussions may give abusive adults undue influence over the proceedings (Geddis, 1993). Yet the public disclosure of information about violence to the wider family can break the silence on which much child abuse is sustained. The provision of information by professionals, including the setting of 'bottom lines' relating to the concerns and subsequent action if FGC plans are not safe, means that the professionals maintain a key role in monitoring the safety of family plans. Protection can also come from the coordinator excluding any adults who present a threat to the child, or can come from the wider family and community present at the conference; Ban (1993), for example, identifies in practice how an alliance of women across generations can establish coalitions and form power blocs.

Agreement on FGC plans is reached in most cases (Renouf *et al.*, 1990; Lupton *et al.*, 1995; Crow and Marsh; 1997; Smith and Hennessey, 1998). Agreement about resources and family commitment to the plans after the FGC is, however, less clear. There is a concern that, despite the high level of agreement in FGCs, a number of decisions and plans are not being implemented (Paterson and Harvey, 1991; Lupton *et al.*, 1995). There have been problems over a lack of coordination in the ongoing implementation of plans and/or a diminishing commitment of families and professionals in a period after the FGC.

However, national research on FGCs in the UK has shown that children were, in the view of the professionals, considered to be *better* protected by FGC plans, and there was an indication of a reduction in the re-abuse rates compared with other approaches (Crow and Marsh, 1997). There is still, however, a need to understand the long-term effects of FGCs on children and their families, longitudinal research being needed to assess these outcomes (Lupton and Nixon, 1999).

Redefining families and reclaiming social work?

FGCs have been interpreted in many ways – shifting power from professionals to families; diverting children from public care or families from State interference; providing a radical approach to partnership – but perhaps they are just about good social work practice.

FGCs are unusual because they are not easily located in many of the systems and structures within which childcare professionals operate, ones that seek to constrain the autonomy of both families and social workers. Practitioners working in hierarchical and disabling structures will not find it easy to put into practice principles that are absent in their organisations, and managers reluctant to devolve powers to social workers are unlikely to feel comfortable with family decision-making. While social work remains constrained by anxiety over the perceived need for procedural and administrative control, FGCs are unlikely to flourish.

FGCs have been subject to much research scrutiny, but service-user and community groups could have a greater role in influencing research design and defining what they consider to be good outcomes. There are still a number of key research questions on the quality of information presented at FGCs, on what conditions make FGCs most effective and on the long-term effects from the perspectives of the children and families involved. The extent to which good practice is attained will be contingent upon the extent to which families have a real say over the way in which services are delivered and the extent to which the structure enables practitioners and families to work together.

While conservative and orthodox social work continues to overlook the importance of kinship ties, the practice of FGCs has started to re-assert the value of kin, re-defining families in a broader and more positive role. Social work too might be reclaimed if practitioners were enabled to utilise their skills in a creative and collaborative fashion, so that practice and services move much closer to the spirit of the Children Act, with all its good intentions.

Part III

Service-user and Practice Perspectives

20

Issues for Practice

Penelope Welbourne

The transition to practice from learning about practice – a step up or a leap of faith?

By the end of their social work training, newly qualified practitioners may feel well prepared for many aspects of practice. Their value base has been explored and developed, their knowledge of the social context of social work has expanded, and they are equipped with theoretical knowledge and practical skills to help them get to grips with a wide range of areas of social work practice. In theory, there is an answer, or at least an optimal response, to every problem that they are likely to encounter. In practice, however, the information on which to base evaluation and planning is often tentative or provisional, discipline boundaries may be unclear, theoretical guidance may not seem to 'fit' a particular problem area, and resistance by reluctant service-users may threaten to undermine well-laid plans.

Another aspect of social work with the potential to cause anxious supervision sessions and sleepless nights is the relativity and subjectivity of many of the key principles in social work. One example of this is the concept of 'significant harm' from the Children Act 1989. Most social work graduates will be familiar with the concept and have considered the problem of defining the idea of 'significant' in relation to harm to a child. In practice, when carrying out an assessment of a family in which a child is failing to thrive and develop as well as his or her peers, cared for by chaotic but caring parents who hate 'official' intervention in their family life, the social worker will have to decide which of his or her competing values should dominate the assessment. Should it be the 'forensic test' approach indicated by Part IV of the Children Act 1989, or the principle that children are best brought up in their families of origin unless there are compelling reasons for removing them from their parents' care? Where does the boundary between Parts III and IV of the Children Act lie? If you decide to compare the child of the family under assessment with a 'similar child' to help you decide which Part(s) of the Act should inform your approach to this family, how do you identify the 'similar child'?

Interprofessional discussion can be very helpful if the basis of the discussion is clear to both agencies. A social worker who identifies the developmental issues as falling within the remit of the health visiting service, talking to a health visitor who sees the problem as a 'social' one that the social worker should 'do something' about, is unlikely to have a positive discussion leading to an improvement in services to the child. The child's safety is similarly unlikely to be enhanced unless the members of the two agencies can clarify what they expect of themselves and of the other agency, and can negotiate a way forward that does not leave interdisciplinary 'gaps'.

All of these areas of complexity and lack of clarity cause difficulty, conflict and stress. It is a significant component of the job for some social workers, particularly those working in areas where the level of need is great, resources are tightly rationed and there is a resulting focus on statutory intervention. Having said that, all the issues raised above can, and do, arise in most social work settings involving children and families.

It might even be said that a social work setting in which these issues and conflicts do not arise is one in which there should be some review of practice and values. Social work as a profession deals with new, challenging and unique situations every time a piece of work is undertaken. Without the dialogue that results from conflict, analysis and reflection on practice, individual workers' and the organisation's development may grind to a halt.

How does it feel on the 'front line', and how do social workers cope?

There are a number of ways in which social workers new to practice might expect to be supported, and ways in which they can help themselves to cope with the pressures of work in what is arguably a hostile environment. First, every social worker has a right to good-quality supervision on a regular basis. There can be few agencies or teams in which aspirations relating to supervision are met in practice. There are hundreds of valid reasons for cancelling planned supervision sessions. New deadlines loom associated with court hearings or emergency action to protect a child, illness or leave leads to a long break between sessions. Despite these obstacles, each agency has a responsibility to provide adequate supervision to its staff, and when it is not provided, each worker has a responsibility to apply pressure to ensure it is made available. As a social worker, you have the right to share the burden of responsibility for decision-making and case-planning with someone with experience and a degree of detachment from the families who make up the social worker's caseload. You also have the right to discuss any anxieties you may have, including any anxieties for your own welfare. This is very pertinent for social workers involved in exercising statutory powers, who may provoke a strong feeling of hostility in their clients. You have the right to have someone proactively concerned about your ability to cope with the task in hand, and consider your professional development. You therefore have the right to moan, memo and, if need be, make an official complaint if this support is not forthcoming.

One of the many pitfalls of working in a situation where there is pressure on everybody and everything, especially time, is that the things that can sustain and support the stressed worker are the ones that are often jettisoned first. Finding the time for self-protective activities such as supervision and consultation helps to reduce pressure and aid the development of good professional practice for the individual and the agency.

Many social workers would probably rate peer group support very highly when asked about their own coping mechanisms. A good start to surviving in social work and deriving enjoyment and satisfaction from the work is to have the good fortune to be a member of a team in which there is an ethos of mutual support and sharing of thought about the most difficult cases. While this is not a substitute for supervision, it is very noticeable how much difference it makes to workers when they are part of a friendly, facilitating team. This will unfortunately not be much comfort to those who know from experience how professionally isolating the membership of a team in conflict can be, but it is a good reason for those in teams subject to internal tension to look for ways of improving the situation.

Statutory social work is not likely to be an easy task – and it is arguable that it should always feel a challenge in that the weight of responsibility for a child's future associated with the task is awesome. One needs confidence in the quality of the decision-making process that preceded the initiation of statutory intervention. Were all the possible alternatives fully explored? Was the family assessed fairly, with due respect to their race, culture and other individual factors? Does the worker fully understand why the proceedings are being brought at this point, agree with the analysis that underlies it and participate fully in that process? That groundwork needs to be done well in order that workers may have the confidence that they are pursuing a legitimate aim, with all their questions addressed and their ambivalence having been explored. This may take time, but it is an essential preliminary to taking on the task ahead.

Second, there should be professional support – legal advice, help in preparing information about the family to shape it into legal 'evidence', someone to talk the social worker through the process of court proceedings and giving evidence in court. There should be the confidence that the social worker will not be left alone to deal with the hearing itself or the issues it raises.

Confidence that the task of obtaining a statutory order (such as a care order) in respect of a child is a legitimate one and necessary in the child's interests, together with the confidence that goes with adequate support in the task, can make it a challenge with rewards as well as difficulties. It demands flexible thought about the best way of helping children when their families fail them, and a degree of rigour and reflection since practice is under scrutiny by the outside world in the persons of the guardian *ad litem*, family legal advisors and judges or magistrates. Children's cases under Part IV of the Children Act 1989 are very often settled outside the courtroom, the social worker's role being to work towards a consensus through which the child can be safe and protected, but the family's strengths and potential for supporting the child are fully explored. The pressure of court proceedings and the influence of persuasive legal advice will often stimulate parents to re-evaluate their position. They may decide to comply with the request for further assessment and treatment, which may in turn lead to an unanticipated outcome – a supervision order rather than a care order and removal from the family, for example. Even in cases in which there is no potential for such a positive outcome, there can be the satisfaction of having undertaken a difficult task, done it well and prevented ongoing child abuse or neglect.

Sadness for the parents who 'lose' their children through social work intervention, and anxiety for the future of a child who is now dependent upon the State for his or her quality of parenting, is real, valid and an appropriate response. This is part of the emotional landscape of social work: learning to manage the personal and professional implications of one's actions is a task that assumes critical importance once training ends and practice as a social worker begins. The reward of the job lies in the belief that each piece of work undertaken is done as well as one can, leading to the most positive outcome possible for the children and families involved – and some personal professional development along the way.

21

The Challenges of Care and Control: Experiences and Observations from an Approved Social Worker

Jeanette Henderson

Introduction

The role of an ASW is wider than undertaking Mental Health Act 1983 assessments, although much mental health work is in some way related to the Act. The implementation of mental health legislation requires more than a factual knowledge of the law and is bound up with ethical and professional dilemmas. Is it possible, for example, to detain someone formally in hospital against his or her will in an *empowering* manner? I found this one of the most challenging aspects of my role as an ASW, requiring me to confront personal and professional ethics. In child protection practice, there is an adult–child relationship, the protection of the child being the central feature of the role; in statutory mental health work, the interaction is between adults – the worker and the 'patient'.

The person alongside the professional

In Mental Health Act assessments, I have confronted people who reminded me of my family, friends and myself – to assess an older woman of a similar age to my own mother or grandmother, for example, affected me as a person as well as a professional. To a greater or lesser extent, most of us will feel distress and pain at some time in our lives. We often deal with these feelings and move on with our lives. However, mental distress is not something that is experienced only by others, by 'them', by people who use the services of welfare agencies. It happens to doctors, social workers, nurses – and their families and friends – as well (Perkins, 1996; Jones, K.S., 1998; Mathews and Lindow, 1998).

From a professional point of view, I have learned from every assessment I made. To come face to face with the pain in someone's life demands a response that respects the humanity of the people involved. The learning, challenge and complexity of the role make it both demanding and fulfilling. An essential component of an assessment is the period of reflection that follows the decision once it has been taken – whether or not it is to apply for formal detention. Applying to detain someone against his or her will is not a decision to be taken lightly or without concern. The ability to take such a decision is one thing, but it must be underpinned by an awareness of rights and the ethical context of the role. I have never felt wholly comfortable with ASW work – it provides a stark contrast between the caring and controlling aspects of social work – and I constantly questioned my practice and looked for ways to make the assessment as respectful and dignified for the service-user as possible.

The Mental Health Act is currently under review, and the future role of ASWs in formal assessments is uncertain. In this chapter, the focus is particularly on the Revised Code of Practice that accompanies the Act, since it relates to the *implementation* of the law as given in the Mental Health Act 1983. It is probably not possible – or desirable – fully to separate the personal from the professional, and that is perhaps recognised by the Code. The Code begins with guiding principles that include respect and the recognition of basic human rights. As will be briefly considered below, the situations that confront the ASW are not clear cut (but which part of social work is?) so they present a challenge to personal values and professional judgment.

In statutory mental health work, the law is interpreted by those involved in an individual assessment using their professional experience and judgment. It is possible that a different group of people, another GP, psychiatrist and ASW, would take an alternative decision. An assessment in one part of the country, for example, may have an outcome not possible in another. In some areas, there may be a range of facilities available that are more acceptable to some people experiencing a period of acute distress (Campbell, 1996) and that enable a person to stay in the community.

Anyone detained under the Act has the right to appeal to a Mental Health Review Tribunal made up of three people – legal, medical and lay members. The tribunal receives reports from medical, nursing and social work professionals, and the patient may be legally represented. The patient is interviewed by the medical member of the tribunal prior to the hearing. One of the tasks for the ASW when making an assessment and writing the social circumstances report required by the tribunal is to consider all the circumstances of the case. How much of this is then reflected in the final report is a matter for the individual ASW. As well as outlining the circumstances leading up to admission and the current situation, a recommendation to the tribunal and details of discharge planning, the ASW should consider:

> the patient's home and family circumstances, including the attitude of the patient's nearest relative or the person so acting;
>
> the opportunities for employment or occupation and the housing facilities which would be available to the patient if discharged;
>
> the availability of community support and relevant medical facilities;
>
> the financial circumstances of the patient. (Mental Health Tribunal Rules 1983 Sched. 1, Pt. B, paras 2–4 quoted in Eldergill, 1998)

This is a daunting task, especially when an ASW may only have three or four days' notice of the need for a tribunal report and may not know or have previously met any of the people involved.

Law alongside practice

What is said and what is left unsaid, the *process* of the assessment as well as the outcome, may give an indication of the experience of the implementation of mental health legislation for the person being assessed. The statements in a social circumstances report following a Mental Health Act assessment do not necessarily give an account of the decision-making process and the dilemmas that may have faced the ASW. Assessments are not neat and tidy – as ASWs we deal with people in the midst of great distress, pain and fear. There may, for example, be a debate about the appropriateness of detention in the first place – could someone's response to his or her circumstances be interpreted in another way? Joint assessments are to be preferred unless there are 'good reasons' for separate interviews (DoH/Welsh Office, 1999, Code of Practice, para. 2.3). It is up to the ASW, who has the responsibility for coordinating the assessment, to decide what constitutes a 'good reason' and weigh this against the recommendations in the Code of Practice. The following two case studies (describing real-life situations, although the names of those involved have been changed to preserve confidentiality) relate particularly to the assessment and admission process.

Case Study

Mary was a quiet, almost timid, 67-year-old woman whose husband had recently died. Since his death, Mary had become confused and withdrawn, refusing to eat or accept help. All of the professionals involved were concerned that Mary's mental health had deteriorated to such an extent that she should be admitted to hospital as soon as possible. Everyone – including Mary's son (her nearest relative) – was available to meet at Mary's warden-controlled bungalow in the early afternoon. The community psychiatric nurse had visited earlier in the day when Mary refused hospital admission. The community psychiatric nurse planned to return that afternoon, and Mary's son had agreed to go to his mother's home to let the professionals in. At 2 pm, an ASW and a colleague, the consultant psychiatrist, the community psychiatric nurse and the GP arrived. The community psychiatric nurse and Mary's son stayed in the hallway, leaving the four others – consultant, GP, ASW and colleague (all male) – and Mary in her tiny front room.

There are certainly occasions on which there is a high degree of risk to those involved during an assessment (although Mary's case was not one of them). The person involved may be very reluctant to meet with, and may be hostile towards, the professionals involved. The circumstances may be dangerous and hold a risk of violence for the ASW. It is not unknown for other involved professionals to depart after an assessment, leaving the ASW in an isolated and vulnerable position. In such circumstances, the support and assistance of a colleague may be invaluable. Some agencies have responded to these risks by introducing policies whereby two ASWs attend *all* assessments rather than considering the particular circumstances of the situation.

It was this local authority policy that all ASW assessments should be undertaken in pairs in view of the risk posed to individual ASWs during the assessment process. Were there 'good reasons' in this case to undertake a separate assessment, or have fewer people involved at the same time? It might be argued that to have one single interview when all involved were present would be less distressing for Mary. The process would be quicker, and it would give the professionals the opportunity to discuss the situation there and then. On the other hand, the sheer number of people in her home could be distressing and lead to greater confusion and anxiety for Mary. This might have been amplified by the fact that most of the people involved were men and strangers to Mary.

Admission to hospital

Let us stay with Mary's case for the next step in the process of assessment and admission. As was noted above, assessments are not neat and tidy, nor is there only one dilemma in each situation. Section 6(1) of the Mental

Health Act 1983 gives 'sufficient authority for the applicant, or any person authorised by the applicant, to take the patient and convey him to hospital'. This may involve asking for police assistance or using ambulance transport, depending on the circumstances of each individual case. When someone is particularly distressed, the decisions may be more clear cut, if, for example, the situation makes the need for police assistance a matter of urgency, but this is not always so. In Mary's assessment, we face some more difficult decisions.

The assessment has taken place and a decision has been made that Mary should be formally detained in hospital under s.2 of the Act for a period of assessment. Mary has not agreed with this decision, has refused to leave her home and has become more distressed, shouting and demanding that everyone leave because she must make her husband's tea. Rather than ask for police assistance, the ASW has requested that the GP call for an ambulance, hoping that by the time it arrives Mary will agree to go to hospital. The ambulance arrives. The two ambulance workers ask Mary whether she would like to go for a ride with them to the shops. Mary says that would be better than going to that awful hospital, gets her coat and goes to leave with the ambulance workers.

So Mary could walk from her home into the ambulance believing she was being taken to the shops, or the ASW could send for police assistance and Mary could be carried from her home to a police car, knowing she was going to hospital. A complex and difficult decision needs to be made. Which would protect Mary's human rights and treat her with respect? During the assessment is not the most appropriate time for the ASW to think through such dilemmas. I would argue that such issues need a long and careful consideration to enable the ASW to identify his or her own personal and professional ethical response to such situations and dilemmas. If honesty is the central value, Mary must be told that she is not going to the shops but to the hospital. If dignity is key, Mary could walk out of her home with a mistaken belief about her destination. The law requires that Mary is told she has been formally detained under a section of the Act, will be taken to hospital and has rights of appeal.

Nearest relative

Susan is a 19-year-old woman who lives alone in a bedsit, has been involved with mental health services for the last year and has recently been an in-patient at the local psychiatric hospital. Doctors have diagnosed both depression and anorexia, and are concerned that Susan may need to be admitted formally to hospital under s.3 of the Act. As part of the assessment process, the ASW (who has known Susan for some time) must consult Susan's nearest relative, her father Eric.

A list of people who may be the nearest relative is given in s.26 of the Act, and the ASW must use this list to identify the person he or she is required by law to approach. The ASW is required to consult with the nearest relative when considering an application under s.3 (for treatment that may last for up to six months). Once consultation has taken place, an application under s.3 may not proceed if the nearest relative objects. It is, however, the consultation rather than a possible objection that is the subject here.

Several years ago, Susan disclosed a history of physical and emotional abuse by her father, of whom she lives in fear. Susan does not want the ASW to contact any family members – especially her father. Susan's father lives nearby, and the ASW has details of his address and telephone number. A joint interview is planned for the following afternoon. The law is very clear that consultation should take place unless it appears to the:

> social worker that in the circumstances such consultation is not reasonably practicable or would involve unreasonable delay. (Mental Health Act 1983 s.11(6))

Debate about the meaning of 'practicable' has led to writers such as Richard Jones referring to a range of cases including employment and adoption law, to state that:

> These cases strongly suggest that it would not be 'practicable' for an approved social worker to consult with a nearest relative if such consultation would have an adverse effect on the patient's situation by, for example, causing significant emotional distress to the patient or by placing the patient at risk of harm. (Jones, 1999)

So where does that leave the ASW? Would consulting the nearest relative be 'practicable' in this case?

Conclusion

The situations briefly outlined above give an indication of the type of dilemma that an ASW may face in the course of a single day. An assessment may take several days, or an ASW may undertake more than one during the course of that day. Any day in the life of an ASW is different from the one before it. In a similar way, all ASWs are different. The dilemmas above are mine, although they are shared by many ASWs with whom I have spoken. In my past practice as an ASW and a trainer of ASWs, I always returned to the fundamental issue of implementing the law in an ethical way.

This is a continuing process that follows initial training and practice as an ASW. Reflection and continuing professional development are, I suggest, an essential component of the ASW role. I was once told that when we have the law, we have enough to practice – ethics don't come into it. It is my argument in this chapter that ethical practice is essential to a distressed person's experience of the law. It is doubtful whether formal detention in a psychiatric hospital can be a positive experience for many, but it is perhaps possible to shape the experience of admission into a less negative one. And maybe that is the best one can hope for.

22

Working with Children: A Guardian Ad Litem*'s Experience*

Ann Dale-Emberton

In this chapter, I explore some of the practice dilemmas for guardians *ad litem* working on behalf of children. This will include a consideration of how a balance, if any, can be achieved between the child's wishes and feelings, and child's best interests.

In order to safeguard the interests of a child, the guardian *ad litem* has a number of powers and duties enshrined by legislation (Children Act 1989) and two sets of Court Rules (the Family Proceedings Rules (1991) Part IV and the Family Proceedings Courts (Children Act 1989) Rules 1991). Guardians *ad litem* need to draw on different theory and knowledge bases, as well as to develop a range of skills, so that they can undertake the various tasks that are incumbent in the role. Broadly speaking, the tasks include investigating the background to the case; accessing information by reading and analysing various files and documents, and critically evaluating them; information-gathering through conducting interviews with the child in a sensitive and age-appropriate way, as well as with their parents, relatives, carers and other professionals; managing the case in order to avoid unnecessary delay; advising on the allocation of the case to the appropriate court and ensuring that those with parental responsibility are aware of the proceedings; as well as negotiating and mediating skills. The guardian also needs to be aware of the child's cultural, ethnic and religious needs and how these can be promoted. A crucial task is assessing and commenting on the local authority's care plan for the child, including their recommendations to the court.

The guardian is an independent worker and, besides having the skills, knowledge base and experience outlined above, also needs well-developed report-writing abilities, thus ensuring that reports are well evidenced and reflective. The role can, at times, be isolating and stressful so it is important that guardians work in partnership with the solicitor whom they have instructed, as well as having the opportunity to access independent consultants/experts or to review the case by consulting with a colleague. Many Panels have established protocols for regular peer review between guardians, which guardians perceive as beneficial insofar as they offer the guardians the opportunity to gain a broader perspective, as well as reflecting on their practice.

In order to illustrate the work of the guardian, I will draw on a case study involving four children, whom we shall call Stacey (9), Emma (4), Lucy (3) and Marcia (7 months). All the names have been changed in order to preserve confidentiality.

Case Study

By the time the local authority made an application for interim care orders (Children Act 1989 s.38), Stacey, Emma, Lucy and Marcia had been separated from their parents for five months. The family had been known to the social services department for eight years, with active ongoing social work intervention for the past four. The children's names had been placed on the Child Protection Register in the category of 'at risk of emotional abuse', latterly including Marcia.

Records indicated that there had been a multi-professional approach (doctor, community psychiatric nurse, psychiatrist, social worker, health visitor and education social worker) to working with the family, all the professionals working collaboratively, with the prime objective of helping the parents to address long-term problems that affected their functioning and had a negative affect on the children's development. Among the problems identified were: incidents of violence by the father towards the mother; the mother frequently leaving the family; evidence that father could not cope during her absence; both parents being in contact with the mental health services; a lack of school attendance by Stacey; as well as inappropriate methods of physical disciplining by the father. Despite considerable assistance and resources, there was no consistent improvement in the quality of the care that the children received.

The parents separated following the mother being severely assaulted by the father, resulting in her being hospitalised. The father was charged with grievous bodily harm, for which he was to stand trial. Following this incident, all four children were initially cared for by a paternal relative for a few days, but the relative indicated that she was unable to care for the three older children any longer. Another relative agreed to care for Stacey. Emma and Lucy were accommodated by the local authority in foster care and, Stacey and Marcia with relatives under Children Act 1989 s.20. It had been envisaged that, once the mother recovered from her injuries, she would resume care of the children.

Case Study (cont'd)

Approximately two months after the incident, the father, who had taken an overdose, disclosed to his psychiatrist that he and his partner had sexually abused Marcia by subjecting her to oral sexual abuse. This disclosure was reported to the Child Protection Co-ordinator, who set up an investigation under the child protection procedures. There had been concerns expressed by the foster carer that Emma and Lucy were exhibiting sexualised behaviour, both individually and in their play with one another. At this time, the children also began to make disclosures of sexual abuse to their foster carer. They revealed that they, together with their elder sister, had been exposed to incidents of sexual abuse perpetrated by both parents. Interviews with all three older children were conducted under the child protection procedures, with additional police and child protection interviews with both parents, but there was insufficient evidence to proceed with a prosecution. In the interviews, the parents denied their joint involvement in the abuse of the children. Stacey was steadfast in her refusal to reveal any information to the police or social workers, and was very loyal to both parents.

Against this background of concerns and inconclusiveness of the enquiries, the local authority instituted care proceedings. Their application was to safeguard the children as well as to prevent the children being removed from the voluntary arrangements. They needed time to carry out assessments to decide whether or not it was safe to return the children to either parent. An interim care order was granted to the local authority.

During the course of my preliminary enquiries, which included a perusal of the social services files and discussions with the children, parents and different professionals who had first-hand knowledge of the children's situations, additional concerns were raised with me about the children's lives, which indicated that they had been exposed to long-term physical and emotional neglect. Incidents had been documented separately over a lengthy period of time, but it was not until these had been considered cumulatively that the full extent of the children's plight emerged. The parents' ability to cater long term for their children's needs thus needed further investigation.

There was an agreement between the various parties and the court that certain assessments of both the parents and the children were essential before any decision could be made. As well as the social worker assessments, these included a risk assessment by a forensic psychologist who specialised in assessing risk, or potential risk, in sexual abuse allegations. In order to obtain a clearer view of the parents' mental health status, as well as the violence and interdependence between the parents, a referral was made to a forensic psychiatrist.

During the period when the assessments were being undertaken, I saw the children regularly, keeping them informed of what was happening in an age-appropriate way. In the interests of good practice, I was able to see the

Case Study (cont'd)

children in a variety of different settings, as well as observing them in contact sessions with their parents and also with their siblings. In order to gauge their wishes and feelings, I used, as well as direct communication, a variety of techniques including trigger drawings, games and toys, such as puppets, to explain and explore situations with them. Through this, I was able to gain a comprehensive picture of the children and their attachments, which enabled a full assessment of the individual needs of each child, what was in her best interests and how these could be promoted in future.

One of the roles of the guardian *ad litem* is to empower the children to talk about their experiences and to have these taken seriously. This must be done in a sensitive, child-focused way, working at their pace. It is important to value their experiences in a non-judgmental way. The direct work with the children helped them to begin to trust me and to gain confidence in order to express their views and feelings about their experiences. As the sessions progressed, Emma and Lucy began to feel freer in what they told me. Often, without any prompting, they would spontaneously disclose information to me about their experiences of abuse while in the care of their parents. They graphically described various incidents of what happened, who was involved and what they had to do, as well as what they observed in their parents' relationship, particularly the violence. From their vivid accounts, it became clear that all the children had been exposed to extensive sexual abuse by both parents.

When children make such a disclosure, it is important to remember the boundaries of the guardian's role. He or she is not the child's therapist, and the role is time-limited. It is therefore important that systems are set up to ensure that the children receive ongoing support from their key social worker or carer in order to deal with the effects of the trauma that they have experienced and the disclosures they have made. A dilemma throughout working with these children was that the older three all frequently expressed their wish to return to their mother's care. At contact sessions, the children showed joy and excitement when they saw their parents. There was a good interaction between them, with clear evidence that the children had established a good bond and trust with their mother in particular.

During the course of the assessments, the father made a partial admission that he had sexually abused the children, but he maintained that he had been coerced into this by his partner. Throughout my meetings with the mother, she resolutely denied any involvement until an interview shortly before the final hearing, when she made an admission that she had also been involved, confirming much of the information that the children had given me. She claimed she had done so under duress because of her partner's violence towards her and that she could no longer cope with his excessive sexual demands.

Case Study (cont'd)

At an expert's meeting there was complete agreement that it was too risky for the children to return to either parent as both required considerable therapeutic work in order to address their abuse of the children, and there was no guarantee that treatment would be successful. Focusing on the children's ages and need for stability and permanency, it was felt that the possible timescale of such treatment programmes would not meet the younger children's developmental needs. During the course of my investigations, I explored the possibility of kinship placements within the extended family, who were assessed by the family placement team. Discussions with family members, however, revealed that they did not consider the sexual abuse of the children to be a serious issue, tending to minimise this as well as the trauma that the children had experienced from many years of exposure to violent incidents and neglect. There was no confidence that the extended family would in future protect the children so placement within the family was not recommended.

The report I prepared for the court fully documented the interviews I had had with the children. On the first day of the hearing, the parents made a number of admissions to their counsel, partially admitting to some of the sexual abuse described by the children. The nature of their admissions meant that the threshold criteria was met in relation to each child (s.31). Care orders were made on all four children, with a proposed care plan of adoption for the three younger children, with inter-sibling contact.

The guardian *ad litem* is entrusted with a complex task that is time limited and focuses on the needs of the child. During the investigative process, the guardian gains the trust and confidence of the child and listens fully to his or her wishes and feelings, yet the guardian's function is also to provide an independent assessment to the court to enable them to determine what outcome will protect the child from further abuse or negative experiences. When a child is unable to remain in the care of his or her birth family, the guardian has the responsibility of weighing up what alternatives there are on offer and recommending to the court which option can provide the child with the security and consistency needed in order to promote the child's overall development. Sadly, the recommendations do not always coincide with the voiced views of the child. A dilemma for guardians *ad litem* is that they are no longer involved in the support of the child with regard to the consequences of their recommendation once the final order has been made.

23

The Official Solicitor and Children Cases

Peter Harris

Origins and nature of the office

The Official Solicitor is the guardian *ad litem* or litigation friend of last resort. His office can be traced back to mediaeval times since the State has always recognised the need for the representation of an incapacitated person when a benevolent relative or friend cannot be found to act on his behalf. The Official Solicitor to the Supreme Court became a statutory office in 1981, although the representation of children in family proceedings has been one of the principal functions of the office since the 1970s, mainly through the appointment of the Official Solicitor as guardian *ad litem* in wardship cases. When local authorities began to use wardship as a means of taking children into care, the Official Solicitor began to deal with care proceedings, and his role as guardian *ad litem* in complex children's cases has continued ever since. No woman has ever been appointed, so the male gender is used throughout.

Overview of functions

It is the aim of the Official Solicitor:

1 by his intervention in proceedings in a representational role or otherwise

2 in the absence of any other appropriate person or agency

3 in as economical, effective and expeditious manner as practicable

to perform duties which have as their purpose:

(a) the prevention of a possible denial of justice to any individual party to proceedings (including safeguarding the liberty of the subject)

(b) safeguarding the welfare, property and status of persons under legal disability or at a disadvantage before the law

(c) the facilitation of the administration of justice (as investigator, confidential advisor to the judges and others or by instruction of counsel as *amicus curiae*).

As the foregoing indicates, the office deals with a wide variety of cases, representing not only children, but also adults under a mental incapacity. This chapter, however, deals primarily with his role in children cases.

The Official Solicitor is assisted by about 100 staff, all civil servants in the Lord Chancellor's Department, some 11 of whom are lawyers, four of these, including the Deputy Official Solicitor, working virtually exclusively on children cases. There are five children divisions, each headed by a divisional manager with five or six case workers. None are social workers, although all have received training in child development, child protection and the law relating to children, as well as in interviewing children. They also carry out the functions of a solicitor in the conduct of each case, under the supervision and guidance of the lawyers, dealing with the correspondence, instructing experts and counsel and attending court.[1]

Appointment

The Official Solicitor is invariably invited to act by the court, although his appointment might be suggested by counsel or the solicitors for one of the parties. The invitation will be made because the court is concerned that, unless the child is separately represented, his or her interests will not be adequately safeguarded in private law proceedings, or, where care or other public law proceedings have been transferred to the High Court, that the complexities of the case would be better dealt with by the Official Solicitor than a panel guardian *ad litem*. (In public law cases the Official Solicitor may accept appointment only in the High Court.)

If the criteria for his appointment are not met, the appointment will be declined by the Official Solicitor, and in about 30 per cent of references appointment is declined, usually after seeing the court file which is always sent to him. The criteria for accepting appointment are set out in a Practice Note published by the Official Solicitor. These include: where there is, or are, a significant foreign element; conflicting or controversial medical evidence; a need for expert evidence where the child is ignorant of the truth of its parentage or a psychiatric assessment is required of a child who is refusing to have contact with a parent; some other proceeding in which the Official Solicitor is already acting, or will act, for the same child; and exceptionally difficult, unusual or sensitive issues.

Children cases

Investigation

After a consideration of the court file, an acceptance of appointment will be filed in court. The issues having been identified, perhaps with a clarification from the court or the legal advisers of the parties, a plan for the way in which the Official Solicitor's enquiries will be conducted will be made. The usual course of an investigation is then for the caseworker to arrange to interview all the individuals who may have a view relevant to the child's situation and future welfare. Enquiries may need to be made with a variety of agencies, typically schools, GPs, the health visitor, social services and the police, from whom reports, medical records and other documents may be sought. The nature of the cases with which the Official Solicitor deals frequently requires the advice and assistance of an expert witness, the need for which will be identified at a very early stage.

Before children or parents are visited they are sent one or more of the leaflets (for child and parents) explaining in broad terms and age-appropriate language who the Official Solicitor is and what he does. The caseworker will see the child in virtually every case in order to assess the family situation and, most importantly, to ascertain the child's wishes and feelings. In a very few cases, the child will not be interviewed, for example where the child is unaware of the true identity of an absent parent. It is a matter of good practice not to intervene unnecessarily in the life of the child, and in such cases there is no benefit to the child from being interviewed by a number of strangers when no proper explanation can be given of why he or she is seeing them. The child will, in any event, be seen by the caseworker in the family home.

If at any time the child asks about having his or her own solicitor, the case worker will, whatever the age of the child, always explain what may be done. If the child is obviously competent, the caseworker should explain that if the child takes a view different from that of the Official Solicitor, he or she has the right to ask the court to let him or her have another solicitor. If the child has not asked about a solicitor, the case worker should, provided he or she thinks that the child has an understanding of the issues and may have the capacity to take a full part in the proceedings, offer a brief explanation of the child's right to ask the court to allow him or her to have a different solicitor.

Once the assessment of the child's capacity has been made, the next step is to ascertain the child's perception of priorities and, following that, the weight to be given to the views of the child. These are very much questions of judgment: the younger the child, the more likely it is that his or her priorities will differ from those of an adult, if only because the child's view of time and ability to predict probable outcomes may be limited by his or her intellectual capacity, emotional immaturity and lack of experience against which to test its judgment. The Official Solicitor's approach is therefore that care must be taken not to burden children with what they may perceive as a need to make choices, or to assume responsibilities which are beyond their capacity, and which are properly for the adults or the court to address. Some children, even quite young children, have a remarkably sensible ability to understand this and will say quite explicitly that the conflict between the adults is not their business and that they want the judge to decide. But a child can also be protective of a parent and may have a mistaken view of his or her responsibility for the situation, even believing that the situation may be his or her fault. Protecting the child from assuming such responsibility is part and parcel of proper representation.

In a great many cases, children will also want an assurance that the views that they do wish to express are made known to the judge. The practice followed in the Official Solicitor's office is always to give that assurance, and either to invite children to write down what they want the judge to know, or to show them the caseworker's record of the interview so that they can be sure that their views have been noted accurately. The court will be reluctant to allow children to attend the hearing, but it is open to the Official Solicitor to invite the court to allow them to be present for at least part of the judgment so that they can hear from the judge why a particular course has been decided upon, although this occurs in only a few cases. Invariably the Official Solicitor's representative will report back to the child the judge's decision and how it was arrived at. This is especially important where there is intractable hostility between parents and the child may, as a consequence, be misinformed and confused about the result. It is equally important where the decision is contrary to the child's wishes so that he or she may be given a careful explanation of why those wishes cannot be met.

The weight that should be given to children's views obviously depends upon the capacity to understand the issues and their intellect, maturity and insight. Assessing a child's capacity is a matter of judgment, but one very important factor that must always be borne in mind is the extent to which the child has, or may have, been – for want of a better term – 'tutored' by a parent. As we know from experience, children are on the whole very loyal to, and can be quite protective of, their parents. They will often tend to adopt the line of the person with whom they live, whether out of a sense of loyalty and the needs of the parent which the child may seek to meet, or out of a sense of self-preservation. It is quite striking, on occasion, to see a child resolving a conflict of loyalty by taking up the position of the parent with whom the child lives.

Report

The Official Solicitor is always required to file a report of his investigations, and that usually contains a description of the family and any other parties, the proceedings, the sources of information and the background to and history of the case, an account of interviews with the parties and the child or children, a synopsis of relevant information from schools, social services, health professionals and so on, a summary of the findings and opinion of any expert instructed, and finally conclusions and recommendations. The report is drafted by the caseworker and is submitted for consideration, amendment if necessary and approval by the Official Solicitor or his Deputy. It is then sent to the court and to the other parties.

At the hearing the Official Solicitor instructs counsel to appear on his behalf as guardian *ad litem*, but invariably the only witness he will call is an expert witness if one has been instructed. The expert is very frequently a child and adolescent psychiatrist or a child psychologist, as evidence may be required on the child's mental and emotional state, the nature and quality of her or his relationships with the significant adults, or whether the child has been sexually abused. The expert witness will always make a report and be called to give evidence at the hearing. Depending on the nature of the issues, other medical experts may be instructed – in cases of physical or sexual abuse or neglect, for example, a paediatrician or perhaps a paediatric radiologist. Counsel may cross-examine witnesses called by the other parties. The child only attends court in exceptional circumstances and is never called to give evidence.

Other cases

It is important to bear in mind that the Official Solicitor represents children (and incapacitated adults) in many other sorts of litigation, for example personal injury claims, Inheritance Act claims and disputes over deceased persons' estates and family trusts. It is possible for such issues to be present in children's cases (for example, Inheritance Act and criminal injury compensation scheme claims when one parent kills the other). Even where the Official Solicitor is not involved in the children proceedings, it may be desirable to invite him to consider whether he should act in other matters, such as those mentioned above on behalf of the child. The same principle also applies in respect of a person under a mental disability, particularly when there is a possibility of proceedings being taken by the local authority against the individual (or vice versa).

Future

In 1998, a consultation paper was circulated by the Lord Chancellor's Department, the Home Office, the DoH and the Welsh Office on the future of court welfare and guardian *ad litem* services. As a result of consultation, ministers announced in May 1999 that they had approved in principle the amalgamation of the Court Welfare Service arm of the Probation Service, the guardian *ad litem* panels and the children divisions of the Official Solicitor's Office. Work is being undertaken by the Lord Chancellor's Department to carry forward the integration of the three services into a Children and Family Court Advisory and Support Service.

This will be constituted as a non-departmental public body, responsible to the Lord Chancellor. It is envisaged that the new service will come into operation in April 2001. The Official Solicitor will then lose his responsibilities for representing children in family cases, although he will retain his responsibility for representing mentally incapacitated adults in such cases. He will continue to represent children in other sorts of litigation mentioned above under 'Other cases', and he may exceptionally represent a child in family proceedings where, for example, there is a conflict of interests between siblings, each requiring separate representation.

Note

1 The Official Solicitor welcomes enquiries and has a help line on 020 7911 7127.

24

The Children Act 1989: Dilemmas and Issues in Family Proceedings

Duncan Gore

A court welfare officer perspective

This chapter will begin with an overview of the main principles underlying the court approach to decision-making in family proceedings and go on to look at the current legal system, considering whether it offers the most appropriate means for resolving parental disputes about children after separation or divorce. It will also highlight some key issues for practice in the light of the author's experience as a court welfare officer working with children and families for a number of years.

Courts dealing with applications under the Children Act 1989 are required to act in a way ensuring that parents are encouraged to make decisions about their children themselves; the court should only intervene or make an order when it is absolutely necessary. The courts should also have regard to the principle that there should be a minimum of delay in dealing with cases relating to children and their welfare. The overriding principle guiding decision-making is that the welfare of the child is paramount.

The legal system

Solicitors, mediators and marriage guidance counsellors help a significant number of parents who are considering seeking orders in respect of their children, before they enter the legal system. When an application has been made, the majority of cases will be heard in either the family proceedings or the county court. Once a court is in receipt of an application, the parties and their representatives are usually invited to attend a conciliation appointment or directions hearing. Court welfare officers are frequently asked to be present at such meetings to assist the parents in their negotiations. The conciliation meetings or directions appointments are used where possible to explore the major issues in the case and to determine whether they can be resolved without the court becoming involved. If this process is successful, the parents often find that their involvement with the legal system is temporarily halted (for example, where they agree that contact should be tried for a few months and the matter be brought back to court to review progress). If a final agreement is reached, their involvement is likely to cease altogether.

Where the parents continue to be in dispute or there are concerns about the children's welfare, the court will order the court welfare officer to prepare a report. This usually takes about 10 weeks to prepare. It involves the court welfare officer speaking with the parents, their children and any other individual or organisation (such as the children's GP or school) who might be able to help the court welfare officer consider what is best for the children involved in a case. The completed report is sent to the court and the parents' legal representatives in advance of another directions hearing. If the parents continue to be in dispute after reading the report, the case progresses to a final hearing in which the court will hear evidence, determine whether an order is to be made in the case and, if so, which order best meets the interests of the children involved. It is important to keep in mind that although the courts, court welfare services and lawyers are all working to budgets and within tight time frameworks, some cases still take some time reaching court. Those cases which go to a final hearing can be in the system for up to a year before any order is made.

How successful is the current system in meeting the needs of families and their children?

Although the figures vary both regionally and over time, it is clear that a substantial number of families are removed from the legal system at each stage and only a very small proportion become involved in final hearings. As well as the issues related to the time it takes for decisions to be made in such cases, there is a further problem confronting these families. The courts currently respond to the family's continuing conflict by obtaining additional reports, arranging further hearings and/or making a range of orders. While such measures can lead to issues being resolved, there are still a significant number of cases that remain intractable. In these cases, the court can sometimes find itself not only in possession of a substantial amount of information in the form of various reports and statements, but also having to consider how its orders can be enforced. The threat of a fine or imprisonment for ignoring or disobeying an order sometimes forces a reluctant parent to accept it. The possibility of imposing such a penalty is, however, to heighten the tension between the parents and place the children involved in an even more difficult position.

The wide range of emotions that parents experience when they go through the process of divorce or separation means that they may at times feel apprehensive, confused, angry, frightened, anxious, distressed or guilty. Where these emotions are very intense or there is an imbalance of power within the family brought about by domestic violence, it is not surprising that the parents often find it impossible to work together in the best interests of their child. It is recognised that children can also experience periods of insecurity, anger, sadness and confusion when their parents are separating and that being caught up in the legal system can make the experience a more painful one.

Adjusting to the end of a relationship and dealing with the emotional and practical problems that arise will take adults and children a varying length of time. It could be questioned therefore whether the principle of minimum of delay in dealing with such cases is appropriate for all families. A further question is whether families with deep-rooted and seemingly intractable problems should be allowed to continue going through what is essentially an adversarial system. Although there is an emphasis on negotiation and conciliation, it must be remembered that lawyers are there to represent their clients' interests. This means that they sometimes struggle to act in a way that is of benefit to the whole family and, in particular, the children involved. It is hoped that the existence of a more broadly based role for court welfare officers within the Children and Family Court Advisory Service will help to alleviate this problem.

One way in which the current system attempts to help families experiencing problems is by way of a family assistance order (s.16 Children Act 1989). These orders are made with the consent of the parties and involve a court welfare officer or social worker trying to assist and advise a family. They are not, however, extensively used and there is no requirement for the person responsible for supervising the order to report on how successful or unsuccessful it has been. The low level of uptake in relation to family assistance orders may be the result of the court welfare service's current funding being geared to assessments and the provision of reports to the court as opposed to the support of families through various forms of social work-based interventions.

Practice issues

The following list highlights some key practice issues for court welfare officers and families involved in separation or divorce:

- identifying cases where children and parents would benefit from advice and support from an independent agency
- recognising when support is needed for families (children particularly) experiencing continuing problems post-separation
- understanding the importance of listening to children while at the same time being aware that this may allow parents to transfer completely their responsibility for making important decisions, as well as recognising the implications of this for children
- being aware that one or both parents may try to draw their children into any dispute they are having with the other parent
- practising a more proactive approach to work with children than is currently undertaken; in the current system of private family law, children are usually only seen once by the court welfare officer when a report is being prepared
- being more aware of the impact of domestic violence on children and the victims.

Conclusion

There have been calls by professionals and academics for some reform of the legislation in order to meet the best interests of children whose parents are involved in a dispute. In particular, there have been suggestions that there be a presumption against contact in cases where domestic violence is a significant issue, and/or that the impact of domestic violence should become one of the considerations in the welfare checklist. More generally, it is argued that families experiencing divorce or separation require greater independent advice and support, both during and after the process, in order to achieve a workable and effective, lasting solution to their problems.

25

Probation Officers' Work

Sarah Chand

The role of the probation officer has changed and developed over the years, in line with changing government policies and society's views of offenders. From the early days of police court missionaries, whose purpose was to assist those who had transgressed the law, to today, when the probation officer is regarded far more as an enforcer of court orders, we had always had a unique role in working *with* offenders rather than simply punishing them. In this chapter, I will provide a personal perspective upon the current issues facing probation officers, based upon my own experience as a practitioner and countless discussions with colleagues.

Role of the probation officer

What exactly do probation officers do? In his foreword to the Probation Circular 3/2000, *Probation Service Objectives and the Home Secretary's Priorities and Action Plans for the Service 2000–01* (Home Office, 2000b), Jack Straw wrote that 'The probation service has a key role to play… as a law-enforcement agency at the heart of the criminal justice system'. The two objectives defined in the circular are:

- to reduce re-offending and protect the public, in particular by effective enforcement of sentences in the community
- to provide the courts and others with high quality information and assessment to assist them in sentencing and other decisions.

Probation officers work with offenders aged 18 and over, those younger than 18 being dealt with by YOTs (although these teams also contain seconded probation officers). Their aim was traditionally to 'advise, assist and befriend', harking back to the days of police court missionaries. The change in how the role is now perceived by the government is well encapsulated in the proposed name change: from the Probation Service to the

Community Punishment and Rehabilitation Service for England and Wales. This clearly reflects the swing from 'helping' the offender to refrain from criminal activities, often on the basis of welfare needs, to punishing offenders through supervising and enforcing their sentence, the focus being very clearly on their specific offences and relevant criminogenic factors. Paul Boateng, Minister for Prisons and Probation, is quoted in *National Standards* (Home Office, 2000a) as saying 'We are a law enforcement agency. It's what we are. It's what we do.' This shift has been driven by the government's determination to have evidence of the effectiveness of probation supervision, evidence that can be used to assuage society's fears about escalating crime.

Reports

Probation officers have always provided reports of some nature, initially verbal and later written, to the courts. In 1991, pre-sentence reports were introduced, as defined by s.3(5) of the Criminal Justice Act 1991, replacing social enquiry reports. The latter were felt to be too 'woolly', providing a large amount of information about the offender that the court did not necessarily need to know but often skating over the offence. Pre-sentence reports were designed to focus very specifically on the offence, an analysis of why the crime had been committed, the offender's attitude to their behaviour, the impact upon the victim, providing relevant personal information, assessing the risk of both re-offending and of causing harm, and proposing a sentence to the court. Over the past nine years, the time allowed for the preparation of these reports has been shortened, currently standing at a maximum of 15 working days.

Despite this, the Narey Report in 1997 recommended that the speed of justice should be increased and procedural delays be reduced (Narey, 1997). This ensures that the link between offence and sentence is clearer to the offender, and means that the offender may be subject to supervision more speedily, thereby offering faster protection to the public. To implement the recommendations in that report required a substantial change in how the criminal justice system processed its work, initial pilots for certain offences beginning in October 1998.

For the Probation Service, it has led to the introduction of the specific sentence report, a shortened version of the pre-sentence report. This is designed for offences that will require no more than a short community sentence (also taking into account previous convictions and other factors) and is prepared the same day as it is requested, which is often at the first court hearing. Although there are obvious benefits to this system (less expense to the tax-payer, a saving of probation resources and a faster dispensing of justice), the reality has become more problematic. In the sentencing process, specific sentence reports can be inappropriately requested by magistrates wishing to make orders not covered by specific sentence reports (for example, conditions of treatment that require full assessment and consent). Sometimes, sentences are imposed on the basis of specific sentence reports that are later, after a more thorough assessment, found to be unsuitable, thereby increasing the rate of breach and the number of applications to revoke orders. It is, however, early days for these reports, and the situation will undoubtedly improve. Thankfully, the guidance to the courts remains that they should request a report of some sort prior to sentence, even though it is no longer a legal requirement.

Sentences

The range of sentences available to courts for adult offenders is quite lengthy, the majority requiring an input from the Probation Service. Those that probation officers are not required to supervise are absolute and conditional discharges, fines, compensation, senior attendance centre orders, curfew orders, suspended sentences and terms of imprisonment of less than 12 months for adults (an adult in this context being defined as someone 21 years or over at the time of sentence). This leaves us with probation orders, combination orders (probation and community service orders combined), suspended sentence supervision orders, youth custody (of any length for offenders aged between 18 and 21) and adult imprisonment of 12 months or over. In addition, each service provides groupwork programmes added as conditions of probation or combination orders (for example, offending behaviour, alcohol, drugs and sex offending) and supervises conditions of residence at probation hostels.

As was described earlier, the meaning of supervision has changed substantially over the past 30 years: 'From the beginning of the [twentieth] century until the early 1970s, the aims of the services were unequivocally rehabilitative, and their work was focused consistently on less serious offenders' (Her Majesty's Inspectorate of Probation, 1998). The *National Standards for the Supervision of Offenders in the Community* (Home Office, 2000a) now describe the purpose of community sentences as being to:

provide a rigorous and effective punishment;

reduce the likelihood of reoffending;

rehabilitate the offender, where possible; and

enable reparation to be made to the community.

While the *National Standards* are actually guidelines for the probation service rather than law, they are the markers by which all probation work is judged and are thus seen by both the government and probation officers as being extremely important. The dilemma arises over the issue of punishment. I do not regard myself as being employed to punish an offender – that is the role of the court in sentencing – yet by supervising that order, I feel pushed into that position. This is shown particularly well by enforcement and breach.

Enforcement

As the push for demonstrating effectiveness and accountability has gathered pace, the enforcement of orders has become increasingly important. Research has demonstrated that consistent enforcement leads to a greater compliance with orders, and thus is one of the key performance indicators defined by the Home Office for services. The *National Standards* (Home Office, 2000a) require as a minimum that a standard letter of explanation be issued for each failure, a standard warning letter will be issued after the first unacceptable failure, and breach proceedings will be instigated after, at the latest, the second unacceptable failure, which is a tightening-up of the procedures laid out in the previous edition of the *National Standards* (Home Office, 1995). Although I do not doubt the veracity of the research, and indeed have personal experience of compliance improving after a breach hearing, this rigid position does not allow for the difficult, often chaotic lifestyle led by many offenders, or for those many with literacy problems who cannot read the standard letters (which are not designed to basic literacy or dyslexic needs). Furthermore, when faced with an individual who is, overall, making excellent progress, it is a hard decision to return him or her to court for a second failure within 12 months.

Of particular concern is the proposal that offenders on benefit may have that benefit reduced by 40 per cent upon allegation of breach of a community sentence. Should the breach be proved, one part of the punishment may be a continued reduction in benefit for a set period of time; should it not be proved, the offender will be reimbursed, but he or she has of course in the meantime had to manage on a much reduced income. Given that the majority of offenders are receiving benefit and already have financial problems, the fear of causing even greater hardship and thereby increasing the risk of financially motivated offending is likely to mean that probation officers will be reluctant to instigate breach proceedings. Should this proposal be passed, there is clearly an issue relating to how this reluctance will be managed when balanced against the priority of rigorous enforcement.

Throughcare

One area of probation work not concentrated upon in this chapter is that of throughcare and its proposed changes. Although there is currently substantial work being undertaken between both prison and probation services, this is being developed further with the idea of the 'seamless sentence'. The consultation document *Joining Forces to Protect the Public* (Correctional Policy Unit, 1998) indicated the direction of closer working, and this is being taken forward through a number of initiatives, such as the national use in both the prison and probation services of the assessment tool Offender Assessment System. Given the traditionally very different aims of the services and how they deal with offenders, this appears to be yet another indication of the shift towards punishment and 'correctional' work.

Conclusion

Over the past 30 years, there has been a substantial change in how the probation service perceives itself and how it has been perceived by others. Changing government policies, a demand for accountability and proven effectiveness, reduced resources and an increasing caseload have had a huge impact upon the service. The scope of this chapter is too limited to provide greater detail of the above issues, or to list others with which probation officers are grappling. I hope, however, to have provided an idea of the work undertaken by probation officers and some of the current issues in working with adult offenders.

26

Account of a Magistrate who Sits in the Youth Court

Stuart Vernon

Magistrates sitting in the youth court are a central element in the administration of the youth justice system. Each petty sessional area will appoint a youth panel every three years with members chosen from the whole bench of magistrates for the area. Youth panel magistrates are chosen for being 'particularly well qualified to deal with juveniles', and they must receive induction and refresher training specific to their jurisdiction in the youth court. It is recommended that justices aged over 50 should not be appointed to the panel for the first time. The retirement age for justices sitting on the youth panel used to be set at 65, although this was raised to 70 in 1991.

Youth court magistrates are involved in the same range of work as those sitting in the adult court. This work includes hearing and determining prosecutions against children and young people aged 10–17; sentencing those who plead guilty or are convicted after a trial; making a decision on applications for bail; enforcing fines; and determining issues arising from breaches of community sentences. Legal and procedural advice is available from the Clerk to the Justices and other court clerks, but decisions on fact, law and sentence are ultimately the responsibility of those youth magistrates dealing with a particular matter.

Lay magistrates sitting in the youth court are therefore faced with the same matters and questions as they encounter in the adult courts but with the added responsibilities and dilemmas that arise when dealing with children and young people. While all those appearing in the youth court are held to be personally responsible for their crimes, the age range of 10–17 inevitably encompasses significant differences in maturity and vulnerability. The challenges arising from such diversity have also to be placed alongside difficult issues concerning parental responsibility and the application of the principles of proportionate sentencing established by the Criminal Justice Act 1991. The complexity of the 'youth justice equation' is regularly compounded by new legislation reflecting the increased politicisation of youth justice.

A brief survey of the major legislative provisions and principles will give an indication of the challenges facing youth court magistrates. The Criminal Justice Act 1991 established a principle of proportionate sentencing that applies to the youth courts as well as the adult courts. Sentencers have to determine issues of offence seriousness and then reflect the seriousness of an offence in the chosen category of sentence and in the individual choice of sentence within each category. Conclusions on seriousness reflect a consideration of aggravating and mitigating factors and will often be influenced by the content and proposals contained in pre-sentence reports. The Act also contains provisions concerning parental responsibility so that youth court magistrates have to decide whether to order the attendance of parent(s) at court, whether to impose fines and compensation orders on parents, and whether to impose parental bindovers. Each decision may be significant and is subject to legislative powers and duties that apply differentially to those aged under 16 and to those aged 16 and 17.

The Criminal Justice and Public Order Act 1994 extended the range of parental bindovers, legislated for the reduction of sentences where there had been a plea of guilty, and allowed magistrates, including those sitting in the youth court, as well as juries to draw appropriate inferences from the decision of a defendant to remain silent when questioned in the police station and when appearing at trial.

Nevertheless, there were, until the implementation of the Crime and Disorder Act 1998, relatively few fundamental principles to inform youth court magistrates in their work. The sentencing guidelines issued by the Magistrates' Association do not apply in the youth court, and few of the sentencing guideline cases decided in the Court of Appeal deal with children and young people. The youth court is, however, subject to an important welfare principle established in s.44(1) of the Children and Young Persons Act 1933:

> Every court in dealing with a child or young person who is brought before it, either as an offender or otherwise, shall have regard to the welfare of the child or young person, and shall in a proper case take steps for removing him from undesirable surroundings, and for securing that proper provision is made for his education and training.

The impact of this provision has been tempered by the historical tensions in the administration of youth justice between welfare and justice, treatment and punishment, and care and control. Youth court magistrates are not immune from this historical legacy, their decisions reflecting the range of these positions rather than any universal commitment to the welfare of the child or young person. Ambivalence about 'welfare' as a fundamental value of the youth justice system has also been historically linked to a concern among the youth court magistracy about the role of 'social work' agencies in the administration of sentences imposed in the youth court. New appointees to the youth panel will still encounter hostility among their colleagues to 'social workers' and their commitment to 'welfare', as well as arguments against comment and proposals in the pre-sentence report that are perceived as excusing personal responsibility for offending.

Each new generation of youth panel magistrates is subject to a socialisation by those already serving on the panel. This process of socialisation has tended to transfer and inculcate an understanding of youth crime and the youth justice system that, although diverse, encourages the acceptance of change as a technical challenge rather than a chance to discuss the value base of youth justice. New youth justice legislation is seen to require new knowledge and skills rather than a commitment to any value base. This pragmatism has allowed many youth court magistrates to implement and administer a youth justice system that has changed considerably in the last 15 years without any real challenge to changing values and politics.

The Crime and Disorder Act 1998 and the Youth Justice and Criminal Evidence Act 1999 represent the most recent legislative changes to youth justice, their provisions being radical enough to suggest that youth court magistrates are facing a period of real challenge. The youth court is and will be required to administer a significant range of new orders within a system that is now subject to a statutory aim. Section 37 of the Crime and Disorder Act provides:

> (1) It shall be the principal aim of the youth justice system to prevent offending by children and young persons.
>
> (2) In addition to any other duty to which they are subject, it shall be the duty of all persons and bodies carrying out functions in relation to the youth justice system to have regard to that aim.

Youth court magistrates are in the front line for the delivery of the aim, not only by reason of their role as a central agency of the youth justice system, but also because of the individual duty imposed by s.37(2) above.

The complex equation of proportionate sentencing, personal and parental responsibility, maturity and vulnerability referred to above will now itself be subject to another imperative, the principal aim of preventing (re-)offending. By declaring this to be a 'principal aim', government is indicating that the prevention of offending should underpin all the work of youth court magistrates.

There is some evidence that government may be unsure about the ability of youth panels of lay magistrates to deliver a 'new' youth justice system. Section 48 of the Crime and Disorder Act provides that stipendiary magistrates may sit alone in the youth court. This development may indicate a move toward the professionalisation of the court element of the youth justice system; the referral order provisions of the Youth Justice and Criminal Evidence Act can be interpreted as a similar indicator.

These provisions, which are due to be implemented in 2002, originate from the White Paper, *No More Excuses* (Home Office, 1997), which suggested a radical reform of the function and organisation of the youth court:

> The purpose of the youth court must change from simply deciding guilt or innocence and then issuing a sentence. In most cases, an offence should trigger a wider enquiry into the circumstances and nature of the offending behaviour, leading to action to change that behaviour. This requires in turn a fundamental change of approach within the youth court system.

Further to this objective, the 1999 Act provides for the referral by the youth court of a particular group of offenders to youth offender panels. Referral orders will be the normal sentence for offenders who, on their first appearance in the youth court, plead guilty, except where the court proposes to make an absolute discharge, the offence is one for which the sentence is fixed by law or the court is proposing to make a custodial sentence or a hospital order under the Mental Health Act 1983. Offenders will be referred to the youth offender panel for the purpose of agreeing a youth offender contract between the offender and the panel. The terms of the contract will be supervised by the YOT. The panel will consist of a member of the YOT and two other persons who are not members of the team.

The youth justice reforms of the 1998 and 1999 Acts are significant and reflect the acceptance by government of the principles of restorative justice:

> The Government considers that it will be necessary to reshape the criminal justice system in England and Wales to produce more constructive outcomes with young offenders. Its proposals for reform build on principles underlying the concept of restorative justice:
>
> - *restoration:* young offenders apologising to their victims and making amends for the harm they have done
> - *reintegration:* young offenders paying the debt to society, putting their crime behind them and rejoining the law abiding community; and
> - *responsibility:* young offenders – and their parents – facing the consequences of their offending behaviour and taking responsibility for preventing further offending. (Home Office, 1997)

The work of youth court magistrates is increasingly challenging. Traditional quasi-judicial skills must now be utilised in a youth justice system that is complex, one subject to the increasing influence of managerialism and professionalisation in the criminal justice system as well as to the vagaries of populist politics. A clearer value base, derived from the Crime and Disorder Act and the Human Rights Act, may also challenge the preconceptions of some members of youth panels. These are interesting times for youth court magistrates.

27

Young People in Care

Ruth Hayman

This chapter is a first-hand account of a young person's experience of the care system

Issues for young people in care

Moving around a lot is one of the real issues for young people in care, especially as it can affect your education. Because of all the moves I made in my final year at school, I did not manage to get the grades I needed to go on to further education. I took a year out and then went to sixth form college and re-sat some of my exams. I had help and support from my social worker and the key worker at the hostel where I was living. That and the support from my friends, plus my own determination, meant that I passed everything with high grades. If you move a lot, it also means that your friends live far away from you and it can be difficult to get to see them, especially when there are restrictions about sleep-overs.

Another issue for children and young people in care is that you get stereotyped – by teachers and by professionals. Also, if someone at school finds out you are in care, they start spreading rumours about you and about your family; the bullying isn't really dealt with. You just have to prove to your peers that you are still the same person as before you went into care and just wait for the bullying to stop. You get bullying in the children's homes as well, especially if you want to get on with your life in your own way. Sometimes you are allowed to take refuge in the office, but staff mostly ignore it and you have to get on with it.

Support for young people in care

Having a key worker who has been allocated a time to work with you each week is important. You need someone who respects you as much as you respect them and who will listen to you about any problems you may be facing. You need someone who encourages you with your school work or even leisure activities. You need someone who cares for you – a social worker, foster carer, support worker – someone who is also your best friend. For example, the last foster carer I had would close the kitchen door and allow me to talk to her alone without any distractions when I was feeling low – which was most of the time then. Angie would see the good in me as well as the bad but would always tell me that I would have fewer bad days than good days and that I would forget about the bad ones. To this very day, I believe in what she said, and although I very occasionally have a bad day, the good ones definitely outnumber them.

Young people would have a better experience in care if their social worker could spend quality time with them on a regular basis. There are a lot of other things that could make it better, such as being able to go clothes shopping without being told what you are and are not allowed to buy, or being able to go to the cinema without the staff from the children's home and the minibus, which labels you. Having someone who will give you a hug whenever you need one would help, especially at times like Christmas when you do not have a family around.

It is very difficult to make a complaint if you are in care. You do not want to seem ungrateful, but at the same time you might really want something to change. My social worker hardly ever came to see me when I was in the children's home, and I wanted to have somebody new allocated to me. The manager of the home said I should write a complaint, so I did, and although I did not get a new social worker, things did improve a bit. I found it quite difficult to know how to write the complaint and had to have help with the wording so that people would know what I was trying to say. I think that young people should be able to record a complaint on an audio cassette so that there is not the difficulty of writing it.

Education: in care and after leaving care

Getting young people to go to school is very important. They often enjoy it when given the right teaching. It helps to have someone you can associate with at school, such as a teacher or a support teacher employed to come into the school and sit with you through your lessons to help you do the work. After you leave care, it is a very different kettle of fish altogether. If you really want to carry on with your education, you have to really want to do it and be very determined. I felt that I had no support from my social worker at the time to go into further education, and that she did not really care at all what I did as long as I kept out of her way and did not land her with any paperwork. But I worked really hard to build up close relationships with the tutors at college, and now, if I am in trouble or having difficulty, my personal tutor will try to help with homework problems, and my teachers always have time to go through my work with me. There is also a student welfare officer if I get into problems with housing or finance, and they will contact my social worker to ask for advice.

Reviews

I did not have the confidence to speak out in reviews because my parents were there and I could never say what I really wanted. The foster carers and social workers always seemed to go off at a tangent, talking about stuff I did not really understand and leaving me out. The questions in the review booklet are the same every time. I think they should be made relevant to the child or young person's age rather than being the same year in and year out. Sometimes, it would have been better not to have been there but to have had someone else speaking on my behalf.

Leaving care

I was told that I would have to leave care at the age of 17. It was only three months since I had come out of the adolescent psychiatric unit and I was feeling very vulnerable. I felt as if there was no support for me. There were no supportive lodgings (family placements where you learn how to live independently) in the area where I wanted to live, so I had to move into a hostel. It was being used as a brothel and consequently closed down, so I had to find somewhere else to live. Things would have been much easier if my social worker had visited me on a regular basis to discuss the problems I was having. Having someone to help fill in forms or telephone the benefit agency when your Giro does not come would also make things easier to cope with. You need the kind of help that any parent would give their child when they leave home.

I was very lonely after I left care, and I was suffering from chronic fatigue. I used to be scared that something would happen to me while I was on my own and that no one would ever know about it. It is hard to find your feet when you move to a new area: you worry about money and where your next meal will be coming from. Social services can sometimes give you a food voucher if you have started work and you are waiting for your first wages to be paid. But I think that young people receive very little support when they leave care; often it is because it is deemed that you are out on your own now and you have to look after yourself.

Consulting with young people in care

Young people and children are sometimes consulted – this usually happens when they are old enough to understand what all the social work jargon means. Consultation should be made more user-friendly for all ages. It is important to listen to the views of children and young people, and to take into account what they want. Professionals should discuss issues before making hasty decisions, especially if the child or young person disagrees with them. I think social workers still find it hard to take advice from a young person on what will work and what will not. Sometimes I am listened to, and sometimes I am not. It usually depends on who is doing the listening. I feel I could be listened to more carefully and have people actively changing things I have suggested instead of politely nodding their heads.

What can social workers do?

I would say that social workers should try to spend quality time with the young person and take time to listen to what they have to say. They should make sure that, if the young person has to move, he or she gets on well with the new foster carers or carers in the children's home prior to moving. Social workers should try to build up a rapport with the young person. They should try to gain their respect and allow the young person to participate in decision-making. This would transform the experience of young people in care and help them to feel more in control of their own lives.

28

The Development of Advocacy Services with and for Children and Young People

Judith Timms

Introduction

Advocacy services for children and young people looked after by local authorities have developed over the past 20 years as part of a grass roots movement that recognised the extreme vulnerability of young people looked after and leaving care, and sought to ensure that their voice was heard when decisions were made about their lives.

Many of the major children's charities – the Children's Society, NCH Action for Children, NSPCC and Barnardo's – now have advocacy projects in different parts of the country, but services have in general developed in a piecemeal fashion. This is largely because there is no statutory recognition of the role of advocate.

Although s.26 of the Children Act 1989 introduced the possibility of children and young people looked after by local authorities making complaints or representations about the services that they receive, there is no statutory recognition of the need for children to have help in initiating and participating in such procedures. Advocacy is mentioned but not encouraged by the Children Act Regulations. The position is as stated in Volume 4 of the Children Act 1989 *Guidance and Regulations* para. 4.17:

> Advocacy as a service to the child as part of child care service provision is not ruled out by these Regulations nor is it ruled out if a responsible authority wishes to provide such a service to support the child in this or other procedures. (DoH, 1991)

Volume 3 of the *Guidance and Regulations* is a little more positive in outlining situations in which the involvement of an independent advocate might be appropriate. In some situations, the position of the child may be an unhappy one. The child may be dissatisfied with the current arrangements for care or the absence of progress in achieving a plan for the future. He may dislike and distrust his carers and those in authority who have responsibility for him. He may feel that his views are ignored or never sought and that he has no realistic opportunity to complain or challenge the validity of the legal processes that affect him. He may then disclose that he is being abused by his carers. In such a bleak scenario, the child has an urgent need for skilled advocacy. This is not a role that the independent visitor is expected to play. Instead, the independent visitor must be able to recognise the needs of the child in such serious situations and, with the child's agreement, draw these concerns to the attention of the child's social worker or, if necessary, a more senior officer in the social services department. In certain cases, it may be appropriate to refer the matter to one of the voluntary organisations that specialises in advocacy (DoH, 1991, Volume 3).

The role of the advocate is to ascertain the wishes and feelings of children and young people and ensure that their voice is heard in all decision-making forums, both in and out of court. It also means being proactive in ensuring that children and young people receive their fair share of the resources that they may need in order to fulfil their full potential as adults and citizens of the future.

The concept of advocacy – a changing culture

Health and welfare services were traditionally provided to all client groups as part of a process of benevolent 'paternalism' in which doctors, nurses, social workers and other professionals exercised their professional judgment on behalf of patients who expressed their gratitude for services received and who were not generally encouraged to think that they knew better than those who were making the decisions about them rather than with them. The introduction of the internal market for welfare provision, bringing with it the new 'contracted-out' world in which health and social services buy services from one another through the operation of an internal market, led to a recognition of the importance of clients' rights, advocacy and complaints procedures as central elements in quality control.

It could in many ways be said that the statutory requirements in the Children Act 1989 and s.50 of the NHSCCA 1990 for each local authority to establish procedures for considering any representations, including any complaints, acted as a catalyst for service-users, including children and young people, to have increasing recourse to the services of an advocate. The essential right of the consumer to question decisions and to choose between different services is an essential ingredient in a participatory model of service provision and has been stressed in a number of major reports. The Wagner Report made the following recommendation:

> Each local authority shall have a clear and well-publicised complaints procedure and comparable measures shall be taken by private and voluntary agencies. People who require assistance in presenting their complaints should have the services of an advocate or personal representative, who is entirely independent of those providing the service. (NISW, 1988)

The change in attitude and organisational culture required for professionals and members of powerful bureaucracies to acknowledge and facilitate the participation of service-users in service provision, to consult them in the development of those services and to facilitate and empower them to make use of complaints procedures is considerable. Nowhere was the culture clash more obvious than in children's residential services, the introduction of statutory complaints procedures under s.26 of the Children Act being viewed with suspicion and unease by many staff members.

Moreover, children as service-users and the bearers of rights are in a particularly vulnerable position as they are dependent upon the good offices of adults to enable them to exercise their rights. Children making a complaint fear that it may lead to a withdrawal of affection or services, or to more active victimisation or reprisal. The experience of the National Youth Advocacy Service shows that it is virtually impossible for a child or a young person to complain effectively without an independent advocate to support him or her. Even with an advocate, it is a tortuous obstacle course that one often hesitates to encourage the child to negotiate. Experience has demonstrated that the s.26 complaints procedures are simply not robust enough to provide an adequate safeguard to the child complainant. Many children are not even aware of the existence of complaints procedures.

What do children complain about?

Overwhelmingly, the largest single problem for children 'looked after' is multiple changes of placement within the system with little regard for their own wishes, education, family or peer group ties. It is not unusual to see children who have been moved 10, 15, even 20 or more times. Other complaints include:

- physical, sexual and emotional abuse
- unjust punishments
- rough handling by care staff
- breaches of confidentiality (personal information being left lying around)

- educational problems, problems of re-entering the system after a move and a lack of positive planning about education – sometimes there is not even a decision to dispute
- not being treated as a person of worth, including unfair or demeaning treatment and being held up to ridicule by other children or staff
- having their wishes and feelings ignored. Children complain that review meetings are sometimes used as a forum to criticise them.

The position of children and young people looked after and leaving care

In the last 25 years of the twentieth century there were an increasing number of inquiries into the abuse of children in residential care, culminating in the appalling catalogue of abuse over a 20-year period revealed in the inquiry into the abuse of 600 children in North Wales, chaired by Sir Ronald Waterhouse and published in March 2000 in *Lost in Care* (DoH/Welsh Office, 2000). They have led to an increasing recognition of the vulnerability of children and young people, who have a right to expect more from their corporate parents than the dismal outcomes set out in Sir William Utting's Safeguards review published in 1997 (DoH, 1997b).

Outcomes

- 75% leave care without any academic qualifications.
- 50% leaving care after the age of 16 are unemployed.
- 17% of young women leaving care are pregnant or already mothers (25% according to National Children's Bureau research in 1999).
- 23% of adult prisoners and 38% of young prisoners have been in care.
- 30% of young single homeless have been in care.

Characteristics of looked-after children:

- The number has halved in 20 years – there are now approximately 50,000 children looked after in England, two-thirds of whom are aged over 10.
- An estimated 75% have a mental health problem.
- There is a greater incidence of physical and learning disability.
- A high level of previous physical and sexual abuse and physical and emotional neglect is seen.
- 'Care' status is an additional stigma.

Responding to Sir William Utting's Safeguards review in November 1998, Frank Dobson, then Secretary of State for Health, acknowledged that:

> the whole system has failed. Too many children taken into care to protect and help them have received neither protection nor help. Instead they have been abused and molested. Many more have been let down, ignored, shifted from place to place, school to school, and often simply turned out to fend for themselves when they turned 16. (DoH, 1997b)

He then announced a three-year £375 million programme of improvement and investment in children's services under the title of Quality Protects.

The first Quality Protects circular, published in the spring of 1999, identified 'establishing mechanisms to amplify the voice of the child' and allowing a 'greater participation of children in care planning' as key priorities, but it failed to make any specific reference to the need to provide children with access to independent advocacy services. At this stage, the providers of advocacy services to children came together as the Children's Advocacy Consortium and, in June 1999, issued the following joint position statement:

> Every local authority should have a children's rights and advocacy service as part of the Quality Protects programme and every child looked after should have a statutory right of access to an independent advocate. These services should be provided according to an agreed standard.

The statement was supported by the National Youth Advocacy Service, Voice for the Child in Care, the Children's Rights Officers and Advocacy Association, the Children's Society, the NSPCC, NCH Action for Children (Scotland), the Boys and Girls Welfare Society, the Who Cares? Trust, ChildLine, Barnardo's and First Key.

The basis of the Advocacy Consortium's concern was the lack of government commitment to the national funding and development of independent and confidential advocacy services and great variations in the regional and local availability, method and quality of service. The members of the Advocacy Consortium produced the position statement in the hope that the provision of advocacy services for young people looked after by local authorities could be discussed and carried forward at a national level, with a view to exploring a central system of funding that would be both fair and equitable to local authorities as well as to the vulnerable young people who needed the voice and safeguards that an independent advocacy service could provide.

The second Quality Protects circular, published in October 1999, states, at para. 8.5:

> particular attention should be given to the involvement of young people collectively and to enhancing their individual voices, for example, through the development of independent advocacy services.

The Circular still failed to provide any enlightenment about future funding mechanisms for advocacy services and to define the criteria that the DoH would be applying to decide whether or not the advocacy services provided were truly independent, but it nevertheless constituted a significant step forward. The impact of the Quality Protects circular was also significantly emphasised by Recommendation 4(d) of the Report of the Inquiry into Abuse in North Wales (DoH/Welsh Office, 2000), which recommended that social services departments should 'ensure that recourse to an independent advocacy service is available to any complainant or affected child who wishes to have it'.

The Leaving Care and Care Standards Bills, before Parliament at the time of writing, both have the potential capacity to introduce a statutory right to independent advocacy services for children looked after and leaving care, amendments to that effect having been proposed. The outcome is still unclear, but the question of advocacy is now firmly on the political agenda.

National standards in advocacy with children and young people

The DoH has commissioned the National Youth Advocacy Service to develop National Standards in Advocacy, which are due to be published late in the year 2000. There are ten standards:

1 Advocacy led by children and young people

2 Commitment to children's rights

3 A service which is well publicised, non-discriminatory, easy to use and prompt

4 Confidentiality

5 Independence

6 Involving children and young people in the service

7 An effective and easy-to-use complaints procedure

8 Good management

9 Recruitment of staff

10 Training, support and supervision of advocates.

Of these standards, independence and confidentiality are those most valued by the young people using the services.

Conclusion

In the past 20 years, advocacy with and for children and young people has developed from a fringe activity to something that is becoming an essential part of mainstream social work provision and an integral part of quality assurance. Effective and swift advocacy has an important proactive and preventative potential to identify children who are falling through gaps in the service provision and ensure that the outcomes for them are the best, rather than the minimum, that can be achieved (for a further discussion see Timms, 1995).

29

The Court of Protection

Denzil Lush

Introduction

There are two ways of looking after the property and financial affairs of mentally incapacitated people. One is a system whereby a court appoints a manager to look after someone's property and finances. The other is a document, known as an Enduring Power of Attorney, in which people appoint someone in advance to manage their financial affairs in the event that they may become mentally incapacitated at some time in the future. The Court of Protection operates these two schemes under Part VII of the Mental Health Act 1983 and the Enduring Powers of Attorney Act 1985 respectively.

The Court of Protection's jurisdiction covers only England and Wales. Similar schemes are operated in Scotland by the Sheriff Court and the Accountant of Court, in Northern Ireland by the Office of Care and Protection, and in Ireland by the Office of the Wards of Court. In this chapter we shall look briefly at both of the schemes in England and Wales, explore their respective strengths and weaknesses, and consider various proposals to reform the existing legislation.

The Court of Protection

The Court of Protection[1] is an office of the Supreme Court, and its titular head is 'The Master', which is simply another word for a judge. The court's function is to protect and manage the property and financial affairs of mentally incapacitated people.

The court and Public Trust Office look after the affairs of approximately 22,000 people (known as 'patients') under the Mental Health Act 1983. They fall into four distinct client groups:

- the elderly mentally infirm, mainly with Alzheimer's disease or multi-infarct dementia. Seventy per cent of the court's patients are aged 70 or over, 75 per cent of these being female

- people with mainstream mental illnesses such as schizophrenia and hypomania
- people with learning difficulties
- people who have suffered traumatic brain damage as a result of an accident or assault and have been awarded compensation for their personal injuries.

The number of people in this last group has grown considerably during the past 20 years, partly because of medical advances in accident and emergency treatment, partly because of the increased volume of traffic on the roads and partly because of the growth of a litigation culture. The largest damages awards managed by the court are in excess of £4 million.

In addition, the court registers approximately 10,000 Enduring Powers of Attorney each year, the vast majority of which have been created by older people. The average age of the donor when a power is registered is 87.

The Court of Protection has 'power over the purse' but it does not have 'power over the person'. In other words, it can make decisions relating to a person's property and finances but it cannot make medical decisions or personal decisions, such as where a person should live and with whom he or she should have contact.

Receivership under the Mental Health Act

If someone is incapable, by reason of mental disorder, of managing and administering his or her property and affairs, and has not made an Enduring Power of Attorney, it may be necessary to apply to the Court of Protection for an order under the Mental Health Act appointing a receiver to act on their behalf.

The forms for applying for the appointment of a receiver can be obtained free of charge from the Customer Services Unit at the Public Trust Office. The following forms should be completed and returned to the Public Trust Office:

- two copies of the application (form CP1)
- the medical certificate (form CP3), in which a registered medical practitioner certifies that the patient is incapable, by reason of mental disorder, of managing and administering his or her property and affairs
- the Certificate of Family and Property (form CP5)
- a cheque for the commencement fee, currently £200, made payable to 'Public Trust Office'.

On receiving these forms, the Public Trust Office will return one copy of form CP1 marked with the date and time when the court will consider the application. Unless the court directs otherwise, no attendance on that date will be necessary, the appointment of a receiver being purely a paper transaction. An attended hearing will be necessary only if someone (perhaps the patient or a relative) objects to the application for any reason.

If the patient's assets amount to less than £10,000, the court can, instead of appointing a receiver, make a 'short order' authorising a suitable person to manage those assets, and generally speaking it need no longer be involved in that patient's affairs.

In most cases the court appoints a receiver to deal with the day-to-day management of a patient's affairs, and it has a complete discretion as to whom it appoints. There is no formal order of priority, although it has traditionally preferred to appoint relatives – mainly because they are on the spot and aware of the patient's needs.

Members of the patient's family make up 63% of receivers, 13% are solicitors, and 8% are office-holders with local authorities, usually the Director of Social Services. In about 10% of cases, the Public Trustee is appointed as the 'receiver of last resort', often where the patient is aggressive or violent, has been the victim of financial abuse or comes from a particularly unstable family background.

The receiver is required to present an annual account on every anniversary of the order appointing him or her. Where an order is to be made appointing anyone other than the Public Trustee or a professional receiver, the receiver may be required to obtain a security bond to cover any fraudulent mismanagement. A small premium is payable, which can be recovered from the patient's estate.

A receiver is entitled to the reimbursement of his or her reasonable out-of-pocket expenses, such as postage, telephone calls and travelling expenses, but is only allowed to be paid for acting as receiver in exceptional circumstances, usually if he or she is a solicitor, accountant or other professional person.

Receivers have only the powers that are conferred upon them by the first general order or subsequent orders of the court. Generally speaking, they have access to the patient's income, which they are expected to apply for the patient's maintenance, but any dealings with capital and gifts must be authorised in advance by the court.

A fee is charged for the services that the court and the Public Trust Office provide. In addition to the commencement fee of (currently) £200, there are various individual transaction fees, and an annual administration fee based on the patient's annual income.

Since 1970, the court has had the power to make a will (commonly known as a 'statutory will') on behalf of a patient who is incapable of making a valid will for him- or herself. About 250 statutory wills are made each year. Case law has established that, when it exercises this function, the court has to assume that:

- the patient is experiencing a brief lucid interval
- the patient has a full knowledge of the past
- the court is making a will for this individual patient, with his or her own personal preferences, prejudices and peculiarities, rather than for a hypothetical, ordinary reasonable person
- the patient is being advised by competent solicitors
- the patient adopts a broad-brush approach towards the distribution of his or her estate.

Where a patient's capacity has improved sufficiently to enable him or her to be restored to the management of his or her own affairs, an application can be made to the court for an order determining proceedings. Relatively few such orders are made – on average about 100 a year – compared with over 6,000 new applications a year for the appointment of a receiver.

Enduring Power of Attorney

An Enduring Power of Attorney is a document in which an individual ('the donor') appoints one or more other persons to be his or her attorney(s). Unlike an ordinary Power of Attorney, which is automatically revoked when the donor becomes mentally incapacitated, an Enduring Power of Attorney endures – or remains in force – after the donor becomes mentally incapacitated, but only if it is registered with the Court of Protection. Once the power has been registered, it cannot be revoked by the donor unless the court confirms the revocation.

An Enduring Power of Attorney must be in the form prescribed by the Lord Chancellor. The prescribed form consists of three parts. Part A contains some explanatory information. Part B, which is signed by the donor, contains the appointment itself. In Part C, the attorney(s) accept the appointment. Unless the donor specifically states that it is not to be used until he or she has become mentally incapacitated, the power comes into effect as soon as it has been signed.

If the donor wishes to appoint more than one attorney, the appointment must be either joint (in which both or all the attorneys must act) or joint and several (which allows any one attorney to act independently). Sixty per cent of donors appoint only one attorney, 34 per cent appoint joint and several attorneys and only 6 per cent appoint joint attorneys.

The prescribed form gives the donor the choice of conferring on the attorney general authority in relation to all his or her property and affairs, or specific authority in respect of a separate area of his or her affairs, such as a business or a particular account; 98.5 per cent of donors confer general authority on their attorneys.

When the attorney has reason to believe that the donor is, or is becoming, mentally incapable of managing his or her affairs, the attorney must apply for the power to be registered with the Court of Protection. The legislation does not specifically require the donor to be medically examined for this purpose.

Before making the application to register the power, the attorney must give notice (on the prescribed form EP1) of his or her intention to apply for registration to the donor personally and to at least three of the donor's closest relatives. There is an order of priority of relatives entitled to receive notice: (1) the spouse, (2) children, (3) parents, (4) siblings, (5) grandchildren, (6) nephews and nieces, (7) uncles and aunts, and (8) cousins.

The donor and the relatives have 28 days during which they may object to the registration of the power. There are five grounds on which they may file a valid objection:

- that the instrument is not valid as an Enduring Power of Attorney
- that the power no longer subsists
- that the application is premature because the donor is not yet becoming mentally incapable
- that fraud or undue pressure was used to induce the donor to create the power
- that, having regard to all the circumstances, the attorney is unsuitable to be the donor's attorney.

If there are no objections, the instrument is registered, with a date stamp and court seal, and returned to the attorney. If there are objections that cannot be resolved amicably, the court will impose a solution at an attended hearing. The number of applications that actually result in such a hearing is fewer than one per cent, the most common ground of objection being that the attorney is unsuitable.

When an Enduring Power of Attorney has been registered, the court generally has no ongoing involvement in the management and administration of the donor's affairs. This is the essential difference between receivership under the Mental Health Act on the one hand, and Enduring Power of Attorney on the other. Under the former, the court has a continuing responsibility to supervise the receiver. Under the latter, however, the management of the donor's affairs is firmly vested in the attorney, the court needing to intervene only if a problem arises.

If there is a problem with a registered Enduring Power of Attorney, the court can give various directions and can require the attorney to render accounts, furnish information and produce documents. If necessary, it can revoke the power and bring the attorneyship to an end.

Attorneys acting under an Enduring Power, whether registered or unregistered, have limited authority to make gifts of the donor's assets.

They may only make seasonal gifts, or presents on a birthday, wedding or wedding anniversary, to people related to or connected with the donor, provided that the value of each such gift is not unreasonable in the circumstances. The donor may, if he or she wishes, include a clause in the power that prohibits the attorneys from making any gifts at all.

What's wrong with receivership?

In alphabetical order, Court of Protection proceedings are:

- *Archaic*: There is much out-of-date terminology, such as 'patient', 'receiver' and 'Master'.
- *Bureaucratic*: The court and the Public Trust Office are not especially unapproachable, slow or inflexible, but they do have procedures, and procedures involve time and expense.
- *Centralised*: The court is based in London and has no regional presence whatsoever. This aggravates a common perception that it is distant and remote.
- *Disempowering*: Once people become patients, they are deprived of the right to manage their own property and finances, even though they may still retain the capacity to enter into a particular transaction, make a particular decision or manage a particular account.
- *Expensive*: The court and Public Trust Office provide a high degree of protection, but at a price. To finance the infrastructure, a patient has to pay an annual administration charge based on his or her income.
- *Financial*: The court only has jurisdiction over patients' property and financial affairs. It has no say over medical decisions or personal questions, such as where to live or with whom to have or not have contact. At present, these matters can only be addressed by the Family Division of the High Court by means of a declaration.

What's wrong with Enduring Powers of Attorney?

Enduring Powers of Attorney also present a number of problems. First, there is what has been described as a widespread failure to register. An Enduring Power can be operated as soon as it has been signed by the donor. Some attorneys see little point in applying to register the power, particularly if they think that it will expose them to some sort of scrutiny.

Second, the legislation actively invites relatives to object to the registration of a power. These objections are numerically greater and more acrimonious than objections to the appointment of a receiver – mainly because it is generally known that receivers are subject to much closer supervision by the court than are attorneys.

Third, although Enduring Powers of Attorney are more user-friendly than a receivership, they are also more abuser-friendly. Financial exploitation occurs in between 10 and 15 per cent of cases involving registered powers, the level of abuse being considerably higher with unregistered powers that ought to have been registered. Attorneys have been known to distribute a donor's estate as if he or she were dead, and frauds involving sums of over £1 million are not unprecedented.

The final problem – common to both Enduring Powers of Attorney and receivership – is that, once the power has been registered, donors have no more right than patients to be involved in the management of their own affairs, even though they may still retain the capacity to make a particular decision.

Proposed reforms

The Law Commission was set up in 1965 for the purpose of promoting the reform of the law in England and Wales. In 1989, it began an investigation into the adequacy of legal and other procedures for making decisions on behalf of mentally incapacitated adults. Four discussion papers were circulated before the final report, *Mental Incapacity*, was published in March 1995 (Law Commission, 1995). The report contains a draft Mental Incapacity Bill.

The draft Bill proposes that the present Court of Protection will be abolished and replaced by a superior court of record, which may possibly still retain the name of the Court of Protection. The new court will have jurisdiction over property and financial matters, personal decisions, and medical decisions, thereby addressing the criticism that the current jurisdiction is confined to financial affairs. The court will consist of nominated district judges, circuit judges and High Court judges, sitting at any designated venue in England and Wales, thus addressing the problem of centralisation.

Receivership under the Mental Health Act will be abolished. In its place, the new court will appoint managers with powers comparable to those of an attorney. It is intended that there should generally be a hands-off approach towards the supervision of managers, who will have direct access to both the capital and income of a patient. As a result, much of the existing bureaucracy will be dismantled, and patients will no longer need to pay an annual administration fee to fund its infrastructure, thereby addressing the criticism that the present scheme is both bureaucratic and expensive.

The Enduring Powers of Attorney Act will be repealed. Instead, it will be possible to make a Continuing Power of Attorney under which the attorney can make any financial, personal or medical decisions that the donor is incapable of making him- or herself at the time the decision needs to be made. It will not be possible to use a Continuing Power unless it is registered, thus overcoming the problem of failure to register an Enduring Power. The donor's relatives will no longer have an automatic right to object to the registration of the power, which in theory should reduce the number of contentious hearings.

In a policy statement, *Making Decisions*, published in October 1999 (LCD, 1999), the government stated that it intends to introduce legislation to implement these proposals as soon as Parliamentary time allows. In anticipation of this legislation, the Lord Chancellor has announced that the Public Trust Office will cease to exist, with effect from 1 April 2001. Some of its functions will be transferred to the Court Service and the Official Solicitor, others being taken over by a new Mental Incapacity Support Unit.

In March 2000, the Scottish Parliament passed the Adults with Incapacity (Scotland) Act 2000, implementing recommendations made by the Scottish Law Commission that are very similar to those made by the Law Commission in England and Wales. These developments north of the border will be observed with great interest by those of us in the south.

Note

1 The Court of Protection and the Public Trust Office are both housed in the same building: Stewart House, 24 Kingsway, London WC2B 6JX (tel. 020 7664 7300).

30

Partnership in Action: The New Challenge of the Youth Justice Reforms and Youth Offending Teams

Helen Watson

Introduction

This chapter will provide an overview of the reforms of the youth justice system as set down in the Crime and Disorder Act 1998, and a personal perspective from a manager of one of the 10 pilot teams on what it is really like operating in the new partnerships. The pilot operated from October 1998 for 18 months to the end of March 2000. A number of issues will be raised about the new legislation, in particular the positive benefits of many professionals working together in one setting. The discussion will also highlight some of the challenges and complexities in this arena.

The context for the reforms

The Audit Commission publication *Misspent Youth* (1996) identified a number of problems in the youth justice system as follows:

- prosecution through the courts was a slow process
- not enough was being done directly to address offending behaviour
- the agencies involved did not coordinate their efforts
- little was done to prevent crime in the first instance.

The indictment was scathing and set the scene for the Labour Party in opposition's blueprint for the changes now occurring – *Tackling Youth*

Crime, Reforming Youth Justice (Labour Party, 1996) – to be fully implemented from May 1997 onwards, when the Labour Party came into government. A number of consultation papers were published by the Home Office in Autumn 1997, culminating in a White Paper in November 1997 *No More Excuses: A New Approach to Tackling Youth Crime in England and Wales*, which sets down in detail the new approach (Home Office, 1997). This was closely followed by the publication of the Crime and Disorder Bill in December 1997 and its passage through Parliament, culminating in its enactment at the end of July 1998. The Crime and Disorder Act 1998 contains the reforms.

The youth justice provisions in the Act focus on the following objectives and principles:

- a clear strategy for preventing offending and re-offending by children and young people
- a framework for agencies to deliver youth justice services through multi-agency YOTs
- a Youth Justice Board for England and Wales to set standards for and monitor the performance of the system
- early intervention with children and young people to stop them being drawn into crime
- children, young people and their parents accepting responsibility for their actions
- reducing the delay in the youth justice process.

The framework for managing the new youth justice system

Part III of the Crime and Disorder Act 1998 makes provision to provide a seamless way of working with young offenders in the community through multi-agency YOTs. This approach is entirely about agencies working in partnership, pooling their skills and resources to best effect. The aim of this new structure is set down in the Crime and Disorder Act, being to prevent offending by children and young people.

Several agencies are required in legislation to commit resources to the Youth Offending Service. Section 38 of the Crime and Disorder Act places a duty on local authorities with social services and education responsibilities, in cooperation with police forces, probation services and health authorities, to ensure that appropriate youth justice services are available in their area. Each YOT must include at least one representative from education, social services, health, police and probation, but may also include individuals from other agencies or organisations. In Sunderland, for example, the housing department has seconded a housing development worker into the service to strengthen the work of the department in the crime prevention arena. Relevant youth justice services that YOTs are required to undertake are defined as:

- the provision of an appropriate adult service, undertaking police interviews with children and young people
- the assessment of children and rehabilitation programmes associated with final warnings (which will replace cautioning)
- bail support services for children and young people on court bail
- the placement of children and young people on remand in local authority accommodation
- the provision of court reports or other information
- the supervision of community sentences and court orders
- the supervision of the detention and training order, both in custody and following release from custody.

Chief Executives of local authorities chair the new multi-agency Chief Officer Steering Groups, tasked with driving through the new reforms.

Pivotal within this new framework is a national body set up to monitor the delivery of youth justice services – the Youth Justice Board for England and Wales. This body was established in September 1998 and is responsible for driving through the youth justice reforms. The Youth Justice Board also has oversight of the performance of youth courts across England and Wales, will monitor and publish benchmarking information on speeding up the criminal justice process, and has also taken responsibilities for the commissioning and purchasing of places in secure facilities for young people who offend. The Youth Justice Board advises the Home Secretary on national standards, will monitor the performance of the new system, will identify, promote and disseminate good practice, and, through its work, will ensure a greater consistency and effectiveness in working with young offenders.

One of the first pieces of work undertaken by the Youth Justice Board has been the development of a structured assessment model to assess criminogenic risk and need in young people who offend. This is called the ASSET assessment tool and is comprehensive and holistic in its approach. This was piloted in selected areas such as Sunderland and was rolled out nationally in April 2000.

The aim and objectives of the Youth Justice Board may be set down as follows:

To prevent offending by children and young people by:

- the swift administration of justice so that every young person accused of breaking the law has the matter resolved without delay
- confronting young offenders with the consequences of their offending

- intervention that tackles the particular factors that put a young person at risk of offending
- punishment proportionate to the seriousness and persistence of the offending
- encouraging reparation to victims by young offenders
- reinforcing the responsibilities of parents.

A number of these themes can be traced through interventions that are now available for young offenders and those at risk. Each YOT is required to set down in its Youth Justice Plan its local targets, which will assist the realisation of these national objectives.

Crime and Disorder Act 1998 measures

The new interventions are as follows:

- reprimands and final warnings
- the reparation order
- the action plan order
- the parenting order
- the detention and training order
- the child safety order (Family Proceedings Court).

In Sunderland we have been piloting:

1 the parenting order: designed to support parents whose children may be at risk of, or actually, offending, or not attending school

2 the child safety order: a preventative order designed to intervene swiftly and briefly with children under the age of 10 (under the age of criminal responsibility) to 'nip offending in the bud' at the earliest opportunity.

In the 18 months of piloting from October 1998 to the end of March 2000, we have had 93 parenting orders and 2 child safety orders made by the court.

The experience of piloting

The pilot has been a steep learning curve for all concerned – Youth Offending Service staff, magistrates and others linked with the reforms. The partnership has, however, blossomed, and seamless service delivery has developed. By way of illustration, a youth justice social worker would in the past have held sole case responsibility for a case and would have involved other agencies where possible. Now, those agency representatives are sitting in the same room with skills to call upon with immediate effect. Education, health, housing and related concerns can now be immediately redressed from within the resources of the team. Staff, meanwhile, are learning at first hand about the skills of other professionals. Myths and stereotypes about different professional groups (for example, police officers disliking 'woolly' social workers and social work stereotypes of anti-youth police officers) have been questioned as staff have learnt to have respect for and trust their colleagues, and to pool information (s.115 Crime and Disorder Act 1998) in order to prevent offending by children and young people.

Some onerous issues have been encountered along the way and acknowledged, if not fully resolved. Pay and leave entitlement differences across professional groupings have been a source of some discomfort – social workers appear to lose out on both fronts. Equally, some professionals, particularly qualified social workers, have not taken kindly to others taking on some of their tasks, for example pre-sentence report preparation, seeing this as a potential dilution of their professionalism. This is not so, being merely the pooling of skills across the team, although obviously some boundaries can never be crossed – police officers, for example, cannot act as 'appropriate adults'. A potential skills shortage has also been identified, some vacancies proving hard to fill.

In Sunderland, we have three multi-agency teams, each team member being responsible and accountable to the team manager of the respective team. As Head of the Youth Offending Service (YOT Manager), all team managers are accountable to myself, and I carry responsibility for the service and its development. I am also directly accountable to the multi-agency Chief Officer Steering Group locally for the performance of the service, and, through quarterly data returns and the preparation of an annual strategic plan, to the Youth Justice Board. The performance management agenda is very demanding, YOTs being measured against 32 performance indicators, and league tables have not been ruled out for the future.

Professionals seconded into YOTs face very real challenges, and a number of issues have arisen. One pilot area, for example, was faced on day one with a police officer asking where his tear gas canister could be safely stored during office hours! We have had issues about whether police officers should wear uniform on duty (with its pros and cons – the possibility of negative responses from young people versus providing absolutely no doubt about the particular powers conferred on that individual to arrest and so on) and what roles police officers in particular should undertake in the team. This is still subject to negotiation – pre-sentence report writing is not an option, but work with final warnings and the victims of crime is legitimate.

Another danger in multi-agency working can arise from the setting of agendas for seconded YOT staff by managers in partner agencies who may not be totally familiar with the government agenda and who may see their own agency goals as a higher priority. This has at times been difficult, resulting in some fairly terse discussion at the Chief Officer Steering Group. A final danger must be highlighted – the very real risk of YOTs becoming a dumping ground for any children and young people perceived to be either 'in need' or 'at risk', whether this is a crime prevention activity, work with parents or work with convicted offenders.

Information-sharing can be a hot potato in YOTs. Different professionals may initially be uneasy about sharing confidential information. The Crime and Disorder Act 1998 helps here – s.115 enables information to be shared across boundaries for the purpose of preventing offending. The way forward is through information-sharing protocols. The six local authorities in Tyne and Wear and Northumberland are currently drawing up a regional information-sharing protocol binding upon all YOTs in those areas, the police, probation services, and the education and health authorities. We have used a commonsense, pragmatic approach to information sharing, which has so far worked well.

The current youth justice reforms and the development of YOTs mark a radical shift in policy and practice in the youth justice arena. The focus is now firmly on early intervention in the lives of children and young people on the fringes of offending in order to divert them from repeat offending; on offering targeted, focused interventions that tackle risk factors and are based on research findings (that is, what works); on intervening swiftly, intensively and surely; and on monitoring and evaluating everything that is done. This is a shift from the previous emphasis in the youth justice system on 'welfare'-based orders or punishment. Some workers have found this move to a new work ethos and culture extremely difficult, to such an extent that, in some pilot areas, previous social services Youth Justice Service staff have moved on.

The new agenda does offer some real benefits for children, young people and their families. Interventions are much more focused, utilise the skills of a diverse range of professionals who now operate from one base, and are firmly evidence-based. The basis of early intervention, nipping offending in the bud at the earliest opportunity, is a case in point. In Sunderland, one of our two child safety orders was made on a five-year-old child who had been involved in repeat offending with teenagers. We were able to intervene and to work closely with the child, the parents and the school to prevent further offending through putting together an additional package of support at school, working with both parents on parenting orders and building a strong relationship with the child. Parenting orders provide a second example of new benefits. While such orders may initially be met with anger, hostility and resentment, parents usually adapt to the parenting group and enjoy the support that can be offered by skilled facilitators and other parents who may also be reeling with the challenge of parenting adolescents who offend and/or are not attending school. A number of parents have spoken graphically and movingly to the media (for example on Radio 4's programme *You and Yours* and in the article by Maureen Freely in the *Guardian* newspaper on 29 September, 1999) about the benefit of the order for them personally, their children and also younger siblings coming up behind.

We have had parents on parenting orders say to us that they wished they had received help and parenting support many years earlier when their child was six – not now when he was a 15-year-old persistent offender. The following quotations illustrate the positive nature of the comments received:

> I found it useful to talk to someone outside my family who listened to how I felt.
>
> I did not feel as though I was being punished for his crime… as I was shown much kindness.
>
> I feel more confident with Darren… It has changed our lives because we can [now] talk to each other.

The new restorative justice agenda is also welcome, firmly placing work with victims and reparation at the heart of the reforms.

A promising beginning has been made in this new world of multi-agency partnerships. Every local authority area in England and Wales has had a YOT since April 2000, and the new Crime and Disorder Act 1998 measures were rolled out nationwide in June 2000. The reforms should make a real difference to children, young people, their families and the wider community.

31

Piggy in the Middle: Good Practice and Interpreters

Nicki Cornwell

I am a white British woman with a background in social work; my first language is English, my second one French. In the part of London in which I live, the influx of asylum-seekers and refugees from French-speaking parts of Africa has resulted in an unprecedented demand for French interpreters, and I have recently taken advantage of that need to move into the role of interpreter. My services are requested and paid for by health and local authority departments.

The people for whom I interpret have health, education and social needs in addition to problems of poverty and housing, and they are vulnerable through their uncertain status in this country. They potentially face many issues of racism and discrimination. In my role as interpreter, I have been present at their face-to-face encounters with professionals from health, housing, education, social service and advice units.

Moving from a social work role to that of an interpreter has provided me with a fascinating insight into the communication between professionals and users. I will try to explain what these are; then I will use those insights to illuminate the problems faced by those of us who act as interpreters between the two.

Contact with professionals

People often feel frustrated in their contacts with professionals by the amount of jargon that is used. Lay people find it difficult to understand what is going on in law courts, users complain of social work jargon, and patients of incomprehensible medical language. Professionals have a responsibility for decoding professional jargon, and when they do so, they are acting as interpreters between themselves and other English-speaking people. Interpretation doesn't always involve a foreign language. And there are other instances of interpretation between people who speak the same language, as in signing, or the use of Braille.

Professional–user communication

As a social worker, when you make an initial contact with a user, you try to build a bridge between you that is strong enough to carry communication both ways. If either of you lack confidence that the structure is sound, communication will be subject to misconceptions and misinterpretation.

It is probably fair to say that as well as the 'what-do-you-want-from-me/my-agency?' questions, there are three basic areas on which to focus. First, the professional has to explain what the agency can offer. This is a tricky operation. If you jump the gun, you will prevent the user telling you what the trouble is; if you do not do it, you leave the user confused. My experience of interpreting suggests that professionals do not pay enough attention to the need to explain their role and that of the agency.

Second, there is the negotiation of differences. All users have their own perspective on the agency, the professionals, the problems they face and the help they need, these perspectives rarely coinciding with professional definitions of the three. If the user's perspective is swamped, or can only be expressed as a form of conflict, communication between professional and user is not likely to be productive. Factors of race, culture, age, gender, sexual orientation, class and language subtly affect the positioning between professional and user, adding another layer to differences of perspective.

The third area, the development of trust, depends largely on the successful negotiation of the other two. It is crucial for bridging communication between professional and user.

Professional–interpreter–user communication

The use of an interpreter further complicates the process of communication, meaning that three sets of trust have to be established instead of one. In addition, however neutral the interpreter, there is an added layer of difference of gender, class, race and so on that can trigger a potential collusion between any two of the three. When two people are involved in a conversation that the third cannot understand, the third person is quick to feel excluded and suspicious. I am sure that professionals often find it hard to trust interpreters who are of the same ethnic origin as the user, and that users perceive interpreters and professionals who speak the same language and come from the same culture as being on the 'same side'.

As an interpreter, you stand at the intersection between the professionals and the users of their services. You have a responsibility for facilitating communication, but your control over the script is minimal. It soon becomes apparent when professionals are in productive contact with users, and when they use pre-programmed and threadbare replies. It is hard to know when to translate word for word, when to paraphrase and when to offer an explanation. Interpreting as word for word translation does not achieve the interpretation of meaning, which is something rather different: a Tamil Asian, for example, had understandably but mistakenly filled in the costs of childcare as the cost of the child's food, nappies and clothes.

As an interpreter, you need the trust of both user and professional. At best, interpreters can be effective PR agents, helping users to have confidence in the professionals and the services they offer. Yet that can be difficult to achieve. I was embarrassed by a health visitor who interrogated a woman about the family health history with little explanation of why the information was needed. It was clear that there was a reluctance to answer questions, particularly about the man from whom the woman had separated. I found the questions invasive. Who knows what the woman's previous experience of persecution and torture may have been. Did she think that a failure to give the correct information might result in expulsion?

Why use an interpreter?

The use of an interpreter is both an equal opportunity and an access issue. People who cannot access services because they cannot communicate in English should be offered the use of an interpreter, and written material should be translated, where necessary. It is good anti-discriminatory practice to use interpreters and translation services, and it is important to raise this issue with agencies if an interpreting or translation service is needed but is not yet available.

Using a relative or a member of the same community may result in information being suppressed for fear that it will reach the wrong ears. The use of a child or a partner may also be inappropriate. I have interpreted for an HIV investigation in which it was clearly undesirable to ask a woman about previous partners in the presence of her current partner.

When does the use of an interpreter enter the legal arena rather than the good practice one? One example is that, in Wales, bilingual services are an expected response to the Welsh Language Act.

The pitfalls of using interpreters

I have found that professionals often develop a strange pattern of communication when they are faced with a user who does not understand what they say. They begin to talk in disjointed phrases instead of sentences, rather as they would speak to a small child. I have done this myself. Yet this is much more difficult for the user to understand and much more difficult to translate. Similarly, long speeches that make several points put pressure on memory and make language harder to retrieve. Both cliches and jargon, too, are difficult to translate from one language into another. I was stumped by the health visitor who said, 'He's a lovely child; enjoy him.' It's a very English thing to say; there isn't a French equivalent. Through my head went the exhortations of waiters to enjoy one's meal – 'Mangez bien!' – while the puzzled mother waited to hear what the health visitor had said.

Then there is the famous 'does-she-take-sugar-with-her-tea' syndrome: the consultant turns to me and says, 'Does she have any pain in her abdomen?' It is extraordinary how prevalent this way of behaving can be, despite attempts by the media to publicise the issue. I think that people are rendered uncomfortable or even distressed by the blank look of incomprehension that passes over someone's face, and they respond by defining the other person as stupid.

Best of all are those professionals who maintain eye contact with the user and produce clear, straightforward sentences. (As professionals, shouldn't they be doing this anyway?) By all means turn to the interpreter for translation, but look back to the user for the response. And if you know a few words of the user's language, try them out. I think it must be music to the ears of those who wonder if anyone is going to be able to communicate with them.

It is worth remembering, however, that asylum-seekers and refugees can also be people with mental illnesses, disabilities and learning difficulties, or have their own idiosyncratic ways. I interpreted for one person who had a meandering short story approach to any answer and was in danger of being perceived as uncooperative because he was using the situation as a social encounter. Making an assessment through the medium of an interpreter thus has the potential for going badly wrong.

It can also be easier to disguise poor professional practice when an interpreter is used. A GP who is Catholic repeatedly failed to answer the patient's question about how and where to obtain an abortion; he kept offering a pregnancy test and a second opinion with one of his colleagues in the same practice (also Catholic).

On another occasion, I found myself in the strange situation of having to translate advice given by a health visitor that directly opposed the views expressed by the midwife for whom I had translated the week before. Both were giving advice on whether the new mother should ask her landlord to make her homeless. I know that professional opinion does not always agree, yet I was surprisingly put out by the situation. I came to the conclusion that I had unwittingly agreed with the first advice offered, and then felt somewhat abashed appearing to support the second source of advice. So much for neutrality!

Power issues

There is no getting away from the fact that there is an imbalance of power between professionals and users, and ways of minimising the effects have been well charted. Working in partnership, the use of negotiation, providing access to information and advice, and seeking to empower users while being prepared to be an advocate when it is appropriate are all means of loosening the tendrils of professional power. However, the use of an interpreter is crucial when there is a language issue. One woman told me that she hides the extent to which she is able to understand English in case she is told that she does not need an interpreter.

What effect does the use of an interpreter have on the balance of power between user and professional? It is usually the professional who pays for the interpreter's services, but interpreters have a professional code of neutrality to adhere to. Making sure that the user's voice is heard is seen as part of the professional role of interpreter. In addition, the onus is on the interpreter to take up issues about racism and discrimination if and when they occur. Furious with the inflexibility of the rules applied to asylum-seekers, I wrote a letter to *The Times*; it wasn't published, but at least it relieved my anger.

Conclusion

Interpreting a foreign language highlights issues of communication. I realise how great are the opportunities for misunderstanding between two people who apparently speak the same language, and how we all of us need to be interpreters in our communication with others, wise to differences of culture and perspective.

32

Elder Abuse

Jacki Pritchard

Researching elder abuse

There has to date been limited research into the subject of elder abuse within the UK, unlike North America, where research has been extensive (Pritchard, 1999). Elder abuse is only just gaining recognition in this country, a continuing problem being the fact that it is not statutory work. Consequently, it is often not given the priority it deserves, and securing funding for research into this subject area can prove to be very difficult.

Much of the research concerned with elder abuse has focused on what constitutes elder abuse and the definitions of abuse. A comprehensive review of research in English-language countries was undertaken by McCreadie (1996), who states, 'How abuse is defined is clearly crucial to what is discovered about it'. In the 1980s and early 1990s, most of what was written about elder abuse came from committed individuals such as Mervyn Eastman (1984; for a more recent review of key issues see Slater and Eastman, 1999), who were pioneering to raise public awareness about elder abuse. The majority of studies that have been undertaken have focused on:

- prevalence
- incidence
- the characteristics of cases: age, gender and ethnicity.

There has never been a national survey regarding prevalence, so research has been based on the findings of small projects that have been carried out locally. In recent years, the focus has been on policy development as more agencies have started to develop their own policies and procedures.

Sadly, what is lacking is the undertaking of qualitative studies; such research is being carried out in other fields – child abuse and domestic violence, for example. One would hope that such methods of research will eventually be used more in the elder abuse field. There are many difficulties implicit in undertaking research on a 'sensitive topic' because of the ethical issues related to gaining access, sharing of information and the effect on victims.

The prime objective for any researcher is to obtain data, whether for a quantitative or a qualitative study. In preparing a research project, a great deal of thought has to be given to how to gain access not only to agencies, but also to victims. Various agencies (for example, social service departments and the police) are likely to collate statistics about victims and abusers, but they may have reservations about sharing this information with a researcher. They are likely to be concerned about the boundaries of confidentiality and the dissemination of findings.

Front-line workers may not wish to divulge information about service-users to someone who is outside the agency. They may also feel threatened by the presence of an outsider viewing and commenting on their work practices (Pritchard, 2000). If the researcher is wishing to interview victims, workers may feel that the research would be an intrusion into a service-user's privacy and that consideration must be given to victim's rights. Other considerations relate to:

- how to identify victims for interview
- getting victims to talk about the abuse they have experienced
- ensuring that the victim is safe when giving an interview, that is, that the abuser will not find out and there will be no repercussions
- ensuring that the researcher has got the necessary skills to deal with disclosures about abuse, the emotional effects of the interview on the victim, and other problems that may arise during the course of the interview
- providing appropriate support after the interview has taken place – for the victim (and for the researcher).

Much thought and preparation needs to go into considering how to undertake research into elder abuse, but it can be done. A key finding from my own recent project is that many victims are willing to talk about their experiences if they know that they have 'permission to speak' (Pritchard, 2000).

Why victims stay in abuse situations

One of the most frequently asked questions is, 'Why does a victim stay?' There is no simple answer, and it is wrong to promote only one theory of why abuse happens and may continue for many years. It is important for anyone working with a victim to become familiar with the different theories and explanations in relation to abuse.

We have learnt over the years that elder abuse is a very complex issue. It was initially thought that elder abuse was a result of carer's stress, that is, that a person who was heavily dependent, either physically or mentally, might cause the carer to lash out in a fit of temper. This is, however, far too simplistic. Current circumstances and conditions may be contributing to the abusive situation, but it is in some cases helpful to look back to the past to see what has happened to both the victim and the abuser. Events or relationships from the past are often the root cause of the current abuse. It is important not to look at elder abuse in isolation (Pritchard, 2000). So why might people stay? In my research the three main reasons for not leaving were:

- nowhere to go
- no money
- the need to keep the family together.

The elder abuse victims talked in depth about why they had stayed (although, by the end of the research project, the majority had left the abusive situation). Their reasons could be summarised as follows:

- *fear:* of not being believed and of the repercussions for themselves or the abuser
- *control:* victims often being terrified of the abuser and the power and control he or she had over them
- *loyalty to the abuser:* based on beliefs that, for example, marriage is until death do you part or that once you have made your bed, you have to lie in it
- *self-blame:* victims blaming themselves for the abuse and/or making excuses for the abuser's behaviour (for example, that he was a victim of child abuse or was unemployed)
- *no-one to talk to:* victims feeling isolated and not knowing whom to turn to for practical advice and support. In the past, it was believed you should keep things to yourself
- a *lack of knowledge:* about agencies, rights, money, benefits and housing.

Needs of older men

The victim of elder abuse was always historically stereotyped as a female aged over 80 (Eastman, 1984), and in general people do tend to think of females as being victims of domestic violence and sexual abuse. It is, however, likely that there are male victims of all types of elder abuse, although many of them may find it hard to disclose the abuse they have experienced. In my recent study, 23 per cent of 126 older people who were identified as victims of elder abuse were male.

When I have run focus groups for women who have been abused, men have come forward to ask if they could also participate. As a result of their involvement in focus groups and personal disclosures to me, I have conducted in-depth interviews with male victims of abuse in order to identify their needs. It seems that, like female victims, if men are given 'permission to speak', they will talk about the abuse they have experienced. I was particularly struck by the way in which the men talked openly about the abuse and seemed very much at ease with me when disclosing what had been done to them.

All the men interviewed were very vulnerable because of their poor physical health and need for help with basic care. Another important factor was the fact that most of them were extremely lonely so had welcomed company or help from outside. Subsequently, carers were able to take advantage of the situation. To summarise, the following needs were identified:

- advice relating to the management of finances, alternative accommodation and divorce
- the assessment of medical problems
- the assessment of mental capacity
- company
- rehousing
- the management of finances
- physical or basic care
- a place of safety
- the protection of the abuser
- reconciliation with the family.

Workers' attitude to working with elder abuse

There is still much ignorance on the part of some social workers concerning elder abuse. This stems from the fact that elder abuse has been a taboo subject for many years, and it is only since the early 1990s that it has gained a higher profile. It is, nevertheless, not statutory work, and in some agencies this work is not seen as a priority, so workers may not be provided with training in this area. Even if a training programme is in place, it is often time limited and not as extensive as a child protection programme.

However, in March 2000 the Department of Health published *No Secrets* (DoH, 2000d) which is guidance on developing and implementing multi-agency policies and procedures to protect vulnerable adults from abuse. *No Secrets* is a significant development in its recognition that adult abuse is an important issue. Elder abuse might now gain a higher profile and attitudes towards working with elder abuse might change. *No Secrets* emphasises the importance of multi-agency working and collaboration in tackling adult abuse. Local multi-agency codes of practice will have to be developed and implemented by 31 October 2001. It also addresses the importance of training, which is crucial in raising awareness among all workers as well as developing the necessary skills in identifying, reporting, investigating and working with abuse in the short and long term.

Anyone who is working with older people needs to understand that elder abuse is a complex issue. It is necessary to have a knowledge of:

- definitions
- signs and symptoms
- theories and methods of working
- policies and procedures
- resources.

Unless workers are trained on this subject, they may not work effectively with the victims and abusers involved in elder abuse cases.

When I train or consult with social workers on elder abuse, I am often faced with negativity and resistance, which I believe is related to a number of factors:

- Workers may find it difficult to come to terms with the fact that elder abuse does happen and that it is very prevalent.
- Some workers may have a personal history of abuse.
- Workers may be suffering burnout (maybe having worked in the child protection field).
- There may be a fear of having to work with abuse in the future, feeling unequipped and lacking in confidence to deal with it.
- Workers may hold the attitude that nothing can be done because there is no satisfactory legal framework in place.
- A reliance on stereotyping, myths and assumptions still exists, for example that most victims want to remain in the abusive situation, that older victims do not want the police involved and that an older person is not going to leave an abusive situation after all those years.

It is true that working with elder abuse is a complex and demanding area of practice, but it has to be emphasised that good practice does exist and victims can be empowered. It must be recognised that social workers do have a crucial role to play in:

- identifying abuse
- investigating abuse
- assessing risk

- identifying needs
- liaising with other agencies
- working with the victim (supporting, empowering and so on)
- possibly working with the abuser
- developing protection plans
- monitoring and reviewing.

My recent research project proved that many elder abuse victims will choose to leave a situation if they are given options and choices, but this takes time. A victim should not be rushed to make a major life decision simply to fit the timescale of local policy and procedure. Agencies have to recognise that long-term work is often a need for many elder abuse victims.

References

Abbreviations:

ADSS	Association of Directors of Social Services
CCETSW	Central Council for Education and Training in Social Work
CRE	Commission for Racial Equality
DETR	Department for the Environment, Transport and the Regions
DFEE	Department for Education and Employment
DHSS	Department of Health and Social Security
DoH	Department of Health
LCD	Lord Chancellor's Department
NACCC	National Association of Child Contact Centres
NISW	National Institute for Social Work
NSPCC	National Society for the Prevention of Cruelty to Children
OFSTED	Office for Standards in Education
PSI	Policy Studies Institute
REU	Race Equality Unit
SSI	Social Services Inspectorate

Advisory Board on Family Law (1999) *Contact Between Children and Violent Parents: The Question of Parental Contact in Cases Where There Is Domestic Violence, Consultation Paper*, London, LCD.

Ahmad, B. (1990) *Black Perspectives in Social Work*, Birmingham, Venture Press.

Ahmad, B. (1991) 'Setting the context: race and the Children Act 1989', in Macdonald, S. (ed.) *All Equal Under the Act? – A Practical Guide to the Children Act 1989 for Social Workers*, London, REU.

Alabhai-Brown, Y. (1999) 'At home with fear', *Community Care*, 12–18 August, p. 12.

Alaszewski, A., Harrison, L. and Manthorpe, J. (eds) (1998) *Risk, Health and Welfare: Policies, Strategies and Practice*, Buckingham, Open University Press.

Aldgate, J. and Bradley, M. (1999) *Supporting Families Through Short Term Fostering*, London, Stationery Office.

Aldgate, J. and Tunstill, J. (1995) *Making Sense of Section 17: Implementing Services for Children in Need within the 1989 Children Act*, London, HMSO.

Aldridge, M. (1994) *Making Social Work News*, London, Routledge.

Alston, P. (1994) 'The best interests principle: towards a reconciliation of culture and human rights', *International Journal of Law and the Family*, Vol. 8, pp. 1–25.

Altman, S. (1997) 'Should child custody rules be fair?', *Journal of Family Law*, Vol. 325, p. 325.

Anderson, W., Furnivall, J. and Lindsay, M. (1998) *Slipping Through the Net: A Study of Issues of Safeguarding in the Inspection Process*, Glasgow, Centre for Residential Child Care.

An-Na'im, A. (1994) 'Cultural transformation and normative consensus on the best interests of the child', *International Journal of Law and the Family*, Vol. 8, pp. 62–81.

Archard, D. (1993) *Children, Rights and Childhood*, London, Routledge.

Aries, P. (1962) *Centuries of Childhood*, London, Jonathan Cape (Pimlico Edition 1996).

Association of Directors of Social Services/Commission for Racial Equality (1978) *Multi-racial Britain: The Social Services Response*, London, CRE.

Audit Commission (1994) *Seen but Not Heard: Co-ordinating Community Child Health and Social Services for Children in Need*, London, HMSO.

Audit Commission (1996) *Misspent Youth: Young People and Crime*, London, Audit Commission.

Audit Commission (1998) *Misspent Youth '98: The Challenge for Youth Justice*, London, Audit Commission.

Bainham, A. (1995) 'The nuances of welfare', *Cambridge Law Journal*, pp. 512–15.

Bainham, A. (1998) *Children: The Modern Law*, 2nd edition, Bristol, Family Law.

Baker, A. (1975) 'Granny bashing', *Modern Geriatrics*, Vol. 5, No. 8, pp. 20–4.

Ban, P. (1993) 'Family decision making – the model as practiced in New Zealand and its relevance in Australia', *Australian Social Work*, Vol. 46, pp. 23–30.

Banks, S. (1995) *Ethics and Values in Social Work*, Basingstoke, Macmillan.

Barker, S.O. and Barker, R. (1995) A study of the experiences and perceptions of family and staff participants in family Group conferences (Cwlym Project), Porthaethwy Gwynedd, MEDRA Research Group.

Barn, R. (1993a) *Black Children in the Public Care System*, London, BAAF/Batsford.

Barn, R. (1993b) 'Black and white care careers: a different reality', in Marsh, P. and Triseliotis, J. (eds) *Prevention and Reunification in Child Care*, London, Batsford.

Barn, R., Sinclair, R. and Ferdinand, D. (1997) *Acting on Principle: An Examination of Race and Ethnicity in Social Services Provision for Children and Families*, London, British Agencies for Adoption and Fostering/CRE.

Barnardo's (1998) *Whose Daughter Next? Children Abused Through Prostitution*, Barkingside, Barnardo's.

Barnes, M. (1997) *Care, Communities and Citizens*, Harlow, Addison Wesley Longman.

Barnett, A. (1999) 'Disclosure of domestic violence by women involved in child contact disputes', *Family Law*, February, p. 105.

Baylies, C., Law, I. and Mercer, G. (1993) *The Nature of Care in a Multi-racial Community. Summary: Report of an Investigation of the Support for Black and Ethnic Minority Persons After Discharge from Psychiatric Hospitals in Bradford and Leeds*, Leeds, University of Leeds.

Beck, U. (1992) *Risk Society: Towards a New Modernity*, London, Sage.

Bell, M. (1999) *Child Protection; Families and the Conference Process, Evaluative Research in Social Work*, Aldershot, Ashgate.

Bennett, G., Kingston, P. and Penhale, B. (1997) *The Dimensions of Elder Abuse*, Basingstoke, Macmillan.

Berridge, D. and Brodie, I. (1998) *Children's Homes Revisited*, London, Jessica Kingsley.

Biggs, S., Phillipson, C. and Kingston, P. (1995) *Elder Abuse in Perspective*, Buckingham, Open University Press.

Bishop, G., Hodson, D., Raeside, D., Robinson, S. and Smallcombe, R. (1996) *Divorce Reform: A Guide for Lawyers and Mediators*, London, Financial Times Law and Tax.

Biss, D. (1995) 'Weighing up the limitations of partnership policies in child protection', *Child Abuse Review*, Vol. 4, pp. 172–5.

Blair, A. (1998) *Leading The Way: A New Vision for Local Government*, London, Institute for Public Policy Research.

Blaug, R. (1995) 'Distortion of the face to face: communicative reason and social work practice', *British Journal of Social Work*, Vol. 25, pp. 423–39.

Boswell, G. (1996) *Young and Dangerous: the Background Careers of Section 53 Offenders*, Aldershot, Avebury.

Bottomley, A. (1984) 'Resolving family disputes: a critical perspective', in Freeman, M.D.A. (ed.) *The State, The Law and the Family*, London, Tavistock.

Bottoms, A.E. (1977) 'Reflections on the renaissance of dangerousness', *Howard Journal of Penology and Crime Prevention*, Vol. 16, No. 2, pp. 70–96.

Bottoms, A.E. (1980) 'An introduction to the coming crisis', in Bottoms, A.E. and Preston, E.H. (eds) *The Coming Penal Crisis*, Edinburgh, Scottish Academic Press.

Bradshaw, J. (1972) 'The concept of social need', *New Society*, 30 March, pp. 640–3.

Brammer, A. (1996) 'Elder abuse in the UK: a new jurisdiction?', *Journal of Elder Abuse and Neglect*, Vol. 8, No. 2, p. 33.

Brammer, A. (1999) 'A fit person to run a home', in Glendenning, F. and Kingston, P. (eds) *Elder Abuse and Neglect in Residential Settings: Different National Backgrounds and Similar Responses*, New York, Haworth Press.

Brammer, A. and Biggs, S. (1998) 'Defining elder abuse', *Journal of Social Welfare and Family Law*, Vol. 20, No. 3, p. 285.

Brandon, M., Thoburn, J. Lewis, A. and Way, A. (1999) *Safeguarding Children with the Children Act 1989*, London, Stationery Office.

Braye, S. (2000) 'Participation in Social Care: An Overview', in Kemshall, H. and Littlechild, R. (eds) *User Involvement and Participation in Social Care*, London, Jessica Kingsley.

Braye, S. and Preston-Shoot, M. (1992) 'Practising social work', quoted in Dalrymple, J. and Burke, B. (1995) *Anti-oppressive Practice, Social Care and the Law*, Buckingham, Open University Press.

Braye, S. and Preston-Shoot, M. (1995) *Empowering Practice in Social Care*, Buckingham, Open University Press.

Braye, S. and Preston-Shoot, M. (1997) *Practising Social Work Law*, 2nd edition, Basingstoke, Macmillan.

Braye, S. and Preston-Shoot, M. (1998) 'Social work and the law', in Adams, R., Dominelli, L. and Payne, M. (eds) *Social Work Themes, Issues and Critical Debates*, Basingstoke, Macmillan.

Braye, S. and Preston-Shoot, M. (1999) 'Accountability, administrative law and social work practice: redressing or reinforcing the power imbalance?', *Journal of Social Welfare and Family Law*, Vol. 21 No. 3, pp. 235–56.

Brearley, C.P. (1982) *Risk and Social Work*, London, Routledge & Kegan Paul.

Bridge Child Care Consultancy Service (1991) *Sukina – an Evaluation Report of the Circumstances Leading to her Death*, London, Bridge.

Brophy, J. (1982) 'Parental rights and children's welfare: some problems of feminists' strategy in the 1920's', *International Journal of the Sociology of Law*, Vol. 7, No. 2, pp. 149–68.

Brown, S. (1990) *Magistrates at Work*, Buckingham, Open University Press.

Butt, J. and Box, L. (1998) *Family Centred, A Study of the Use of Family Centres by Black Families*, London, REU.

Butt, J., Mirza, K., Box, L. and Bignall, T. (1998) Black and Minority Ethnic Children and their Families: A Review of Research Studies for the Social Services Inspectorate, Unpublished.

Caddle, D. and Crisp, D. (1997) *Mothers in Prison,* Research Findings 38, London, Home Office Research and Statistics Directorate.

Campbell, P. (1996) 'What we want from crisis services', in Read, J. and Reynolds, J. (eds) *Speaking our Minds*, Buckingham, Open University Press.

Cantwell, B., Roberts, J. and Young, V. (1998) 'Presumption of contact in private law: an interdisciplinary issue', *Family Law*, April, p. 226.

Carlen, P. and Powell, M. (1979) 'Professionals in the Magistrates' Courts: the Courtroom Lore of Probation Officers and Social Workers', in Parker, H. (ed.) *Social Work and the Courts*, London, Edward Arnold.

Cavadino, P. (ed.) (1996) *Children who Kill*, Winchester, Waterside Press.

Central Council for Education and Training in Social Work (1995) *Assuring Quality in the Diploma in Social Work – I Rules and Requirements for the DipSW*, London, CCETSW.

Childline (1996) *Children and Racism: A Childline Study*, London, Childline.

Children's Society (1999) *One Way Street? Retrospectives on Childhood Prostitution*, London, Children's Society.

Cleaver, H. (2000) *Fostering Family Contact*, London, Stationery Office.

Cleaver, H. and Freeman, P. (1995) *Parental Perspectives in Cases of Suspected Child Abuse*, London, HMSO.

Colton, M., Drury, C. and Williams, M. (1995) *Children in Need: Family Support Under the Children Act 1989*, Aldershot, Avebury.

Connolly, M. (1994) 'An Act of Empowerment?: The Children, Young Persons and their Families Act (1989)', British Association of Social Workers, *British Journal of Social Work*, Vol. 24, pp. 87–100.

Cooper, A. (2000) 'The vanishing point of resemblance: comparative welfare as philosophical anthropology', in Chamberlayne, P., Bornat, J. and Wengraf, T. (eds) *The Turn to Biographical Methods in Social Science*, London, Routledge.

Cooper, A. and Hetherington, R. (1999) 'Negotiation', in Parton, N. and Wattam, C. (eds) *Child Sexual Abuse: Listening to the Experiences of Childre*n, Chichester, John Wiley.

Cooper, A., Hetherington, R., Baistow, K., Pitts, J. and Spriggs, A. (1995) *Positive Child Protection: A View from Abroad*, Lyme Regis, Russell House Press.

Correctional Policy Unit (1998) *Joining Forces to Protect the Public: Prisons – Probation: A Consultation Document*, London, HMSO.

Crow, G. and Marsh, P. (1997) *Family Group Conferences, Partnership and Child Welfare: A Research Report on Four Pilot Projects in England and Wales*, Sheffield, University of Sheffield.

Dalrymple, J. and Burke, B. (1995) *Anti-oppressive Practice, Social Care and the Law*, Buckingham, Open University Press.

Darnbrough, A. and Kinrade, D. (1995) *Be it Enacted: 25 Years of the Chronically Sick and Disabled Persons Act, 1970*, London, Radar.

Davis, G. (1988) *Partisans and Mediators: The Resolution of Divorce Disputes*, Oxford, Clarendon.

Davis, G. and Pearce, J. (1999) 'A view from the trenches: practice and procedure in section 8 applications', *Family Law*, July, p. 457.

Department for the Environment, Transport and the Regions (1998) *Modern Local Government: In Touch with the People*, London, DETR.

Department of Health (1989a) *An Introduction to the Children Act 1989*, London, HMSO.

Department of Health (1989b) *The Care of Children – Principles and Practice in Guidance and Regulations*, London, HMSO.

Department of Health (1990) *Community Care in the Next Decade and Beyond. Policy Guidance*, London, HMSO.

Department of Health (1991) *The Children Act 1989 Guidance and Regulations*. Vol. 2: *Family Support, Day Care and Educational Provision for Young Children*; Vol. 3: *Family Placements*.

Department of Health (1991a) *Care Management and Assessment: Practitioners' Guide*, London, HMSO.

Department of Health (1991b) *Care Management and Assessment: Managers' Guide*, London, HMSO.

Department of Health (1991c) *The Right to Complain. Practice Guidance on Complaints Procedures in Social Services Departments*, London, HMSO.

Department of Health (1995a) *The Challenge of Partnership in Child Protection: Practice Guide*, London, HMSO.

Department of Health (1995b) *Child Protection: Messages from Research*, London, HMSO.

Department of Health (1996) *Focus on Teenagers*, London, Stationery Office.

Department of Health (1997a) *Social Services Inspectorate Reports: Children in Care*, London, HMSO.

Department of Health (1997b) *People Like Us: The Report of the Review of the Safeguards for Children Living Away from Home* (The Utting Report), London, Stationery Office.

Department of Health (1998a) *Modernising Social Services*, Cmn 4169, London, Stationery Office.

Department of Health (1998b) *Objectives for Social Services for Children*, London, DoH.

Department of Health (1998c) *Caring for Children Away from Home: Messages from Research*, London, Stationery Office.

Department of Health (1998d) *The Government's Response to the Children's Safeguards Review*, London, Stationery Office. Local Authority Circular (98) 27.

Department of Health (1999) *The Children Act Report 1995–1999*, London, Stationery Office.

Department of Health (2000) *Protecting Children, Supporting Parents – A Consultation Document on the Physical Punishment of Children*, London, DoH.

Department of Health (2000a) *Framework for the Assessment of Children in Need and their Families*, London, Stationery Office.

Department of Health (2000b) *Assessing Children in Need and their Families: Practice Guidance*, London, Stationery Office.

Department of Health (2000c) *The Community Care (Direct Payments) Act 1996: Policy and Practice Guidance*, London, DoH.

Department of Health (2000d) *No Secrets: The Protection of Vulnerable Adults – Guidance on the Development and Implementation of Multi-agency Policies and Procedures*, London, Stationery Office.

Department of Health (2000e) *The Children Act Now: Messages from Research*, London, Stationery Office.

Department of Health and Social Security (1985) *Social Work Decisions in Child Care: Recent Research Findings and their Implications*, London, HMSO.

Department of Health and Social Security (1988) *Report of the Inquiry into the Child Abuse in Cleveland, 1984*, Cmnd 412, London, HMSO.

Department of Health, Home Office and Department of Education and Employment (1999) *Working Together to Safeguard Children: A Guide to Inter-agency Working to Safeguard and Promote the Welfare of Children*, London, Stationery Office.

Department of Health/Welsh Office (1996) *The Regulation and Inspection of Social Services* (The Burgner Report), London, DoH/Welsh Office.

Department of Health/Welsh Office (1999) *Mental Health Act 1983 Code of Practice*, London, Stationery Office.

Department of Health/Welsh Office (2000) *Lost in Care: Report of the Tribunal of the Inquiry into the Abuse of Children in Care in the Former County Council Areas of Gwynedd and Clwyd Since 1974* (The Waterhouse Report), London, Stationery Office.

Dingwall, R., Eekelaar, J. and Murray, T, (1983) *The Protection of Children: State Intervention and Family Life*, Oxford, Blackwell.

Dominelli, L. (1988) *Anti-Racist Social Work: A Challenge for White Practitioners and Educators*, Basingstoke, Macmillan.

Dominy, N. and Radford, L. (1996) *Living Without Fear*, London, Cabinet Office Women's Unit.

Donzelot, J. (1979) *The Policing of Families*, London, Hutchinson.

Douglas, G. (1994) 'In whose best interests?, *Law Quarterly Review*, Vol. 110, pp. 379–82.

Douglas, M. (1986) *Risk Acceptability According to the Social Sciences*, London, Routledge & Kegan Paul.

Douglas, M. (1992) *Risk and Blame: Essays in Cultural Theory*, London, Routledge.

Doyal, L. and Gough, I. (1991) *A Theory of Human Need*, London, Macmillan.

Drakeford, M. (1996) 'Education for culturally sensitive practice', in Jackson, S. and Preston-Shoot, M. (eds) *Educating Social Workers in a Changing Policy Context*, London, Whiting & Birch.

Dutt, R. and Ferns, P. (1998) *Letting Through Light: A Training Pack on Black People and Mental Health*, London, REU.

Dutt, R. and Phillips, M. (1990) *Towards a Black Perspective in Child Protection*, London, REU.

Dutt, R. and Phillips, M. (1996) 'Race, culture and the prevention of child abuse', in *Childhood Matters*, Report of the National Commission of Inquiry into the Prevention of Child Abuse, Vol. 2, London, Stationery Office.

Dworkin, R. (1980) *Taking Rights Seriously*, London, Duckworth.

Eastman, M. (1984) *Old Age Abuse*, London, Age Concern.

Economic and Social Research Council (1998) *Violence Research Programme*, Middlesex, Brunel University.

Eekelaar, J. (1994) 'The interests of the child and the child's wishes: the role of dynamic self-determinism', in Alston, P. (ed.) *The Best Interests of the Child Reconciling Culture and Human Rights*, Oxford, Clarendon.

Eldergill, A. (1998) *Mental Health Review Tribunals*, London, Sweet & Maxwell.

Elster, J. (1987) 'Solomonic judgments: against the best interest of the child', *University of Chicago Law Review*, Vol. 54, No. 1, pp. 1–45.

Exworthy, M. and Halford, S. (1998) 'Professionals and Managers in a Changing Public Sector: Conflict, Compromise or Collaboration?', in Exworthy, M. and Halford, S. (eds) *Professionals and The New Managerialism in the Public Sector*, Buckingham, Open University Press.

Family Rights Group (1991) *Children Act 1989: Working in Partnership with Families*, London, HMSO.

Farmer, E. and Pollock, S. (1998) *Sexually Abused and Abusing Children in Substitute Care*, Chichester, John Wiley.

Farnfield, S. (1997) The Involvement of Children in Child Protection Conferences – Summary of Findings. Unpublished conference paper, University of Reading.

Feintuck, M. and Keenan, C. (1998) 'Access to Information and the Social Services', in Hunt, G. (ed.) *Whistleblowing in the Social Services*, London, Arnold.

Fineman, M. (1989) 'The politics of custody and gender: child advocacy and the transformation of custody decision making in the USA', in Smart, C. and Sevenhuijsen, S. (eds) *Child Custody and the Politics of Gender*, London, Routledge.

Fineman, M. and Opie, A. (1987) 'The uses of social science data in legal policymaking: custody determinations at divorce', *Wisconsin Law Review*, pp. 107–59.

Fineman, M. (1998) 'Dominant discourse, professional language, and legal charge in child custody decision making', *Harvard Law Review*, Vol. 110, No. 4, pp. 727–74.

Flynn, R. (1998) 'Managerialism, professionalism and quasi-markets', in Exworthy, M. and Halford, S. (eds) *Professionals and the New Managerialism in the Public Sector*, Buckingham, Open University Press.

Franklin, B. (ed.) (1999) *Social Policy, the Media and Misrepresentation*, London, Routledge.

Franklin, B. and Parton, N. (eds) (1991) *Social Work, the Media and Public Relations*, London, Routledge.

Freeman, M. (1983) 'Freedom and the welfare state: child-rearing, parental autonomy and state intervention', *Journal of Social Welfare Law*, pp. 70–91.

Freeman, M. (1995) 'The morality of cultural pluralism', *International Journal of Children's Rights*, Vol. 3, pp. 1–17.

Freeman, P. and Hunt, J. (1999) *Parental Perspectives on Care Proceedings*, London, Stationery Office.

Fryer, R. (1998) *Signposts to Services: Inspection of Social Services Information to the Public*, London, DoH/SSI.

Fuller, L. (1969) *The Morality of Law*, New Haven, Yale University Press.

Furedi, F. (1997) *Culture of Fear: Risk-Taking and the Morality of Low Expectation*, London, Cassell.

Furness, C. (1998) 'Some key issues from research', in NACCC, *Bridging the Break Up*. Report on the conference held to review the work and purpose of contact centres within a legal, policy and practice perspective, London, NACCC.

Garland, D. (1996) 'The limits of the sovereign state: strategies of crime control in contemporary society', *British Journal of Criminology*, Vol. 36, No. 4, pp. 445–71.

Geddis, D. (1993) 'A critical analysis of the family group conference', *Family Law Bulletin*, Vol. 3, No. 11, pp. 141–4.

Gelsthorpe, L. and Morris, A. (1994) 'Juvenile justice 1945–1992', in Maguire, M., Morgan, R. and Reiner, R. (eds) *The Oxford Handbook of Criminology*, Oxford, Clarendon.

Gibbons, J., Conroy, S. and Bell, C. (1995) *Operating the Child Protection System*, London, HMSO.

Glendenning, F. and Kingston, P. (1999) *Elder Abuse in Residential Settings: Different National Backgrounds and Similar Responses*, New York, Haworth Press.

Goldson, B. (1999) 'Youth (in)justice: contemporary developments in policy and practice', in Goldson, B. (ed.) *Youth Justice: Contemporary Policy and Practice*, Aldershot, Ashgate.

Goldstein, J., Freud, A. and Solnit, A. (1979) *Before the Best Interests of the Child*, New York, Free Press.

Guardian (2000) 'Whitehall mandarins "balking" black staff', 15 April.

Guthrie, T. (1998) 'Legal liability and accountability for child-care decisions', *British Journal of Social Work*, Vol. 28, pp. 403–22.

Haggerty, R.J., Sherrod, L.R., Garmezy, N. and Rutter, M. (1996) *Stress, Risk, and Resilience in Children and Adolescents*, Cambridge, Cambridge University Press.

Hall, J.C. (1972) 'The waning of parental rights', *Cambridge Law Journal*, p. 248.

Hall, J.C. (1977) 'Custody of children – welfare or justice?', *Cambridge Law Journal*, Vol. 36, No. 2, pp. 252–4.

Halliday, E. (1998) 'Key issues', in NACCC, *Bridging the Break Up*. Report on the conference held to review the work and purpose of contact centres within a legal, policy and practice perspective, London, NACCC.

Hansard (1988) The Children Act 2nd Reading, 6 December, Col. 488, London, HMSO.

Harris, R. (1996) 'Telling tales: probation in the contemporary social formation', in Parton, N. (ed.) *Social Theory, Social Change and Social Work*, London, Routledge.

Hassall, I. and Maxwell, G. (1991) *The Family Group Conference: An Appraisal of the First Year of the Children, Young Persons and their Families Act 1989*, Washington, New Zealand, Office of the Commissioner for Children.

Haynes, P. (1999) *Complex Policy Planning. The Government Strategic Management of the Social Care Market*, Aldershot, Ashgate.

Heckman, S. (1995) *Moral Voices, Moral Selves*, Cambridge, Polity Press.

Herring, J. (1999a) 'The welfare principle and the rights of parents', in Bainham, A., Sclater, S. Day and Richards, M. (eds) *What is a Parent? A Socio-Legal Analysis*, Oxford, Hart.

Herring, J. (1999b) 'The Human Rights Act and the welfare principle in family law – conflicting or complementary?', *Child and Family Law Quarterly*, Vol. 11, No. 3, pp. 223–55.

Hester, M. and Radford, L. (1996) *Domestic Violence and Child Contact Arrangements in England and Denmark*, Bristol, Policy Press.

Hester, M., Humphreys, C. and Pearson, C. (1994) 'Separation, divorce, child contact and domestic violence' in Mullender, A. and Morley, R. (eds) *Children Living with Domestic Violence*, London, Whiting & Birch.

Hester, M., Pearson, C. and Radford, L. (1997) *Domestic Violence: A National Survey of Court Welfare and Voluntary Sector Mediation Practice*, Bristol, Policy Press.

Hetherington, R. and Sprangers, A. (1994) 'The work of the Flemish Mediation Committee', *Social Work in Europe*, Vol. 1, No. 2, pp. 50–4.

Hetherington, R., Cooper A., Smith, P. and Wilfrod, G. (1997) *Protecting Children: Messages from Europe*, Lyme Regis, Russell House Press.

Hill, M. (2000) 'Inclusiveness in residential child care', in Chakrabarti, M. and Hill, M. (eds) *Residential Child Care: International Perspectives on Links with Families and Peers*, London, Jessica Kingsley.

Hill, M. and Aldgate, J. (1996) *Child Welfare Services – Developments in Law, Policy, Practice and Research*, London, Jessica Kingsley.

HM Inspectorate of Probation (1998) *Evidence Based Practice: A Guide to Effective Practice*, London, Home Office Publications Unit.

Hodgkin, R. (1998) 'Children's voices in the corridors of power: the case for a minister for children', in Utting, D. (ed.) *Children's Services Now and in the Future*, London, National Children's Bureau.

Home Office (1990) *Crime, Justice and Protecting the Public*, Cm. 965, London, HMSO.

Home Office (1995) *National Standards for the Supervision of Offenders in the Community*, London, Home Office Probation Division.

Home Office (1997) *No More Excuses: A New Approach to Tackling Youth Crime in England and Wales* (White Paper), London, HMSO.

Home Office (1999) *Statistics on Race and the Criminal Justice System*, London, HMSO.

Home Office (2000a) *National Standards for the Supervision of Offenders in the Community*, London, HMSO.

Home Office (2000b) *Probation Service Objectives and the Home Secretary's Priorities and Action Plans for the Service 2000–01*, Probation Circular 3/2000, London, HMSO.

Home Office, Department of Health, Department of Education and Science and Welsh Office (1991) *Working Together Under the Children Act 1989: A Guide to Arrangements for Inter-Agency Cooperation for the Protection of Children from Abuse*, London, HMSO.

Home Office, Department of Health, Welsh Office and Department for Education and Employment (1998) *Establishing Youth Offending Teams*, London, Home Office.

House of Commons Health Committee (1998) *Children Looked After by Local Authorities.* Vol. 1: *Report and Proceedings of the Committee*, London, Stationery Office.

Howe, D. (1992) 'Child abuse and the bureaucratization of social work', *Sociological Review*, Vol. 40, No. 3, pp. 491–508.

Hugman, R. (1994) *Ageing and the Care of Older People in Europe*, Basingstoke, Macmillan.

Humphreys, C. (1999) 'Judicial alienation syndrome: failures to respond to post-separation violence', *Family Law*, May, p. 313.

Humphreys, C., Hester, M., Hague, G., Mullender, A., Abraham, H. and Lowe, P. (2000) *From Good Intentions to Good Practice*, Bristol, Policy Press.

Hunt, G. (1998) 'Introduction: whistleblowing and the crisis of accountability', in Hunt, G. (ed.) *Whistleblowing in the Social Services*, London, Arnold.

Hunt, J., MacLeod, A. and Thomas, C. (1999) *The Last Resort: Child Protection, the Courts and the 1989 Children Act*, London, Stationery Office.

Hunter, M. (1999) 'Team spirit', *Community Care*, 17–23 June, pp. 20–1.

Hutton, J. (1999) 'The Minister Replies', in *Quality Projects, Transforming Children's Services*, Issue 2, London, DoH.

Jay, M. (1999) *Living Without Fear: An Integrated Approach to Tackling Violence Against Women*, London, Home Office.

Jones, A. and Butt, J. (1995) *Taking the Initiative: The Report of a National Study Assessing Service Provision to Black Children and Families*, London, REU/National Institute for Social Work/NSPCC.

Jones, C. (1998) 'Social Work: Regulation and Managerialism', in Exworthy, M. and Halford, S. (eds) *Professionals and the New Managerialism in the Public Sector*, Buckingham, Open University Press.

Jones, K.S. (1998) 'The other end of the couch', *Psychiatric Bulletin*, Vol. 22, pp. 515–16.

Jones, R. (1999) *The Mental Health Act Manual*, 6th edition, London, Sweet & Maxwell.

Karban, K. and Frost, N. (1998) 'Training for residential child care: assessing the impact of the Residential Child Care Initiative', *Social Work Education*, Vol. 17, pp. 287–300.

Kelly, G. (1990) *Patterns of Care*, Belfast, Belfast Department of Social work, Queens University.

Kelly, L. (1998) *Domestic Violence Matters: An Evaluation of a Development Project*, London, Home Office.

Kemshall, H. (1998) *Risk in Probation Practice*, Aldershot, Ashgate.

Kemshall, H. and Pritchard, J. (eds) (1996) *Good Practice in Risk Assessment and Risk Management*, London, Jessica Kingsley.

Kemshall, H. and Pritchard, J. (eds) (1997) *Good Practice in Risk Management: Protection, Rights and Responsibilities.* London, Jessica Kingsley.

Kemshall, H., Parton, N., Walsh, M. and Waterson, J. (1997) 'Concepts of risk in relation to organisational structure and functioning within the personal social services and probation', *Social Policy and Administration*, Vol. 31, No. 3, pp. 213–32.

King, M. (1987) 'Playing the symbols – custody and the law commission', *Family Law*, Vol. 17, pp. 186–91.

King, M. and Trowell, J. (1992) *Children's Welfare and the Law: The Limits of Legal Intervention*, London, Sage.

Kingston, P. and Penhale, B. (1995) *Family Violence and the Caring Professions*, Basingstoke, Macmillan.

Kiss, E. (1997) 'Alchemy or fool's gold? Assessing feminist doubts about rights', in Shanley, M. and Narayan, U. (eds) *Reconstructing Political Theory Feminist Perspectives*, Cambridge, Polity Press.

Kumar, S. (1997) *Accountability in the Contract State: The Relationship between Voluntary Organisations, Users and Local Authority Purchasers*, York, York Pubishing Services.

Kundnani, H. (1998) 'The sanction of last resort', *Voluntary Voice*, No. 129, p. 18.

Labour Party (1996) *Tackling Youth Crime: Reforming Youth Justice*, London, Labour Party HQ.

Laming, H. (1998) 'Chief Inspector of Social Services farewell address to the Association of Directors of Social Services spring seminar, April', *Community Care*, 30 April–6 May, p. 1.

Law Commission (1995) *Mental Incapacity,* Cm 231, London, HMSO.

Lawler, J. and Hearn, J. (1997) 'The managers of social work: the experiences and identifications of third tier social services managers and the implications for future practice', *British Journal of Social Work*, Vol. 27, pp. 191–218.

Lawton, A. (1998) *Ethical Management for the Public Services*, Buckingham, Open University Press.

Leat, D. (1996) 'Are voluntary organisations accountable?', in Billis, D. and Harris, M. (eds) *Voluntary Agencies, Challenges of Organisation and Management*, London, Macmillan.

Lewis, J. and Glennerster, H. (1996) *Implementing the New Community Care*, Buckingham, Open University Press.

Lewis, J., Bernstock, P. and Bovell, V. (1995) 'The community care changes: unresolved tensions and policy issues in implementation', *Journal of Social Policy*, Vol. 24, No. 1, pp. 73–94.

London Borough of Brent (1985) *A Child in Trust: The Report of the Panel of Inquiry into the Circumstances Surrounding the Death of Jasmine Beckford*, London, London Borough of Brent.

London Borough of Lambeth (1987) *Whose Child? A Report of The Public Inquiry into the Death of Tyra Henry*, London, London Borough of Lambeth.

Lord Chancellor's Department (1999) *Making Decisions*, Cm 4465, London, Stationery Office.

Lupton, C. and Nixon, P. (1999) *Empowering Practice? A Critical Appraisal of the Family Group Conference Approach*, Bristol, Policy Press.

Lupton, C. and Stevens, M. (1997) *Family Outcomes: Following Through on Family Group Conferences,* SSRIU Report No. 34, Portsmouth, University of Portsmouth.

Lupton, C., Barnard, S. and Swall-Yarrington, M. (1995) *Family Planning? An evaluation of the FGC Model,* SSRIU Report No. 31, Portsmouth, University of Portsmouth.

McCreadie, C. (1996) *Elder Abuse: Update on Research*, London, Institute of Gerontology, King's College.

McCurry, P. (1999) 'Raring to go: the experience of forming youth offending teams', *Community Care*, 21–7 October, pp. 20–2.

Macdonald, S. (1991) *All Equal Under the Act 1989 for Social Workers*, London, REU.

McGoldrick, D. (1991) 'The United Nations Convention on the Rights of the Child', *International Journal of Law and the Family*, Vol. 5, pp. 132–69.

Maclean, M. and Eekelaar, J. (1997) *The Parental Obligation: A Study of Parenthood Across Households*, Oxford, Hart.

Macpherson, W. (1999) *The Stephen Lawrence Inquiry, Report of an Inquiry*, London, Stationery Office.

McWilliams, W. (1987) 'Probation, pragmatism and policy', *Howard Journal of Penology and Crime Prevention*, Vol. 26, pp. 97–121.

Maidment, S. (1984) *Child Custody and Divorce: The Law in Social Context*, London, Croom Helm.

Marsh, P. (1994) 'Family partners: an evaluation of family group conferences in the UK', in Morris, K. and Tunnard, J. (eds) *Family Group Conferences – A Report Commissioned by the Department of Health*, London, Family Rights Group.

Marsh, P. and Crow, G. (1998) *Family Group Conferences in Child Welfare*, Oxford, Blackwells.

Marsh, P. and Fisher, M. (1992) *Good Intentions: Developing Partnership in Social Services*, York, Joseph Rowntree Trust.

Marsh, P. and Triseliotis, J. (1996) *Ready to Practise? Social Workers and Probation Officers: Their Training and First Year in Work*, Aldershot, Avebury.

Masson, J., Harrison, C. and Pavlovic, A. (1997) *Working with Children and Lost Parents,* York, Joseph Rowntree Foundation.

Mathews, S. and Lindow, V. (1998) *The Experience of Mental Health Service Users as Mental Health Professionals*, York, Joseph Rowntree Foundation.

Meager, N. and Doyle, B. (1999) Monitoring the Disability Discrimination Act 1995. Findings from a recent study of cases brought, in *Labour Market Trends*, Vol. 107, No. 9, pp. 477–86.

Millham, S., Bullock, R., Hoise, K. and Hack, M. (1986) *Lost in Care*, Aldershot, Gower.

Minow, M. and Shanley, M. (1997) 'Revisioning the family: relational rights and responsibilities', in Shanley, M. and Narayan, U. *Reconstructing Political Theory Feminist Perspectives*, Cambridge, Polity Press.

Mirlees-Black, C., Mayhew, P. and Percy, A. (1996) *The 1998 British Crime Survey, England and Wales*, London, Home Office Research and Statistics Directorate.

Mirlees-Black, C., Mayhew, P. and Percy, A. (1998) *The 1996 British Crime Survey, England and Wales*, London, Home Office Research and Statistics Directorate.

Mittler, H. (1992) 'Crossing frontiers', *Community Care*, 12 November, pp. 22–3.

Mnookin, R. (1975) 'Child-custody adjudication: judicial functions in the face of indeterminacy', *Law and Contemporary Problems*, Vol. 39, No. 3, pp. 226–93.

Montero, M. (1998) 'Psychosocial community work as an alternative mode of political action (the construction and critical transformation of society)', *Community, Work and Family*, Vol. 1, No. 1, pp. 65–78.

Morris, K. (1995) *Family Group Conferences: An Introductory Pack*, London, Family Rights Group.

Muncie, J. (1999) *Youth and Crime*, London, Sage.

Murch, M. (1995) 'The cross-disciplinary approach to family law – trying to mix oil with water?', in Pearl, D. and Pickford, R. (eds) *Frontiers of Family Law,* 2nd edition, Chichester, John Wiley.

Murphy, J. (1991) 'The welfare principle again an old problem under a new regime', *Family Law*, Vol. 21, pp. 532–5.

Naik, D. (1991) 'An examination of social work education with an anti-racist framework in setting the context for change', in Northern Curriculum Development Project, *Setting the Context for Change*, London, CCETSW.

Narey, M. (1997) *A Review of Delay in the Criminal Justice System: A Report*, London, HMSO.

Nash, M. (1999) *Police, Probation and Protecting the Public*, London, Blackstone Press.

National Institute for Social Work (1988) *Residential Care: A Positive Choice* (the Wagner Report), London, HMSO.

Nazroo, J.Y. (1997) *The Health of Britain's Ethnic Minorities: Findings from a National Survey*, London, Policy Studies Institute.

Neale, B. (2000) Dialogues with children: participation and choice in family decision making, *Childhood*, (forthcoming).

Neville, E. (1999) Domestic Violence: A Police Perspective. Unpublished seminar report.

Nixon, P. (1992) *Family Group Conferences: A Radical Approach to Planning the Care and Protection of Children*, Winchester, Hampshire County Council Social Services Department.

O'Donovan, K. (1993) *Family Law Matters*, London, Pluto.

Ogg, J. and Bennett, G. (1992) 'Elder abuse in Britain', *British Medical Journal*, Vol. 305, pp. 998–9.

Okin, S. (1989) *Justice, Gender, and the Family*, New York, Basic Books.

Olsen, F. (1985) 'The myth of state intervention in the family', *University of Michigan Journal of Law Reform*, Vol. 18, No. 4, p. 835.

Olsen, F. (1992) 'Children's rights: some feminist approaches to the United Nations Convention on the Rights of the Child', in Alston, P., Parker, S. and Seymour, J. (eds) *Children, Rights and Law*, Oxford, Clarendon.

Otway, O. (1996) 'Social work with children and families: from child welfare to child protection', in Parton, N. (ed.) *Social Theory, Social Change and Social Work*, London, Routledge.

Packman, J. (1975) *The Child's Generation Child Care Policy from Curtis to Houghton*, Oxford, Basil Blackwell.

Packman, J. and Hall, C. (1998) *From Care to Accommodation: Support, Protection and Control in Child Care Services*, London, Stationery Office.

Packman, J., Randall, J. and Jacques, N. (1986) *Who Needs Care? Social Work Decisions About Children*, London, Blackwell.

Parker, H. (1989) *Unmasking the Magistrates*, Buckingham, Open University Press.

Parker, S. (1994) 'The best interests of the child – principles and problems', in Alston, P. (ed.) *The Best Interests of the Child, Reconciling Culture and Human Rights*, Oxford, Clarendon.

Parsloe, P. (ed.) (1999) *Risk Assessment in Social Care and Social Work*, London, Jessica Kingsley.

Parton, N. (1985) *The Politics of Child Abuse*, Basingstoke, Macmillan.

Parton, N. (1991) *Governing the Family Child Care, Child Protection and the State*, Basingstoke, Macmillan.

Parton, N. (1996) 'Social work, risk and the blaming system', in Parton, N. (ed.) *Social Theory, Social Change and Social Work*, London, Routledge.

Parton, N. (ed.) (1997) *Child Protection and Family Support: Tensions, Contradictions and Possibilities*, London, Routledge.

Parton, N. and O'Byrne, P. (2000) *Constructive Social Work: Towards a New Practice*, London, Macmillan.

Parton, N., Thorpe, D. and Wattam, C. (1997) *Child Protection: Risk and the Moral Order*, London, Macmillan.

Paterson K. and Harvey M. (1990) *An Evaluation of the Organisation and Operation of Care and Protection Family Group Conferences*, Wellington, New Zealand, Evaluation Unit, Department of Social Welfare.

Pearce, J., Davis, G. and Barron, J. (1999) 'Love in a cold climate: section 8 applications under the Children Act 1989', *Family Law*, January, p. 22.

Perkins, R. (1996) 'Choosing ECT', in Read, J. and Reynolds, J. (eds) *Speaking our Minds*, Buckingham, Open University Press.

Pillemer, K. and Finkelhor, D. (1988) 'The prevalence of elder abuse: a random sample survey', *Gerontologist*, Vol. 28, No. 1, pp. 51–7.

Pillemer, K. and Wolf, R. (1986) *Elder Abuse: Conflict in the Family*, Dover, Auburn House.

Piper, C. (1999) 'The wishes and feelings of the child', in Day Sclater, S. and Piper, C. (eds) *Undercurrents of Divorce*, Aldershot, Ashgate.

Pitts, J. (1988) *The Politics of Juvenile Crime*, London, Sage.

Pitts, J. (1990) *Working with Young Offenders*, London, Macmillan.

Platt, A.M. (1969) *The Child Savers: The Invention of Delinquency*, Chicago, University of Chicago Press.

Policy Studies Institute (1997) *The Fourth National Survey of Ethnic Minorities in Britain, Diversity and Disadvantage*, London, PSI.

Powell, R. (1998) 'Managerial procedure and professional practice in social work', in Hunt, G. (ed.) *Whistleblowing in the Social Services*, London, Arnold.

Preston-Shoot, M. (2000) 'Clear voices for change: messages from disability research for law, policy and practice', in Cooper, J. and Vernon, S. (eds) *Disability and the Law*, 2nd Edition, London, Jessica Kingsley.

Pringle, K. (1998) *Children and Social Welfare in Europe*, Milton Keynes, Open University Press.

Prins, H. (1996) 'Can the law serve as a solution to social ills? The case of the Mental Health (Patients in the Community) Act 1995', *Medical, Science, Law*, Vol. 36, No. 3, pp. 217–20.

Pritchard, J. (1999) *Elder Abuse Work: Best Practice in Britain and Canada*, London, Jessica Kingsley.

Pritchard, J. (2000) *The Needs of Older Women*, Bristol, Policy Press.

Quality Protects Programme 2000/01 (1999a) *Quality Protects Circular (1)*, London, DoH.

Quality Protects Programme 2000/01 (1999b) *Quality Protects Circular (2)*, London, DoH.

Radford, L. (1996) '"Nothing really happened": the invalidation of women's experiences of sexual violence', in Hester, M., Kelly, L. and Radford, L. (eds) *Women, Violence and Male Power*, Buckingham, Open University Press.

Radford, L., Sayer, S. and AMICA (1999) *Unreasonable Fears? Child Contact in the Context of Domestic Violence: A Survey of Mothers' Perceptions of Harm*, Bristol, Women's Aid Federation of England.

Reece, H. (1996) 'The paramountcy principle consensus of construct?', *Current Legal Problems*, Vol. 49, pp. 267–304.

Reece, H. (1996a) 'Subverting the stigmatization argument', *Journal of Law and Society*, Vol. 23, No. 4, pp. 484–505.

Renouf, J., Robb, G. and Wells, P. (1990) *Children, Young Persons and Their Families Act 1989 Report in the First Year of Operation*, Wellington, New Zealand, Department of Social Welfare.

Rhodes, R. (1997) *Understanding Governance: Policy Networks, Governance, Reflexivity and Accountability*, Buckingham, Open University Press.

Ritchie, J., Dick, D. and Lingham, R. (1994) *Report of the Committee of Inquiry into the Care of Christopher Clunis*, London, HMSO.

Roche, J. (1999) 'Children and divorce: a private affair?', in Sclater, S. Day and Piper, C. (eds) *Undercurrents of Divorce*, Aldershot, Ashgate.

Rowe, J., Cain, H., Hundleby, M. and Keane, A. (1984) *Long Term Foster Care*, London, Batsford.

Rutherford, A. (1986, 1992) *Growing out of Crime*, London, Penguin Books/ Winchester, Waterside Press.

Rutter, M. and Rutter, M. (1992) *Developing Minds, Challenge and Continuity Across the Life Span*, Harmondsworth, Penguin.

Ryan, M. (1994) T*he Children Act 1989, Putting it into Practice*, Dartington Social Research Series, Aldershot, Ashgate.

Ryburn, M. (1991) 'The Children Act – power and empowerment', *Adoption and Fostering*, Vol. 15, No. 3, pp. 10–15.

Ryburn, M. and Atherton, C. (1996) 'Family group conferences: partnership in practice', *Adoption and Fostering*, Vol. 20, No. 1, pp. 16–23.

Sawyer, C. (2000) 'An inside story: ascertaining the child's wishes and feelings', *Family Law*, March, p. 170–4.

Schneider, C. (1992) 'Discretion and rules: a lawyer's view', in Hawkins, K. (ed.) *The Uses of Discretion*, Oxford, Clarendon.

Schwehr, B. (1992) 'A complaint about complaining under the Children Act 1989', *Litigation*, Vol. 11, No. 8, pp. 331–5.

Sclater, S. Day and Yates, C. (1999) 'The psycho-politics of post-divorce parenting', in Bainham, A., Sclater, S. Day and Richards, M. (eds) *What is a Parent? A Socio-Legal Analysis*, Oxford, Hart Publishing.

Sevenhuijsen, S. (1998) *Citizenship and the Ethics of Care Feminist Considerations on Justice, Morality and Politics*, London, Routledge.

Shardlow, S. (1998) 'Values, ethics and social work', in Adams, R., Dominelli, L. and Payne, M. (eds) *Social Work Themes, Issues and Critical Debates*, Basingstoke, Macmillan.

Shaw, R. (ed.) (1992) *Prisoners' Children: What Are the Issues?*, London, Routledge.

Shepherd, D. (1995) *Learning the Lessons: Mental Health Inquiry Reports Published in England and Wales Between 1969–1994 and their Recommendations for Improving Practice*, London, Zito Trust.

Simons, K. (1995) 'Critical responses', *Community Care*, 25–31 May, pp. 30–1.

Sinclair, I. and Payne, C. (1989) *The Consumers Contribution: Management and Inspection of Residential Homes for Elderly People*, London, DoH/SSI.

Sinclair, R., Garnett, L. and Berridge, D. (1995) *Social Work and Assessment with Adolescents*, London, National Children's Bureau.

Slater, P. and Eastman, M. (eds) (1999) *Elder Abuse: Critical Issues in Policy and Practice*, London, Age Concern.

Smaje, C. (1999) *Health, Race and Ethnicity: Making Sense of the Evidence*, London, King's Fund Institute.

Smart, C. (1989) *Feminism and the Power of Law*, London, Routledge.

Smart, C. and Neale, B. (1997) 'Arguments against virtue – must contact be enforced?', *Family Law*, May, p. 332.

Smart, C. and Neale, B. (1999) *Family Fragments?*, Cambridge, Polity Press.

Smith, C. (1997a) 'Children's rights: judicial ambivalence and social resistance', *International Journal of Law, Policy and the Family*, Vol. 11, pp. 103–9.

Smith, C. (1997b) 'Children's rights: have carers abandoned values?', *Children and Society*, Vol. 11, pp. 3–15.

Smith, L. and Hennessy, J. (1998) *Making a Difference: Essex Family Group Conference Project; Research Findings and Practice Issues*, Chelmsford, Essex County Council Social Services Department.

Smith, T. (1996) *Family Centres and Bringing up Young Children*, London, Children's Society/HMSO.

Social Exclusion Unit (1998) *Bringing Britain Together: A National Strategy for Neighbourhood Renewal*, London, Stationery Office.

Social Services Inspectorate (1993a) *Social Services Department Inspection Units: The First Eighteen Months. Report of an Inspection of the Work of Inspection Units in Ten Local Authorities*, London, DoH.

Social Services Inspectorate (1993b) *The Inspection of Complaints Procedures in Local Authority Social Services Departments*, London, HMSO.

Social Services Inspectorate (1993c) *No Longer Afraid: The Safeguard of Older People in Domestic Settings*, London, DoH.

Social Services Inspectorate (1994) *Action on Elder Abuse*, London, HMSO.

Social Services Inspectorate (1994a) *Social Services Department Inspection Units. Report of an Inspection of the Work of Inspection Units in Twenty Seven Local Authorities*, London, DoH.

Social Services Inspectorate (1994b) *Second Overview Report of the Inspection of Complaints Procedures in Local Authority Social Services Departments*, London, HMSO.

Social Services Inspectorate (1995) *Social Services Department Inspection Units – Third Overview. Report of an Inspection of the Work of Inspection Units in Nineteen Local Authorities*, London, DoH.

Social Services Inspectorate (1996) *Third Overview Report of the Inspection of Complaints Procedures in Local Authority Social Services Departments*, London, HMSO.

Social Services Inspectorate/Office for Standards in Education (1995) *The Education of Children Looked After by Local Authorities*, London, SSI/OFSTED.

South and East Belfast Trust (1998) *Domestic Violence Guidelines to Good Practice An Interagency Response*, Belfast, South and East Belfast Trust.

Standing Committee E, House of Commons (1996) Official Report, 14 May, col. 304.

Stanko, E. A. and Hobdall, K. (1993) 'Assault on men – masculinity and male victimisation', *British Journal of Criminology*, Vol. 33, No. 3, p. 400.

Stevenson, O. (1995) 'Abuse of older people: principles of intervention', in DoH/SSI, *Abuse of Older People in Domestic Settings: A Report on Two SSI Seminars*, London, HMSO.

Stevenson, O. (1996) *Elder Protection in the Community: What Can We Learn from Child Protection?*, London, Age Concern Institute of Gerontology.

Stone, L. (1977) *The Family, Sex and Marriage in England 1500–1800*, (abridged edition 1979), London, Penguin Books.

Thoburn, J., Murdoch, A. and O'Brian, A. (1986) *Permanence in Child Care*, Oxford, Basil Blackwell.

Thoburn, J., Lewis, A. and Shemmings, D. (1995) *Paternalism or Partnership? Family Involvement in the Child Protection Process*, London, HMSO.

Thoburn, J., Hill, M. and Aldgate, J. (1996) *Child Welfare: Developments in Law, Policy, Practice and Research*, London, Jessica Kingsley.

Thoburn, J., Wilding, J. and Watson, J. (1999) *Family Support in Cases of Emotional Maltreatment and Neglect*, London, Stationery Office.

Thomas, N. (1994) *In the Driving Seat – a Study of the Family Group Meetings Project in Hereford*, Swansea, Department of Social Policy and Applied Social Studies, University of Wales.

Thompson, A. (2000) 'In search of a protector', *Community Care*, 17–23 February, pp. 20–1.

Thornton, C. (1993) *Family Group Conferences: A Literature Review*, Lower Hutt, New Zealand, Practitioner's Publishing.

Timms, J.E. (1995) *Children's Representation: A Practitioner's Guide*, London, Sweet & Maxwell.

Towle, C. (1973) *Common Human Needs*, London, Allen & Unwin.

Tronto, J. (1993) *Moral Boundaries*, London, Routledge.

Tunstill, J. and Aldgate, J. (2000) *Services for Children in Need: From Policy to Practice*, London, Stationery Office.

United Nations (1989) Convention on the Rights of the Child, Geneva, UN.

Universities of Sheffield and Hull (1999) *Youth Offending Teams After One Year: Youth Justice Pilots Evaluation Second Interim Report*, London, Home Office.

Vernon, S., Harris, R. and Ball, C. (1990) *Towards Social Work: Law Legally Competent Professional Practice*, Paper 4.2, London, CCETSW.

Ward, A. (1996) 'Never mind the theory, feel the guidelines. Theory, practice and official guidance in residential childcare: the case of the therapeutic communities', *Therapeutic Communities*, Vol. 17, No. 1, pp. 19–29.

Wellard, S. (1999) 'Inspection in a state of decay', *Community Care*, 7–13 October, pp. 24–5.

Williams, C. (1993) 'Vulnerable victims? Current awareness of the victimisation of people with learning disabilities', *Disability, Handicap and Society*, Vol. 8, No. 2, p. 161.

Williams, P. (1991) *The Alchemy of Race and Rights*, Cambridge, MA., Harvard University Press.

Wilmot, S. (1997) *The Ethics of Community Care*, London, Cassell.

Worrall, A. (1997) *Punishment in the Community: the Future of Criminal Justice*, Harlow, Longman.

Index

D

E

I

L

M

N

Y